THE COLLECTED COURSES OF THE ACADEMY OF EUROPEAN LAW

Edited by: Professor Neha Jain, Professor Claire Kilpatrick, Professor Sarah Nouwen, and Professor Joanne Scott

Assistant Editor: Joyce Davies

The Academy of European Law is housed at the European University Institute in Florence, Italy. The Academy holds annual advanced-level summer courses focusing on topical, cutting-edge issues in Human Rights Law and The Law of the European Union. The courses are taught by highly qualified scholars and practitioners in a highly interactive environment. General courses involve the examination of the field as a whole through a particular thematic, conceptual, or philosophical lens or look at a theme in the context of the overall body of law. Specialized courses bring together a number of speakers exploring a specific theme in depth. Together, they are published as monographs and edited volumes in the Collected Courses of the Academy of European Law series. The Collected Courses series has been published by Oxford University Press since 2000. The series contains publications on both foundational and pressing issues in human rights law and the law of the European Union.

OTHER TITLES IN THE SERIES INCLUDE:

Reframing Human Rights in a Turbulent Era
Gráinne de Búrca

New Legal Approaches to Studying the Court of Justice
Revisiting Law in Context
Edited by Claire Kilpatrick and Joanne Scott

EU Law Beyond EU Borders
The Extraterritorial Reach of EU Law
Edited by Marise Cremona and Joanne Scott

Freedom of Religion, Secularism, and Human Rights
Edited by Nehal Bhuta

EU Administrative Law
Third Edition
Paul Craig

What's Left of the Law of Integration?
Decay and Resistance in European Union Law
Julio Baquero Cruz

EU Legal Acts
Challenges and Transformations
Edited by Marise Cremona and Claire Kilpatrick

New Technologies and EU Law
Edited by Marise Cremona

The Internal Market as a Legal Concept
Stephen Weatherill

Contemporary Challenges to EU Legality

Edited by

CLAIRE KILPATRICK

AND

JOANNE SCOTT

OXFORD
UNIVERSITY PRESS

OXFORD
UNIVERSITY PRESS

Great Clarendon Street, Oxford, OX2 6DP,
United Kingdom

Oxford University Press is a department of the University of Oxford.
It furthers the University's objective of excellence in research, scholarship,
and education by publishing worldwide. Oxford is a registered trade mark of
Oxford University Press in the UK and in certain other countries

First Edition published in 2021

Impression: 1

Published in the United States of America by Oxford University Press
198 Madison Avenue, New York, NY 10016, United States of America

British Library Cataloguing in Publication Data

Data available

Library of Congress Control Number: 2020950506

ISBN 978–0–19–289805–0

DOI: 10.1093/oso/9780192898050.001.0001

Printed and bound by
CPI Group (UK) Ltd, Croydon, CR0 4YY

Contents

Table of Cases

For the benefit of digital users, table entries that span two pages (e.g., 52–53) may, on occasion, appear on only one of those pages.

CJEU CASES (IN NUMBER ORDER)

n. = footnote

General Court Cases (in number order)

Opinions

European Committee of Social Rights

NATIONAL AND INTERNATIONAL CASES

European Court of Human Rights

Germany

International Court of Justice

Netherlands

Portugal

United Kingdom

United States

Table of Legislation

For the benefit of digital users, table entries that span two pages (e.g., 52–53) may, on occasion, appear on only one of those pages.

EUROPEAN LEGISLATION

Treaties and Conventions (in alphabetical order)

International Agreements

Directives (in chronological order)

Regulations (in chronological order)

Decisions (in chronological order)

INTERNATIONAL INSTRUMENTS

NATIONAL LEGISLATION

United Kingdom

Notes on Contributors

Kieran Bradley was formerly a judge in the EU Civil Service, and then Special Adviser to the Court of Justice on Brexit. He is currently a member of a number of international administrative tribunals, and teaches and lectures widely on European Union law.

Evelien Brouwer is a senior researcher/lecturer at the Amsterdam Centre for Migration and Refugee Law at the Vrije Universiteit Amsterdam. Her areas of expertise include EU asylum and migration law and human rights. She has written extensively on the right to effective legal remedies, non-discrimination, and data protection. She participated in different (EU and national) research projects dealing with mutual trust, Schengen, border controls, and the use of databases. In 2019, she was a Fernand Braudel Senior Fellow at the European University Institute (EUI), conducting research on the use of entry bans in Europe.

Bruno De Witte is Professor of European Union Law at Maastricht University, co-director of the Maastricht Centre for European Law, and a part-time professor at the Robert Schuman Centre at the EUI. His main fields of research and publications are: the constitutional law of the European Union; relations between international, European, and national law; protection of fundamental rights in Europe; the rights of minorities, language law, and cultural diversity in Europe; internal market law and non-market values; decision-making and legal instruments of EU law.

Claire Kilpatrick is Professor of International and European Labour and Social Law at the European University Institute and Co-Director of the Academy of European Law at the EUI. She is also the EUI's Dean of Graduate Studies. Before coming to the EUI in 2011, she worked at LSE and before that at Cambridge University. Her interests lie mainly in the law and policy construction of Social Europe, especially the EU's roles. A focus of her recent work is EMU and Social Europe with a particular focus on sovereign debt loan arrangements and legal challenges to those arrangements from those within debtor EU states. Professor Kilpatrick is involved in two research projects at present concerning 'Equality Law in Europe—A New Generation' and 'The Court of Justice in the Archives'. These projects are hosted by the Academy of European Law at the EUI and involve the participation of many EUI researchers.

Joanne Scott is Professor of European Law, Head of the Department of Law, and Co-Director of the Academy of European Law at the EUI. She is currently on leave from University College London, Faculty of Laws, where she taught from 2005 to 2017. Before that she taught at the University of Cambridge, Queen Mary University of London, and the University of Kent. Her research interests lie in the areas of environmental law and climate change law, EU extraterritoriality, new modes of EU governance, and the relationships between different legal orders. Among her recent publications is a co-edited book (with Marise Cremona) on *EU Law Beyond EU Borders: The Extraterritorial Reach of EU Law* (OUP, 2019). Professor Scott was elected as a Fellow of the British Academy in 2013 and a Fellow of the Royal Society of Edinburgh in 2012. Along with Professor Kilpatrick and Professor Marise Cremona, Professor Scott is currently involved in the Academy research project exploring 'The Court of Justice in the Archives'. This project is funded by the EUI Research Council.

Neil Walker holds the Regius Chair of Public Law and the Law of Nature and Nations at the University of Edinburgh. His main area of expertise is constitutional theory. He has published extensively on the constitutional dimension of legal order at sub-state, state, supranational, and global levels, and on the relationship between security, legal order, and political community. Previously he was Professor of Legal and Constitutional Theory at the University of Aberdeen (1996–2000) and Professor of European Law at the EUI (2000–2008). He has an LLD (Honoris Causa) from the University of Uppsala, is a Fellow of the British Academy, and also of the Royal Society of Edinburgh. His most recent books are the monograph *Intimations of Global Law* (Cambridge, 2015) and the edited collections *The Scottish Independence Referendum: Constitutional and Political Implications* (co-editor, Oxford, 2016) and *Sovereignty in Action* (co-editor, Cambridge, 2019). He is presently undertaking a study of the place of law in utopian visions of society within the framework of a Leverhulme Major Research Fellowship.

Ramses A. Wessel is Professor of European Law and Head of the Department of European and Economic Law at the University of Groningen. He has published widely on issues of EU external relations law and the interface between international and EU law. He was the author of the first monograph on the legal aspects of the EU's foreign and security policy (Kluwer Law International, 1999). Recent books include *The European Union and International Dispute Settlement* (Hart, 2017), *Research Handbook on the European Union and International Organizations* (Edward Elgar, 2019), *The Routledge Handbook on the International Dimension of Brexit* (Routledge, 2020), and *EU External Relations Law* (Hart, 2020). Ramses is vice-president of the European Society of International Law and editor of a number of journals and book series, including *International Organizations Law Review*, *European Papers*, *European Foreign Affairs Review*, *ESIL Reflections*, and the *Nijhoff Series on European Union Law*.

List of Abbreviations

ACP	African, Caribbean and Pacific countries
AFSJ	Area of Freedom, Security and Justice
CEAS	Common European Asylum System
CETA	Comprehensive Economic and Trade Agreement, Canada-EU
CFR	Charter on Fundamental Rights
CFSP	Common Foreign and Security Policy
CJEU	Court of Justice of the European Union
CRPD	UN Convention on the Rights of Persons with Disabilities
CSDP	Common Security and Defence Policy
EAW	European Arrest Warrant
ECB	European Central Bank
ECHR	European Convention on Human Rights
ECRIS-TCN	European Criminal Records Information System on Third-Country Nationals
ECSC	European Coal and Steel Community
ECtHR	European Court of Human Rights
EEA	European Economic Area
EFTA	European Free Trade Association
EMU	Economic and Monetary Union
ESM	European Stability Mechanism
EUIPO	European Union Intellectual Property Office
EUPM	EU Police Mission in Bosnia and Herzegovina
Euratom	European Atomic Energy Community
FRD	Family Reunification Directive
GATS	General Agreement on Trade in Services
GATT	General Agreement on Tariffs and Trade
ILO	International Labour Organization
MoU	Memorandum of Understanding
NGO	non-governmental organization
PJCCM	Police and Judicial Cooperation in Criminal Matters
QMV	qualified majority voting
SBC	Schengen Borders Code
SIS	Schengen Information System
TEU	Treaty on European Union
TFEU	Treaty on the Functioning of the European Union
VCLT	Vienna Convention on the Law of Treaties
WTO	World Trade Organization

1

Challenging EU Legality

Claire Kilpatrick and Joanne Scott

1. Introduction

What do we mean when we talk about contemporary challenges to EU legality? Broadly, we have in mind actions or activities that cast doubt on, or sit uncomfortably with, the premises, principles, and norms that underpin the EU's legal order as proclaimed by the Treaties and the authoritative judgments of the European Court. These premises, principles, and norms range from the precisely formulated to the noticeably vague. They include the rules and principles limiting the scope of the EU's competences, and the principles and procedures which govern their exercise. They establish the sources of EU law and a hierarchy of EU law. They include a commitment to the idea of the Treaties establishing a complete system of legal remedies and procedures which grants the Court of Justice of the European Union (CJEU) a wide-ranging power of judicial review. And they include the values on which the EU is said to be founded: human dignity, freedom, democracy, equality, the rule of law, and respect for human rights.

Our understanding of the concept of challenging EU legality has been informed in the first instance by the nature of the EU's responses to the sovereign debt crisis. These responses can assist in elaborating an initial taxonomy of modes of challenging EU legality, and in developing a vocabulary that can help to shed light on the existence of similar phenomena in other areas of EU law. Drawing on earlier scholarship by one of the editors of this volume, we can distinguish between five key forms of challenging EU legality.

The first concerns the emergence of rule of law shortfalls. This would include, for example, institutional actions that do not meet accepted standards of transparency and the emergence of secret EU norms. We see examples of a rule of law shortfall of this kind in the secret letters that the European Central Bank (ECB) sent to Ireland, Spain, and Italy during the sovereign debt crisis. These letters required bailout entry (Ireland in 2010) or laid down conditions for the purchase of government bonds by the ECB (Spain and Italy in 2011).[1]

[1] For discussion, see Kilpatrick, 'Abnormal Sources and Institutional Actions in the EU Sovereign Debt Crisis: ECB Crisis Management and the Sovereign Debt Loans', in M. Cremona and C. Kilpatrick (eds), *EU Legal Acts: Challenges and Transformations* (Collected courses of the Academy of European Law, 2018) 70.

Claire Kilpatrick and Joanne Scott, *Challenging EU Legality*. In: *Contemporary Challenges to EU Legality*. First edition. Edited by: Claire Kilpatrick and Joanne Scott, Oxford University Press (2021). © Claire Kilpatrick and Joanne Scott.
DOI: 10.1093/oso/9780192898050.003.0001

The second type of challenge to EU legality that emerged during the sovereign debt crisis was a reluctance to accept that a particular measure constitutes a legal act that is susceptible to judicial review. A good example of this can be found in the judgment of the CJEU in *Mallis*.[2] Here, the CJEU held that the Eurogroup statement which preceded the conclusion of the Cypriot Memorandum of Understanding (MoU) could not form the subject of an annulment action because it was a political agreement as opposed to a legal act.

A third challenge to EU legality arises as a result of a reluctance to label an actor with the appellation 'EU', thereby allowing this actor to circumvent legality constraints that are embedded in EU law. Again, the CJEU's judgment in *Mallis* offers an example of this, where the Court concluded that the Eurogroup is not a formal EU Council configuration or a body, agency, or office of the EU.[3] Therefore, instruments adopted by the Eurogroup could not be subject to judicial review before the CJEU.

The fourth type of challenge to EU legality arises when an EU norm that is treated as a valid norm within the EU legal order conflicts, or may conflict, with a higher norm, including higher norms protecting fundamental or human rights, as seen in particular during the response to the sovereign debt crisis. The implementation of many of the sovereign debt measures has been found to breach the European Social Charter as well as raising concerns under UN Human Rights Treaties.[4] Although the EU, as a non-state, is not a party to any of these instruments, bar the UN Convention on the Rights of Persons with Disabilities, the link with EU norms and institutions is clear, particularly in the Decisions of the European Committee of Social Rights finding violations of the European Social Charter.[5]

[2] Case C-105/15 P, *Mallis and Malli v. Commission and ECB* (EU:C:2016:702). See, for analysis Craig, 'The Eurogroup, Power and Accountability' 23 *European Law Journal* (2017) 234, at 244: 'The reasoning of the General Court, Advocate General and CJEU reveals the gap between legal form and substantive political reality. It belies the centrality of the Eurogroup to the decision-making process, and its relative autonomy within the EU decision-making scheme. It is illustrative of a more general problem with aspects of EU decision-making, which is the disjunction between power and responsibility.'

[3] Ibid.

[4] See, in particular, the Views by the European Committee of Social Rights on a series of Collective Complaints (CC) from Greek civil society organizations: *Labour law complaints on the first Greek programme, Decisions 23 May 2012* CC 65/2011 *General Federation of employees of the national electric power corporation (GENOP-DEI) and Confederation of Greek Civil Servants' Trade Unions (ADEDY) v. Greece*; CC 66/2011 *General Federation of Employees of the national electric power corporation & Confederation of Greek Civil Servants Trade Unions v. Greece*; five identically worded complaints introduced by a range of Greek pensioner associations, *Decisions 7 December 2012* CC 76/2012 *Federation of employed pensioners of Greece (IKA-ETAM) v. Greece*; CC 77/2012 *Panhellenic Federation of Public Service Pensioners v. Greece*; CC 78/2012 *Pensioners' Union of the Athens-Piraeus Electric Railways (I.S.A.P.) v. Greece*; CC 79/2012 *Panhellenic Federation of pensioners of the public electricity corporation (POS-DEI) v. Greece*; CC 80/2012 *Pensioner's Union of the Agricultural Bank of Greece (ATE) v. Greece*; *Labour law complaint challenging a range of measures across the first and second Greek programmes*; CC 111/2014 *Greek General Confederation of Labour (GSEE) v. Greece*, Decision of 23 March 2017.

[5] This is clear both procedurally, as the European Commission submits written observations (e.g. CC 111/2014 paras 47–53), and substantively (e.g. CC 79/2012 para. 46). 'With regard to the observation made by the Government to the effect that the rights safeguarded under the 1961 Charter have been restricted pursuant to the Government's other international obligations, namely those it has under the loan arrangement with the EU institutions and the International Monetary Fund, the Committee

Our final category of challenging EU legality has previously been identified by one of the editors of this volume as 'liminal legality'.[6] The concept of 'liminal' is used to situate a phenomenon at, or indeed on both sides of, a boundary or threshold. In the context of the sovereign debt crisis, it has been used to describe norms that are applied by EU institutions but which await location within the EU and/or another legal order. Unless and until such norms escape from liminal legality, the standards and procedures according to which their legality may be contested are unclear in highly significant ways.

The concept of liminal legality can be illustrated by reference to the MoUs setting out the conditions that states had to respect in order to be able to obtain sovereign debt loan assistance during the sovereign debt crisis. For example, the status of MoUs adopted as international agreements between euro area states, but in an institutional context that exhibited multiple links to EU law and EU institutions, remains unclear in two ways. It is unclear whether they constitute law and it is unclear whether they constitute EU law and/or international law. This still remains the case some years after the most recent bailout programme ended with the exit of Greece in August 2018.

However, even in relation to MoUs that were clearly adopted under EU law, rather than in the form of international agreements, their characterization as a source of law remained unclear for almost a decade after the last (Romanian) MoU was used. This was finally resolved by the CJEU in *Florescu*, albeit with the somewhat terse and unusual characterization of the MoU as 'mandatory'.[7]

These five forms of challenging EU legality are summarized in Table 1.1.

Looking at this important range of examples taken from the single phenomenon of the sovereign debt crisis, and having regard to the expansive legal scholarship on this theme, we asked ourselves whether such manifestations of challenging EU legality form, or are likely to form, part of a broader pattern in EU law. This led us to widen our search for challenges to EU legality in other areas of EU law. At the same time, we recognized that while our initial taxonomy could provide a useful starting point, other—and perhaps even more important—forms of challenging EU legality could emerge.

In light of this inquiry, we selected two policy areas as promising candidates for exploring contemporary challenges to EU legality. Asylum law and its associated practices was chosen because we considered that it shared features with the sovereign debt crisis, such as the persistence of an exceptional situation over a long

considers that the fact that the contested provisions of domestic law seek to fulfil the requirements of other legal obligations does not remove them from the ambit of the Charter' (CC 111/2014, para. 50).

[6] Kilpatrick, 'The EU and its Sovereign Debt Programmes: The Challenges of Liminal Legality', 70 *Current Legal Problems* (2017) 337.

[7] Case C-258/14, *Florescu and others* (EU:C:2017:448) para. 41.

Table 1.1 Challenging EU Legality: An Initial Taxonomy

Type of challenge to EU legality	Example drawn from the sovereign debt crisis
Rule of law shortfalls	Non-transparent procedures and 'secret' norms
Circumvention of EU legality constraints because no EU legal act	Refusing to label MoUs as (EU) legal acts
Circumvention of EU legality constraints because no EU actor	Refusing to label the Eurogroup as an EU actor
Failure to respect hierarchy of norms	Continuing validity of EU acts that conflict, or may conflict, with higher fundamental or human rights norms
Liminal legality	Instruments that may or may not be part of EU law

period. For example, large movements of asylum-seekers (compared to previous periods); asymmetrical pressure on EU Member States; highly politicized disputes between EU Member States on how to manage the exceptional situation; and breaches of human rights in actions taken by the EU. Common Foreign and Security Policy (CFSP) was chosen because it has traditionally enjoyed a special status in EU law and has constituted an important exception to the 'Community Method'. The exceptionalism that has characterized this area of law has self-evidently led to a hollowing out of the legality constraints that are, in principle, considered standard in other areas of EU law. We therefore anticipated that this area of law would offer important examples of challenging EU legality. However, we were also eager to learn how the positioning of this area of law in relation to legality constraints has shifted over time.

At the same time, we chose two issues which traverse different policy areas. Both of these require the EU institutions, including the CJEU, to navigate the boundaries between the EU legal order and other legal orders, most notably the relationship between EU and international law. The first concerns the status and operation of international agreements in EU law. According to both the Treaties and the CJEU, such agreements occupy a higher position in the EU legal order. They constitute potentially important legality constraints, standing above secondary EU law. The second concerns the question of how EU law manages the exit process and transitional issues arising from the first departure of a Member State from the EU, namely Brexit. To what extent has this process been managed in accordance with both the Treaties and with public international law?

It can be seen from this initial presentation that we are interested in identifying and analysing EU acts, actions, and activities that challenge EU legality. Additionally, however, we are interested in *why* challenges to EU legality seem to have emerged as an important phenomenon. One possible explanation is that the

EU has both moved increasingly into rights-sensitive subject areas and has also confronted exceptional situations—sometimes simultaneously.

On this account, the hypothesis to be explored and fleshed out by this volume would be one where developments challenging EU legality contrast sharply with deeply embedded, long-developed, and incrementally enhanced institutional practices and primary law commitments to what we might call 'standard EU legality'. In 'standard EU legality', the law is an 'agent and object' of EU integration,[8] and the EU is a law-centric, law-abiding, and rule of law based legal order with a substantial and increasingly entrenched commitment to respect fundamental and human rights. 'Standard EU legality' is an important part of the EU's self-image and its claim to legitimacy and authority. Indeed, it is viewed as a key part of its 'normative power'.[9] Our interest is in exploring the paradoxical coexistence of the EU's enhanced spoken commitment to 'standard EU legality' with the simultaneous spread of EU acts, actions, and activities that may pose a challenge to EU legality.

Let us now, however, complicate the picture by acknowledging both standard EU legality and contemporary challenges to this, and by suggesting another way of imagining the relationship between them. Perhaps these should not be viewed as night and day, or as fundamentally oppositional and in tension with each other, but rather as variants of each other, stemming from the same root. The key to understanding how this could even conceivably be so requires us to consider more fully what 'standard legality' means for the EU as a non-standard (i.e. non-state) legal order and a polity of a distinctive kind.

This is the point of departure for Neil Walker's chapter (Chapter 2) examining 'The Theoretical Foundations of EU Law'. He asks, 'given the kind of functions that law in general (and public law in particular) performs in the case of the state—as the bearer, modifier, corrective, or other mediating influence upon the basic political premises of its host polity—does law perform the same or similar functions where the EU is its host?' He makes the case that what we are calling 'standard EU legality' is itself importantly non-standard when compared to the paradigmatic state template for considering law's foundations. That is to say, law as a state-focused steering mechanism is not the same in a non-state domain, even within the EU, which is perhaps the non-state polity which occupies a position closest to the state. Contrasting the normative and expressive functions played by law within the state context, on the one hand, and within the EU, on the other, Walker notes how the relative scarcity of democratic and cultural supports for the EU as a polity has placed a correspondingly heavy burden on law's normative function within the

[8] Dehousse and Weiler, 'The Legal Dimension', in W. Wallace (ed.), *The Dynamics of European Integration* (1990) 234, at 242.

[9] Manners, 'Normative Power Europe: A Contradiction in Terms?' 40 *Journal of Common Market Studies* (2002) 235.

EU to legitimate supranationalism. The law that emerges is a pragmatic problem-solving and results-oriented vision of law: the law that *works*. This differs from other possible bases on which law is understood and received as legitimate within a political order: namely because it is the authorized law (for positivists), the good law (for idealists), or the appropriate law (for culturalists).

Based on his claim that pragmatism is the most convincing basis for law in the EU, he considers that it is the very paucity of other supportive underpinnings (for the making of authoritative or good or appropriate law) that explains why law has been so central to the EU project. Indeed, going a step beyond Dehousse and Weiler's characterization[10] he states, 'EU law has established itself as the *primary* "agent and object of integration" in the supranational context'. EU law serves both the normative function of getting things done, pragmatically, while also serving the expressive function of signifying the EU's achievements and cohesion as a polity. Yet this pragmatic EU law *modus operandi* runs into trouble when more is needed of EU law without the supportive polity underpinnings that lie behind authoritative, good, or appropriate law. Drawing on examples from the sovereign debt crisis, such as liminal legality, Walker suggests, '[t]he more we rely on law to achieve progressive results with unstable democratic and cultural underpinnings the more we depart from certain key virtues of legal formality that also underpin legal certainty and security'.

It seems to us that three important frames for discussing challenging EU legality emerge from this. First, it is entirely possible to hold on to a meaningful analysis of 'standard legality' and 'challenging EU legality' practices as a matter of helpful identification and taxonomy, while also recognizing that the characterization of specific acts, actions, or activities as such may require us to explore more deeply the characteristics and capacities of EU law and the EU legal order. Second, such identification leaves open for discussion and debate the relationship between standard legality and challenging practices, as brothers-in-arms or instead as incompatible opponents, and this will serve to enhance our understanding of the range, characteristics, and evaluation of EU legality practices and of the EU itself. Third, there can be no doubt—and this is set out in eloquent and extensive terms in Neil Walker's analysis—that the EU is not a state. As Walker puts it, it lacks unlimited final authority, originality of collective agency, and primacy of political identity, or—as alternatively conveyed by Walker—it is not a comprehensively self-sufficient and elementary form of political organization: what Oakeshott calls a *societas*. Rather, the EU has narrower competences for stated purposes: what Oakeshott calls a *universitas* or enterprise association.

At the same time, and drawing on Walker's reminder to see all forms of political organizations as hybrids of these two forms, it is clear that the EU has,

[10] See n. 8.

especially from the Maastricht Treaty onwards, moved significantly closer to the *societas* end of this spectrum, with an immensely wider and deeper competence reach. At any rate, even if the EU's version of standard legality may be expected to be different from that of a state, it is not unreasonable to scrutinize EU acts, actions, and activities to ascertain whether the tenets of its version of standard legality have been met. This is the task that the remaining chapters in the volume undertake.

Evelien Brouwer's analysis of EU asylum and migration law (in Chapter 3) brings out beautifully the shifts between standard and challenging EU legality. Since the millennium, the EU has been a primary standard-setter in this field and her starting point is that this Europeanization of asylum and migration law had the distinct advantage of bringing what our introduction terms 'standard EU legality' to bear in this field: 'general principles of EU law, including effectiveness, proportionality and the right to effective judicial protection'.

However, this 'strengthening effect' of standard EU legality has come under strain in recent years for related reasons, which Brouwer identifies and explores. First, this is a result of Member States shifting away from legality themselves, for example by refusing to accept or implement EU asylum and migration law or by making it difficult to apply concepts such as 'mutual trust', which are premised upon a certain assumed baseline of Member State respect for fundamental rights, which frequently can no longer be taken for granted. Second, this can arise from the unclear coexistence of not clearly compatible EU norms. Brouwer provides the example of the co-existence of the Schengen Information System and the more recent centralized system on national decisions relating to criminal convictions of third-country nationals created in 2019 (European Criminal Records Information System on Third-Country Nationals (ECRIS-TCN)), which creates a lack of clarity on the applicable criteria for entry bans. Third, the CJEU has not achieved clarity in its jurisprudence on the application of public order grounds across a range of immigration instruments. Rule of law shortfalls therefore emerge.

Moreover, and core to challenging EU legality, there is the phenomenon of 'deliberate choices of Member States and EU institutions to exclude migration and asylum measures from the applicability of EU law'. This includes the political institutions as well as the Court of Justice. The latter can lend support to the political institutions in excluding the applicability of EU law. The most striking example is the infamous EU-Turkey statement of 2016 that, when challenged by an asylum-seeker who had been returned from Greece to Turkey, was found not to have been adopted by the European Council but rather by the Member States in an intergovernmental agreement.[11] Brouwer gives the further example of the CJEU finding that the EU Visa Code provides no basis for issuing humanitarian

[11] Case T-192/16, *NF v. European Council* (EU:T:2017:128).

visas, with what Brouwer argues is a narrow formalistic and unconvincing set of reasons; the result, however, being to remove this from EU law to the realm of national sovereignty.

She concludes therefore that this large and complex field of law contains a mix of practices, some upholding standard EU legality, while others—many of recent vintage—challenge EU legality.

Ramses Wessel's chapter (Chapter 4) tells an absorbing story of exceptionalism and normalization in EU CFSP, and the uncertain line that divides the two. It highlights the evolving, legally ambiguous, and technically complex nature of this important area of EU law. Wessel focuses on three main issues: the status of CFSP decisions as legal acts; the jurisdiction of the CJEU to evaluate the legality or validity of legal acts in the area of CFSP; and choice of legal basis in relation to CFSP. He demonstrates that each of these issues bears strongly on the degree of judicial scrutiny possible in relation to CFSP measures.

On the question of the legal status of CFSP decisions, Wessel shows that it is important not to be misled by the Treaty on European Union (TEU). While Article 24(1) excludes the use of 'legislative acts' in the context of CFSP, he suggests that it would be mistaken to conclude on this basis that CFSP decisions are not legal acts which are binding on EU Member States. He argues that this exclusion relates to the decision-making procedure (the ordinary legislative procedure) as opposed to the legal nature of the acts adopted. While the adoption of legal acts is relatively rare in CFSP, he suggests that the TEU makes the binding nature of CFSP decisions clear in Article 28(2) and that the CJEU has also acknowledged the 'committing nature of CFSP norms'.

Wessel reaches a nuanced conclusion in his discussion of the jurisdiction of the CJEU to review the legality or validity of CFSP decisions. Based on a close analysis of the text of the EU Treaties and of the case law of the CJEU, he identifies elements of CFSP exceptionalism and of normalization. On the one hand, the CJEU considers the CFSP to be part of the EU's constitutional order and regards some CFSP acts as legal acts that are subject to judicial scrutiny. On the other hand, the CJEU's legality review of CFSP acts remains limited and it cannot provide 'full review'. Therefore, there remains 'a systemic gap in the EU system of legality review'. The exact contours of this gap remain ill-defined, as exemplified by the CJEU's nebulous statement in Opinion 2/13 that 'certain acts, actions or omissions performed in the context of the CFSP fall outside the ambit of judicial review'. Nonetheless, Wessel reaches the conclusion that, at least where individual rights are at stake, as in relation to restrictive measures, the Court has been able to conduct a legality review on the basis of EU values and principles.

In the final part of Chapter 4, Wessel addresses the issue of choice of legal basis in relation to measures concerning external action, including those with a CFSP component. He links this to the theme of legality by suggesting that recourse to a combination of CFSP and non-CFSP legal bases would facilitate fuller judicial review and could thus help to close the CFSP legality gap. He assesses the CJEU's approach to legal basis in relation to CFSP and shows that the Court does not exclude the possibility of combining CFSP and non-CFSP legal bases. However, he points to the fact that there has in practice been a reluctance to combine CFSP and non-CFSP legal bases, notably in relation to the conclusion of internal acts as opposed to international agreements. Wessel observes that there are 67 Council Decisions listed in Eur-lex which combine CFSP and Treaty on the Functioning of the European Union (TFEU) legal bases, all of which relate to international agreements. He concludes, in light of this, that 'combinations of legal bases only partly solve the problem of the restricted legality assessment in CFSP'.

In his wide-ranging and insightful chapter (Chapter 5), Bruno de Witte explores the role of international agreements as 'a multilevel legality constraint' on both the EU and its Member States. Taking international agreements entered into by the EU as his starting point, he demonstrates the EU's openness to international law, exemplified by the direct applicability and primacy of these agreements. Such agreements are incorporated automatically in the EU legal order and become 'a legality constraint within that legal order, due to the recognition, by EU law itself, of the precedence of those international commitments over secondary EU law'.

Nonetheless, de Witte demonstrates in a detailed and compelling manner how the doctrine of direct effect has become 'a filter for legality review' based on international agreements; and how the CJEU has resisted granting direct effect to many significant multilateral agreements. These include the WTO Agreement, the Aarhus Convention, and the UN Disability Convention. In relation to the last of these, de Witte observes that '[t]he least one can say is that [the CJEU] did not make a great effort to ensure the effective enforcement of the sole human rights treaty concluded by the European Union'. De Witte argues that the CJEU has adopted a stricter approach in assessing the direct effect of international agreements as compared to internal EU acts. This is because the CJEU looks not only at the wording of an international agreement but also at its 'nature and purpose'. Where an agreement is not deemed to be capable of conferring rights on individuals, we see judicial exclusion of direct effect. This leads de Witte to consider whether 'it may be more plausible to call the EU legal order a "neo-monist" (in the sense of: "not-so-monist") one'.

While the CJEU has been more open to granting direct effect to bilateral trade and association agreements, even this has been compromised by a 'new trend' of 'political exclusion'. Since 2008, most such agreements, or in one case the Council Decision adopted when signing the agreement, explicitly exclude direct effect. For de Witte, this new trend presents a challenge for the rule of law. 'How to explain and justify, then, the situation whereby precise provisions of an international agreement (which is "higher law" in the EU legal order) cannot serve for reviewing internal EU (or Member State) acts?'

De Witte also explores the role of treaty obligations assumed by Member States as an EU legality constraint. This includes agreements concluded with third countries which may only be relied on to challenge the validity of EU law where the agreement in question has been 'integrated into primary law by reference'. Here, de Witte looks closely at the role of the European Convention on Human Rights and the Convention relating to the Status of Refugees in the EU legal order. He also discusses the role of 'inter se' agreements concluded exclusively between EU Member States. While he tracks the decline of 'parallel' or 'complementary' agreements, he observes the concomitant rise in 'partial' agreements concluded between 'limited groups of EU Member States on subjects closely connected to the operation of the Union'. While such agreements remain subservient to EU law, they raise issues of 'liminal legality' as referred to our earlier taxonomy.

In his rich and fascinating chapter (Chapter 6), Kieran Bradley argues that 'Brexit has challenged the legal and political foundations of the [European] Union in unprecedented ways, and to an unprecedented extent'. Building his arguments upon a close analysis of the text of Article 50 TEU and of the Brexit jurisprudence of the CJEU, he concludes that Brexit transgresses the scheme of the EU Treaties as well as relevant provisions of international law. Bradley's hope is that we can learn from the deficiencies inherent in Article 50 TEU and use the opportunity of the forthcoming Conference on the Future of Europe to amend Article 50 in order to improve it and to 'adapt it, as far as possible to the logic of both Union and international law'.

Notably, Bradley argues that the withdrawal provisions laid down in Article 50 'fly in the face of the scheme of the VCLT and the underlying concern of the international community for ensuring the stability of treaty relations'. Bradley is critical of the 'potential for legal chaos' which Article 50 TEU does not seek to prevent, other than providing for a possible withdrawal agreement. He condemns the largely unconditional nature of the Article 50 TEU withdrawal procedure and contrasts this with the highly constrained default rules set out in Articles 65–68 of the Vienna Convention on the Law of Treaties (VCLT). As interpreted by the CJEU in *Wightman*,[12] Member States not only enjoy an unconditional right of withdrawal but also a right to revoke a notification of intention to withdraw unilaterally. In view of this, he argues that it is only possible to claim that Article 50 TEU was inspired by the VCLT 'in the same way as a child's go-cart was inspired by a Formula One sports car: each has four wheels and assists the occupant in forward motion, though this particular go-cart has neither steering wheel nor brake'.

[12] Case C-621/18, *Wightman and others v. Secretary of State for Exiting the European Union* (EU:C:2018:999).

Given the gulf that separates these different procedures, Bradley doubts whether the EU can be said to be contributing to the strict observance and development of international law as it is required to do by Article 3(5) TEU. In this respect, he does not consider the requirement that a withdrawing state comply with its own constitutional requirements to constitute a meaningful constraint. Interestingly, he points out that even the EFTA Convention has a more balanced withdrawal clause, which makes withdrawal conditional on 'appropriate arrangements and equitable cost-sharing relating to the withdrawal'.

Among the other legality concerns raised by Bradley is that pertaining to the post-Brexit protection of rights that have been established by EU law and which ostensibly had become part of the legal heritage of individuals. This extends not only to citizenship rights but also to other economic and social rights. He illustrates this graphically by reference to a number of cases, including the *RO* case, which concerns the enforcement of European Arrest Warrants issued by the UK. The subject of these arrest warrants argued that he should not be surrendered to the UK authorities due to the fact that his EU rights would no longer be guaranteed in the UK after Brexit. Bradley is rightly troubled by the CJEU's finding that it is sufficient that the subject of the arrest warrants 'should' be able to rely on equivalent rights under UK law. Thus, '*RO* ... imposes an obligation to surrender a Union citizen in circumstances where neither his rights under Union law, nor the possibility of judicial review at Union level of the respect of those rights, is guaranteed during the entirety of his (possible) incarceration'.

Bradley's chapter concludes by looking at the role of the CJEU in enforcing legality constraints during and after the transition period following the UK's departure from the EU. This includes a discussion of the CJEU's role in arbitration proceedings relating to the interpretation and application of the terms of the Withdrawal Agreement. In keeping with the earlier discussion about the protection of individual rights, Bradley points to the phenomenon of a 'qualitative degradation of rights originally created as Union rights'. This degradation may flow from the CJEU's lack of jurisdiction, as in relation to rights protected under Article 2(1) of the Protocol on Ireland/Northern Ireland. However, it may also flow from temporal limitations that result in a diminution of the CJEU's jurisdiction over time, as in relation to EU27 citizens' rights protected under Part Two of the Withdrawal Agreement.

2. Cross-Cutting Themes in Challenging EU Legality

Taken together, the chapters in this volume both invite us to reflect on the nature of the phenomenon of 'standard legality' in the EU legal order and to understand better the contexts in which departures from this take place. On the one hand, the chapters enrich our initial taxonomy of challenges to legality by making visible additional examples that can be used to illustrate the challenges to which the sovereign debt crisis gave rise. The chapters highlight rule of law shortfalls, illustrate the practice of naming acts or actors as 'non-EU' in order to circumvent EU legality constraints, exemplify the phenomenon of liminal legality, and point to disruption of the EU's formal hierarchy of norms. On the other hand, the chapters also assist in further developing this taxonomy of challenges to EU legality by describing distinctive challenges that were less visible, or not visible at all, during the course of the governance of the sovereign debt crisis. We see this, for example, in Bradley's chapter (Chapter 6) when he refers to the phenomenon of degradation of EU citizens' rights in the wake of Brexit; and in the evidence that emerges from different chapters concerning the failure of the EU to contribute to the strict observance and development of international law. Perhaps the most striking addition to the taxonomy drawn from the sovereign debt crisis is what we can term the 'hollowing out' of standard EU legality. This results in particular from narrow formalistic rights-restricting reasoning by the CJEU and is illustrated across the chapters. For example, it can be seen in Brouwer's analysis of the Court's reasoning that the EU Visa Code does not provide a basis for issuing humanitarian visas, or in de Witte's reflection that the Court certainly did not go the extra interpretative mile to ensure effective EU enforcement of the only UN Human Rights Treaty to which it is a party, the Convention on the Rights of Persons with Disabilities. Thus, the chapters extend our lexicon and provide a range of examples of the production and operation of EU practices challenging EU legality.

One of the clearest messages to emerge is the ambivalence of the role played by the CJEU when it comes to reining in the EU's political institutions in order to ensure respect for the EU's version of standard legality. While the chapters do contain examples of the CJEU pushing back against challenges to legality, for example in the area of CFSP, they also suggest that the CJEU has sometimes played a role in sustaining practices that challenge EU legality. Thus, Bradley is critical of the role that the CJEU has played in endorsing an unconstrained reading of Article 50 TEU, Wessel is cognizant of the ambiguity that characterizes the extent of the CJEU's legality review in CFSP, and Brouwer highlights the Court's endorsement of a perspective on the EU-Turkey statement of 2016 that operates to take it outside the boundaries of EU law. The Court also plays a central role in de Witte's account through its repeated denial of the direct effect of multilateral agreements in the EU legal order. This absence of direct effect not only undermines the EU's ostensible commitment to international law but also undercuts the status and effectiveness of legality constraints that are laid down in international agreements and often interpreted by quasi-judicial bodies. This remains true in policy areas in which the EU has a strong spoken commitment to legality, including trade (WTO), environment (Aarhus), and the protection of human rights (UN Disability Convention).

3. 'It's Law, Jim, But Not as We Know it'[13]

Above all, this volume demonstrates that inquiries based on evidence gathered from careful analysis of EU legality practices can shape our understanding of the concepts of legality or the rule of law when it comes to the advanced non-state public legal order that is the EU. Let us conclude with two examples. We have seen that one of the classic EU 'moves' that challenges EU legality is to partially exit the EU legal order in favour of international agreements: the same people sitting at the same table change from the Eurogroup (an EU 'non-body' with considerable decision-making clout) to the governors of the European Stability Mechanism (an intergovernmental agreement). Or the heads of state can meet in the European Council, publish an agreement on paper headed 'EU-Turkey', but maintain that their asylum relocation agreement was not made by the European Council but, rather, by the states agreeing this internationally. Such practices reflect, on the one hand, the normal and often useful flexibility enjoyed by the EU as a Union comprised of states.[14] On the other hand, these practices give rise to discomforting challenges to legality by facilitating EU exit from the advanced legality and human rights controls that have been developed within the EU legal order in accordance with its foundational values.

In this first example, we see clearly that it is 'law but not as we know it', in that the EU legal order, unlike that of a state, provides legal options for internal governance that allow a back and forth between international agreements between some or all EU states and EU law. This is not always problematic in the sense that it challenges EU legality, but sometimes it can be. For example, it is challenging when one of the primary purposes or effects of recourse to a non-EU legal instrument is to sidestep the demanding legality constraints, including human rights constraints, imposed by EU law.

A different kind of example comes from practices that challenge understandings of the values and baselines associated with the rule of law such as non-retrospectivity, promulgation, and access to courts to challenge adopted norms. One might argue that, unlike our first example, this is no longer 'law but not as we know it' but rather 'not law' because the instruments in question fail to meet the criteria that merit recognition of such. When, therefore, the EU acts to obtain outcomes without respecting such values (e.g. secret ECB letters containing normative obligations to act), one reading is that it has straightforwardly failed to respect the rule of law in its actions. However, it might instead be argued that this is holding

[13] From the apocryphal statement by Mr Spock to Captain James T Kirk in the cult series *Star Trek*, 'It's life, Jim, but not as we know it'; in fact the statement comes from a song celebrating the series, available at https://oupacademic.tumblr.com/post/45375455323/misquotation-its-life-jim-but-not-as-we-know-it (accessed 11 November 2020).

[14] See further De Witte, 'A Gentle Criticism of the Metamorphosis Thesis', in H. C. H. Hofmann, K. Pantazatou, and G. Zaccaroni (eds), *The Metamorphosis of the European Economic Constitution* (2019).

the EU to a higher standard than states, and that as an increasingly mature and expansive non-state public order, the EU can and must act using all the 'statecraft' tools it has at its disposal. Not all of these should be evaluated as though the EU must only use standard legality just because this has been the dominant tool historically at its disposal.

A different counterargument is that because the EU is not a state, rule of law values and standards do not fit well with it and need to be adapted to apply to EU acts, actions, and activities by reflecting further on what kind of legal order and polity the EU is, and what kind of law it adopts and deploys. This volume makes a contribution to this by approaching this question not only from the level of theory but also by working back from a range of examples. By meshing these two kinds of analyses together, the hope is to enrich the applied legal theory of EU law and action by providing a set of examples that deepen our understanding of the distinctiveness of the EU's version of standard legality as well as the circumstances and reasons for departure from this. By looking at both 'standard legality' and legality exceptionalism in relation to EU legality, we can shed light both on the nature of the EU as a political organization and more specifically on the nature and role of law within it.

2
The Theoretical Foundations of EU Law

*Neil Walker**

1. Beyond the State

The high modern age, on which the contemporary age of late modernity builds, saw the development of territorially located political societies of an unprecedented size, complexity, and integrative ambition, whose coordination depends on a variety of steering mechanisms. Alongside economics, culture, and science, law offered one such steering mechanism, but one that claimed an overarching organizing capacity as well as a deep normative authority. And so we tend to think of modern law, even more so than earlier forms of law, in suitably society-encompassing and society-coupled terms. Modern law presents itself in intensively and extensively systemic form, as a complexly interconnected whole geared to the complexly interconnected whole of its host territorial political society. Or, to revert to the language of law itself, modern law presents itself as a 'jurisdictionally relative concept'.[1] And, it follows, since the paradigmatic political society—or polity—of modernity has been the modern state, the jurisdiction relative to which law takes shape and reveals its systemic character is typically that of the state.

So today when we come to consider how and why law operates as it does in its manifold settings—what, for reasons I will shortly provide, we may call law's 'theoretical foundations'—we tend to do so within a state-centred framework. This is most pronouncedly so in the case of public law. Our very sense of the 'publicness' of public law, not to mention our appreciation of the myriad aims and methods of the constitutional law, administrative law, and human rights law parts of public law, is closely informed by the self-conception and practice of the modern state as the dominant source and container (if not the originator[2]) of the very distinction between public and private goods, values, relations, and identities, and of the legal architecture and the institutional forms—often framed by a written Constitution—through which that distinction is articulated and refined. Public law, in short, serves mutually supportive normative and expressive functions in the steering

* An earlier version of some of the arguments in this chapter can be found in Walker, 'The Diverse Objects of Public Law: Taking Theory to the Next Level' in E. Fisher, J. King, and A. Young (eds), *The Foundations and Future of Public Law* (2020).

1 N. MacCormick, *Questioning Sovereignty* (1999) 14.

2 See e.g. R. Geuss, *Public Goods, Private Goods* (2003).

Neil Walker, *The Theoretical Foundations of EU Law*. In: *Contemporary Challenges to EU Legality*. First edition. Edited by: Claire Kilpatrick and Joanne Scott, Oxford University Press (2021).
DOI: 10.1093/oso/9780192898050.003.0002

work of state-building and state-maintenance. It both designs a machinery of governance and, at least in some measure, supplies a symbolic resource for the development and sustenance of a framework for putting things in common—a fabric of shared meaning that is both shaped by and facilitates the implementation of the architectural design.[3] This expressive function, which involves the reinforcement of sentiments of belonging and the generation of narratives of identity associated with the Constitution, manifests itself in a variety of ways. These include the commemoration and celebration of the Constitution's emergence, and collective investment in its distinctive content, its key decisions, and its cumulative record of development—as well as the promotion of positive understandings or identifications with Parliament, the higher courts, and other constitutionally endorsed polity-identifying institutions.

Our understanding of private law is also filtered through the lens of the political society of the state. For not only is the very distinction between public and private domains—and the actors, relationships, and dominant values associated with these domains—articulated and stabilized through the state and its law, but the regulation of the private sphere—notably economic and family relations—is also treated as a matter of public policy. This is true not only in the procedurally derivative sense that such regulation will also be a product of general public deliberation and decision, as organized through constitutionally prescribed legislative channels, but, additionally, in the deeper substantive sense that such areas of policy also involve society-integrative projects or at least implicate society-integrative concerns, even if (unlike administrative law) they do not typically involve public institutions as operational actors alongside private actors.[4]

Today, more than ever in the modern age, law, considered in these systemic terms, palpably has more diverse objects, or jurisdictions, by reference to which it is required to perform its societally-integrative, normative, and expressive functions—albeit that such legal orders beyond the state do not supply the exclusive or dominant jurisdiction for a particular territory. Most pertinently for present purposes, beyond the state there is now the supranational level of the EU, complete with its own dense jurisprudence, and with its own incipient European political society and associated public functions. There are also many other international organizations that carry out a more limited number of either general or sector-specific 'public' functions and possess more modest legal jurisdictions to that end;[5] and there are, in addition, increasingly strong claims for a broader globally pervasive and territorially unbounded level of public law, and especially administrative law.[6] As we are focusing upon the EU, however, we may begin with the

[3] See e.g. Walker, 'Beyond the Holistic Constitution?', in P. Dobner and M. Loughlin (eds), *The Twilight of Constitutionalism?* (2010) 291.

[4] See e.g. D. Oliver, *Common Values and the Public-Private Divide* (1999).

[5] See e.g. G. F. Sinclair, *To Reform the World: International Organizations and the Making of Modern States* (2018).

[6] See e.g. N. Walker, *Intimations of Global Law* (2015) ch. 3.

reasonable—indeed unchallenged—assumption that it is the most 'state-like' site and level of law beyond the state in terms of functional range and penetration and of integrative ambition. And on the basis of that reasonable assumption, I would contend, it becomes methodologically plausible for us to view the state template as a point of departure and comparison for our investigation.

Having fixed on this starting point, however, we should not anticipate any particular conclusion. Rather, our attitude should be a suitably agnostic one. Many questions arise concerning the adequacy or even the assistance of a state-centred framework in accounting both for what is distinctive to the EU as a polity and what is distinctive to the law of the EU polity, and these questions need to be addressed with an open mind. To what extent, in the first place, do the deep political or meta-political assumptions we make about the very nature and justification of the form of organized living-in-common peculiar to the state translate to the EU polity level? These concern matters such as the EU's actual or potential democratic credentials, its self-understanding as a distinct political community with a capacity to develop a distinct (rather than merely state-dependent and state-supporting) conception of its public good, and its claim to a domain of final and exclusive authority. And, in the second place, to what extent do the deep assumptions we make about the capacity and proper role of the fundamental ordering mechanism known as law (with its associated normative and expressive functions) in mediating these deep political assumptions translate to the EU level? In other words, given the kind of functions that law in general (and public law in particular) performs in the case of the state, does law—as the bearer, modifier, corrective, or other mediating influence upon the basic political premises of its host polity—perform the same or similar functions where the EU is its host?

It is here that 'theory'—and, more specifically, the notion of 'theoretical foundations'—enters the picture.[7] For the two sets of 'deep assumptions' referred to are themselves, at least in an elementary manner, theoretical in nature—in the sense that we understand theory in the humanities and the social sciences. They are so by dint of their making or implying speculative claims and hypotheses about how—whether by explanation or justification or some combination of the two—we might account for the emergence or sustenance of a particular state of affairs in our human relations. And so we might say that the two fundamental and interconnected questions of the nature and justification of polity-specific law beyond the state (and in the EU in particular)—namely those concerning our deep assumptions about the very nature and purpose of the arrangements of living in common that are

[7] On the use of the notion of foundations to specify a distinct theoretical dimension to the construction—and the study of the construction—of legal and political community, see e.g. P. Craig, *UK, EU and Global Administrative Law: Foundations and Challenges* (2015) 3–4; there he talks of the need to investigate 'conceptual, judicial, theoretical, administrative and regulatory foundations'—each separately but also in their many and complex relations.

fashioned under a polity,[8] and those concerning our deep assumptions about the capacity and proper role of law in ordering and articulating these polity-specific arrangements for living in common (together in either case with the associated methodological question of the extent to which we might rely on a state-centred template in making either of these sets of deep assumptions)—lie within the closely associated domain of political theory (or, at least, of legal theory only *lato sensu*) and legal theory (here, legal theory *stricto sensu*) respectively.[9]

These are, of course, by no means new questions.[10] But in revisiting them in the EU context in what follows I give more emphasis to the question of legal theory (*stricto sensu*)—that is, what I have referred to as the mediating function of law in articulating the order of the political society in question. This is not only because that is my core disciplinary concern. More pertinently, I do so in order to correct what I see as something of an imbalance and also a lack of connectedness in the treatment of the two objects of inquiry. Our understanding of the potential and limits of law—a state-focused steering mechanism adapted to a non-state domain—remains a vital but sometimes neglected complement to political theory in making sense of the distinctive challenges faced by the EU over the course of its evolution and in future prospect.[11] More specifically, I will argue that this approach helps us better understand the relationship between the particular vulnerability of the EU today in terms of its overall legitimacy and the particular vulnerability of its legal order. Notably, the relative scarcity of traditional democratic and cultural supports for the EU polity, and an emphasis instead on the attainment of results, has placed a greater burden on the autonomous role of law—especially as understood in the pragmatic vein—in legitimating supranationalism. It is a burden, furthermore, that law finds increasingly difficult to discharge.

An examination of the theoretical foundations of EU law along these lines can serve a number of different but inter-related purposes. As noted earlier, the work of theory, at least in the applied sense here intended, is to explicate and assess the unexplicated or under-explicated assumptions that do or could drive or influence a particular tendency, or underpin a particular state of affairs in the world of human relations—in this particular case political and legal relations. In so doing, theory

[8] As discussed later, in Section 3, these questions, and the associated questions of political theory, can be further sub-divided into substantive and structural questions; my focus will be on the latter, as those most closely connected to questions of legal order and legal theory.

[9] For this way of understanding the relationship between legal theory and political theory, see e.g. Craig, 'Public Law, Political Theory and Legal Theory' *Public Law* [2000] 211, at 238.

[10] Although in comparing state with non-state sites, there is a tendency (in the UK literature, though less so in the German and French literature) to take for granted and treat only cursorily the paradigmatic qualities of the state and to focus instead on the peculiarities (or otherwise) of the newer non-state sites. Notable exceptions to this trend in the UK tradition include M. Loughlin, *Foundations of Public Law* (2010); N. Barber, *The Constitutional State* (2010).

[11] For an earlier attempt to connect legal and political theory in the context of the EU, see Walker, 'The Philosophy of EU Law', in A. Arnull and D. Chalmers (eds), *The Oxford Handbook of European Union Law* (2016) 3.

can supply an explanatory, an evaluative, and a practical resource. Different theories can be invoked first, and most fundamentally for us, to identify and explain the beliefs that have been invested in the development of particular legal doctrines and broad legal projects. The aim here is to render explicit the kind of candidate frameworks of collective living and of the ordering of collective living within a political community that are often left implicit, but would account for how the law has come to figure in the way that it does. What 'living theories' have influenced the making and the remaking law from the inside, so to speak? Secondly, an exploration of these theories also allows us to evaluate from an outside perspective the adequacy of different candidate conceptions of law in depicting the EU's current legal order. Regardless of how the law actually came to pass and how it has been or, indeed, might even continue to be conventionally understood from the inside, if we adopt the position of the detached spectator what theory or combination of theories provides the most compelling account for the law as it now stands? Thirdly, theory, considered in a more practical and normatively engaged vein—in terms of an elaborated set of beliefs about how law can and should work in its particular polity context—can be a resource for persuasive intervention in the course of legal and political development. It can guide us in the crucial task of choosing one new normative lead over another, or favouring one interpretation or one mode of extrapolation or departure from existing doctrine or structural arrangements over another.

Thinking about the theoretical foundations in this way—as at once an explanatory, an evaluative, and a practical resource—highlights the deep challenge faced by EU legal theory. In terms of explanation and evaluation both the relative weakness of the standard theoretical conceptions in accounting for and justifying EU law and the strong imperative nonetheless to find robust theoretical foundations for this new supranational species of law stand out, creating a tension that must be addressed head-on when we come to consider legal theory as a practical resource in the here and now.

2. Candidate Conceptions of Law

What, then, are the different conceptions of the capacity and role of law, and public law in particular, in articulating and giving effect to any particular vision of the polity? After treating that preliminary issue, we proceed to ask what is distinctive (from the state) about the political form and structure—the basic conditions of and for living-in-common—of the EU. Then, putting these two pieces together, we ask which of the candidate conceptions of the role of law, or, rather, which combination of conceptions, has become most prominent in the EU context, in light of the development of its distinctive political structural tendencies. And, finally, we consider what the resulting pattern of legal authority today tells us more generally about the legitimacy problems of the EU, and we ask what prospects there are for the invocation of an alternative or additional conception of law that would better address these legitimacy problems.

Our candidate conceptions of law, as earlier noted, should be understood as involving different deep assumptions about the capacity and role of law in the generation and maintenance of a polity. These assumptions connect and roughly correspond to different frameworks of legal theory, and can be elaborated by reference to these. Those who have pursued this line and developed typologies of different operational conceptions of law within the polity and of their underlying theoretical presuppositions have cut the conceptual cake somewhat differently.[12] My own approach draws on these earlier efforts in identifying and examining four main ideal typical categories, although, as we shall see in the concluding section, it also considers a fifth category which emerges from a critique of the limitations of the first four. The four main ideal types are, in turn, *positivism*, *idealism*, *culturalism*, and *pragmatism*. Each theoretical model is associated with a particular mindset—a particular sense of the basis upon which and standard by which law is understood and received within the political order. For the positivist, the focus is on 'the *authorized* law'; for the idealist, it is 'the *good* law'; for the culturalist, 'the *appropriate* law'; and for the pragmatist, 'the law *that works*'. Let us explore each of these.

The positivist narrative is concerned with pedigree—with the identification of an agreed social source on which the authority of law rests and from which all particular laws either directly emanate or upon which they are dependent for their recognition as valid laws.[13] Positivism offers itself as the only or most plausible version of how law, as a human construct dealing with matters over which human subjects have differing and sometimes conflicting interests and evaluations, may nevertheless be successfully devised and applied according to collectively acknowledged and accepted standards of validity. For those who subscribe to some version of 'ethical legal positivism',[14] the focus on authoritative sources identifies various more specific benefits, both 'input' and 'output'. First, on the input side, the pedigree social rule shows how the content and direction of the authorized law can be attributed to a particular political 'author', including (but not restricted to) the collective citizenry whose democratic voice is deemed to be represented in an

[12] See e.g. R. Dworkin, *Law's Empire* (1986) (distinguishing conventionalism, pragmatism, and his own law-as-integrity); Coyle, 'Positivism, Idealism and the Rule of Law', 26 *Oxford Journal of Legal Studies* (2006) 257; Craig (n. 9) (distinguishing positivism and non-positivism); M. Loughlin, *Sword and Scales: An Examination of the Relationship between Law and Politics* (2000) chs 1 and 14 (distinguishing law as Command, law as Custom, and law as Right); B. Tamanaha, *Law as a Means to an End* (2006) (distinguishing non-instrumental conceptions of law (Natural Law and law as Custom) from instrumental conceptions); K. Tuori, *Ratio and Voluntas: The Tension between Reason and Will in Law* (2011).

[13] See e.g. J. Raz, *The Authority of Law* (2nd ed., 2009) 116–20.

[14] See e.g. T. Campbell, *The Legal Theory of Ethical Positivism* (1996).

elected Parliament or through some other constitutionally prescribed law-making procedure.

Secondly, on the output side, the emphasis on law as a purposive and normatively precise intervention available from a determinate and supremely authoritative source indicates a consistency and concentration of law-making means that can aid rational planning and co-ordination of legal policy.[15] Thirdly, also on the output side, positivism's certainty over law-making sources provides a basis for the legibility, transparency, calculability, predictability, and reliable effectiveness of law; that is to say, certainty and clarity of input enables (but by no means ensures) certainty and clarity of output—features allowing individuals and groups to orient their conduct towards the law and its co-ordinating properties and also to hold law-makers and law-executors to account for the quality of their laws and the fidelity of their execution respectively.

Fourthly and finally, as one more significant output feature linked to legal positivism, we can indicate a connection to the virtues of legal formalism, understood as a commitment to 'autonomous conceptualism'[16] in judicial and broader legal decision-making. Legal formalism models law as a self-contained, internally consistent system; one where correct legal answers may be given to any question by reference to the logic of that system, and where resort need not be had to morally or socially controversial external values. While there is certainly no *necessary* connection between positivism's source-based foundationalism and a legal system's display of formal properties,[17] there are significant complementarities that facilitate their co-existence. Legal positivism's disciplined approach to the proper sources of law provides one important way in which the formalist distinction between system-internal and system-external factors can be generated and sustained. More concretely, while their reasons differ, the two approaches share a preference for the legal system to be inhabited by a dense structure of rules or other general precepts organized in a clear internal hierarchy. For the positivist, this protects the pedigree connection between the particular legal disposition and the foundational rule, while for the formalist it prevents 'gaps' that would require to be filled by politically and morally contentious system-external considerations. In brief, through its links to legal formalism, positivism attracts some of the benefits associated with a conception of law as 'autonomous'[18] from—or at least as perceived as autonomous from—the often divisive cultural forces and ideological preferences that inhabit the wider political domain.

The idealist narrative supplies the most obvious contrast with the positivist narrative. Justifying law according to general moral standards, legal idealism is

[15] See e.g. S. L. Shapiro, *Legality* (2011) ch. 5.

[16] Cox, 'An Interpretation (and Partial Defense) of Legal Formalism', 36 *Indiana Law Review* (2003) 56, at 59.

[17] See e.g. Leiter, 'Positivism, Formalism, Realism', 99 *Columbia Law Review* (1999).

[18] See e.g. Fiss, 'The Autonomy of Law', 26 *Yale Journal of International Law* (2001) 517.

historically most prominently associated with the natural law tradition. For the idealist, law should reflect, reward, or be otherwise conducive to ways of communal living according to criteria of moral excellence or defensibility. These criteria may be discovered by reference to the immutable and supposedly objectively correct precepts of religious or other metaphysical belief systems, as in the still powerful natural law tradition, or developed through alternative, more constructivist forms of ethical insight, reasoning, or communication.[19] But in any case, the legitimate authority of law depends upon its pursuit of a generally affirmable conception of the good life.

The culturalist narrative values law as an expression of custom or tradition particular to the political community in question. Unlike the positivist narrative, law is not just a jurisdiction-specific activity as a matter of authoritative design, but also because it reflects a jurisdiction-specific background culture. Evolving over generations, and supplying an adjustable, experience-led practice that becomes a key part of the societal matrix, law-as-culture distils, refines, and contributes to the ethical life of the community. Yet unlike the idealist narrative, law's legitimacy under the culturalist narrative is not connected to universalizable conceptions of the good, but depends on its appropriateness as an expression of the way of social being peculiar to its host community.[20]

The pragmatic narrative is (variably) influenced by a broader philosophical tradition which privileges those forms of knowledge of the world that are associated with agency within it, and which are generated or refined through the exercise of agency.[21] With its focus on practical engagement, pragmatism distances itself from the foundationalist assumptions associated with the first three narratives. It turns away from the positivist reliance on the insuperability of a broadly acknowledged social pedigree rule, as also from the universal moral foundations of the idealist and the thick societal foundations of the culturalist. For pragmatists, the contribution of law depends instead on particular context and on the capacity of legal regulation to grasp and offer secure yet adaptable solutions to problems in light of the contingencies and uncertainties peculiar to that context.

So understood, pragmatism is a very broad church. It includes a wide range of contemporary schools of thought, from legal realism to the economic analysis of law, and—for those for whom pragmatism's vital contextual knowledge base is intimately tied to the inclusiveness of its law-generative procedures and the always provisional and corrigible character of its normative conclusions—even democratic experimentalism.[22] The pragmatist's orientation is towards effect rather than

[19] As in the work of Ronald Dworkin; see e.g. n. 12.

[20] For a subtle version of the culturalist approach, see Cotterrell, 'The Role of the Jurist: Reflections around Radbruch', 26 *Ratio Juris* (2013) 510–523.

[21] See e.g. Legg and Hookway, 'Pragmatism', in *Stanford Encyclopaedia of Philosophy* (2019), available at https://plato.stanford.edu/entries/pragmatism/ (accessed 11 November 2020).

[22] See e.g. Dorf and Sabel, 'A Constitution of Democratic Experimentalism', 98 *Columbia Law Review* (1998) 267; O. Gerstenberg, *Euroconstitutionalism and its Discontents* (2018) esp. ch.1.

cause, future rather than past. Looking forward, the claims of pragmatism bear some resemblance to those output criteria of the positivist centred on the purposiveness, precision, clarity, and wide-ranging remit of law. Yet, unlike the positivist, the pragmatist is not primarily interested in the general 'rule of law' goods of certainty and consistency of regulation across the community as a whole that law's solid social pedigree and formal autonomy facilitates, but in the more issue-specific benefits that flow from these attributes; on law as a robust and distinctive normative tool that is flexible in shape, versatile in purpose, yet also stably reliable in its effects. For the pragmatist, the worth of law is instrumental rather than intrinsic, as a secure yet supplely adjustable means to a specific end. Law is technique: defined in terms of 'what works', rather than a code of higher norms elevated in accordance with the various foundational premises.[23] And while many would concede a pragmatic 'engineering'[24] or problem-solving role for law—with its pliant and highly versatile capacity for normative design—at the micro-level of contemporary public policy, a key question concerns the terms on which a more root-and-branch version of pragmatism might come to coexist with or displace law's more common general operational conceptions. This is nowhere more so than in the circumstances of the EU, as we shall see.

3. The State and the EU: Structural Variation

A. The Three Peaks of Constitutional Statehood

The identification of the aforementioned background circumstances brings us to the question of the distinctive assumptions associated with the EU as a supranational polity, and so to the prior domain of political theory. If political theory is the primary locus of conceptions of how we do and should organize our living together in political communities, we can draw a further distinction between *substantive* and *structural* questions. Substantive questions concern normative assumptions and choices about the priority to be given to particular values and aspirations in the making and sustaining of political community; for example the distinction between liberalism and republicanism, or between secular and theocratic states, or between Marxism and social democracy. Structural questions concern *not* the basis of our living together in terms of human values and aspirations but the shape and locus of the political community in which we do our living together, including the concentration or dispersal of authority, overall jurisdictional

[23] See e.g. Butler, 'Legal Pragmatism: Banal or Beneficial as a Jurisprudential Position?', 3(2) *Essays in Philosophy* (2002) 14; for an explanation of the roots of modern legal instrumentalism and a thoroughgoing account of its problems, see Tamanaha (n. 12).

[24] D. Howarth, *Law as Engineering* (2013).

scope, and the terms of overlap or intersection with other political communities. These structural questions have from the outset arisen in the context of the constitutional state too, in particular through the federal question which was so central to the deliberations in Philadelphia on the first modem constitution that led to the formation of the United States of America in 1789. Yet they have become more salient in the context of post-state polities, where variation from the statist norm in polity shape and in inter-polity relations becomes much more pronounced. What is more, because they are concerned with matters pertaining to the basic architecture of the polity that are typically addressed in the ordering register of law, it is just these structural conditions and arrangements, more directly than substantive purposes and aspirations, that closely engage the different theoretical conceptions of the role and capacity of law within the polity. And so it is not only appropriate but also, in the context of the EU's post-state polity, particularly fruitful to focus on structural questions when exploring the significance of the contribution of legal theory, taking the state as a key point of departure and comparison.

Why, then, in basic structural terms, is the EU *not* a state, at least not as understood in any of our familiar registers of modern legal and political thought? It is because the EU lacks the crucial features of *unlimited final authority*, *originality of collective agency*, and *primacy of political identity*[25] that became associated with the constitutional state from the late eighteenth century onwards as the high modern phase of the global system of states began to take shape.[26] The core idea of a final authority not subject to limits beyond itself refers back to an older, pre-modern notion of sovereignty. This holds that there exists one supreme ordering authority for a territorially located polity—an authority that defers to and is limited by no other internal or external authority and to which all other authorities must instead defer. The other two core statist ideas, however, are of more recent vintage. Originality of collective agency refers to the notion that such state sovereignty be the product of a prior *pouvoir constituant* or constituent power. This understanding crystallized with the eclipse of the mediaeval understanding of the sovereign subject as personal and dynastic and its gradual replacement by an impersonal, institutional, and constitutionally grounded and articulated conception of sovereignty.[27] Constituent power in this new conception would typically reside in 'the people' or a similar abstract collective such as 'the nation', itself conceived of as a non-derivative and unencumbered source. For its part, primacy of political identity refers to a deep aspect of political culture—to the idea that the framing public persona of the members of

[25] For an earlier treatment, see Walker, 'The European Union's Unresolved Constitution', in M. Rosenfeld and A. Sajo (eds), *The Oxford Handbook of Comparative Constitutional Law* (2012) 1185–1208.

[26] See e.g. Walker, 'When Sovereigns Stir', in B. Leijssenaar and N. Walker (eds), *Sovereignty in Action* (2019) 31–64.

[27] See e.g. Skinner, 'A Genealogy of the Modern State', 162 *Proceedings of the British Academy* (2009) 325.

the political community is precisely their membership of that political community. Again, this idea began to achieve maturity only with the emergence of the constitutional state, and is captured in the notion of citizenship that is so central to the vocabulary of the new constitutional state. State citizenship—with only distant roots in the local citizenship of the *polis* of Ancient Greece and Rome, and describing a relationship which is less deferential, more rights-protective, but also more integrative than the 'subjecthood' of mediaeval feudalism—announces a general associative bond through which any more particular political commitments and loyalties, interests, and beliefs are articulated and negotiated and in terms of which other commitments, loyalties, interests, and beliefs are circumscribed.[28]

Not only the foundational constitutional document but also the architecture of public law more generally are key to the articulation and sustenance of these three 'peaks' of unlimited final authority, original collective agency, and primary political identity. Unlimited final authority is a function of the interlocking of an autonomous legal order possessing an unchallenged and only self-limited jurisdictional range, and a set of authoritative political institutions tailored to the pursuit of that legal mandate. Original collective agency is a function of an act or process of self-authorization by which the constituent power is deemed to generate authorship or assume control of these sovereign institutions. Primacy of political identity depends, on the one hand, upon these constitutionally sourced legal measures and institutional orientations that designate the citizen *qua* citizen, and on the other, upon a socio-political culture, itself part product of the symbolic power of the constitutional order as a fount of common meaning, which encourages the *self*-identification of citizens as political community members. What is more, these three elements stand in a relationship of circular support and reinforcement. Sufficient affinity at the socio-cultural level is required to develop the relevant generative processes for the sovereignty-articulating legal and political institutions and for these to be recognized and accepted as self-authorized artefacts, and this institutional accomplishment and event-history in turn reinforces the common bond of citizenship.[29]

How does the EU compare? Precisely because the EU began its life *in relation to* states and has continued to exist alongside states and in close engagement with states, the EU does not and cannot possess these statist features of unlimited authority, original agency, and primary political identity, or at least not in the fullest sense associated with high modern statehood. While states themselves are challenged, altered, and somewhat diluted in their constitutional character by the rise of non-state political entities such as sub-state nations or the EU, states still continue to claim and, in some measure, to possess attributes that are by their nature

[28] See e.g. R. Brubaker, *Citizenship and Nationhood in France and Germany* (1998).

[29] See e.g. Grimm, 'The Achievement of Constitutionalism and its Prospects in a Changed World', in P. Dobner and M. Loughlin (eds), *The Twilight of Constitutionalism?* (2010) 3–22.

Table 2.1 Structural comparison of state and EU

STATE	EUROPEAN UNION
capacity	
comprehensive	partial
elementary	derivative
prior	accessory
nomocratic	teleocratic
spatiality	
exclusive	complementary
monopolistic	competitive
unitary	composite
singular	differentiated
temporality	
accomplished	incipient
determinate	Indeterminate
settled	**unsettled**

exclusive (i.e. unlimited, original, and primary). This precludes an entity such as the EU, which stands in relation to states as something other than a state, from possessing them.

B. Capacity, Spatiality, Temporality

But how might we elaborate the comparative attributes of the EU in more positive terms? In so doing in the somewhat stylized manner summarized in Table 2.1, I do not suggest that these structural questions are by any means *resolved* at the EU level (any more than I claim that the state exhibits the structural features attributed to it in pure form). The sheer range and variation of theoretical output dealing with structural matters in the EU indicates a messier picture. This work tends to go by the name of 'integration theory',[30] itself a somewhat complacently one-sided label, given that in many eyes the contemporary EU lends itself to understanding in less

[30] The three most significant schools of structural thought within integration theory are federalism, neofunctionalism, and intergovernmentalism, but there are countless nuances and variations. For a good recent overview, see S. Saurugger *Theoretical Approaches to European Integration* (2014).

confidently developmental terms, perhaps even as inclining towards 'disintegration'.[31] The aim here instead is to show the conditions of possibility out of which the general structural form of the EU has evolved and may continue to do so. Within these parameters, there is much scope for choice, controversy, disagreement, and reformation in line with rather different visions of the scope and potential of the EU as a polity type—which visions in turn may be connected to different preferences as to the substantive aims of the EU.

Our comparative structural exercise can be organized under three general headings—*capacity, spatiality, and temporality*—each with more specific subheadings. We begin with the fundamental matter of *capacity*, and so with the more restricted breadth and depth of the EU polity horizon. As we have seen, the extensity and intensity of collective action achievable through the high modern state in terms of its peaks of sovereignty, constituent power, and primary citizenship implies a claim on behalf of a community to be the source and container of an authority of an order that is in principle comprehensive and absolute, and so only self-limiting in jurisdictional reach and depth, and to provide the primary political frame of reference for its members. This is reflected in the self-referential character of the state's constitutional posture—its orientation as a *comprehensively* self-sufficient and *elementary* form of political organization, operating through the collective agency of a community of individuals for whom it provides a *prior* political identity. In comparison, the EU possesses both a narrower competence and a less penetrative reach within that narrower competence, and so a jurisdiction only *partial* in scope and effective capacity. The EU is also a polity that, at least as understood in chronological terms, lacks original collective agency and is instead constituted through and *derivative* of the states as the most elementary expression of constituent power, so attracting a political identity secondary and *accessory* to that of state citizenship.

What lies at the root of this most basic set of distinctions? The more restricted capacity of the EU polity in terms of sovereignty, constituent power, and political identity finds its socio-historical explanation in terms of the very rationale of the entity in question. A useful starting point in demonstrating this is Michael Oakeshott's understanding of the history of the political thought and practice out of which the modern state emerged as a tension between two kinds of political association. He characterized each with terms drawn from Roman private law: *societas*, or civil association, on the one hand; and *universitas*, or enterprise association, on the other.[32] Or to use von Hayek's similar and derivative terminology, the distinction lies between *nomocracy* and *teleocracy*.[33] Put simply, the *societas* or nomocracy is based on the acceptance of common rules as grounding an

[31] See e.g. D. Webber, *European Disintegration? The Politics of Crisis in the European Union* (2019).
[32] M. Oakeshott, *On Human Conduct* (1975) 199–203.
[33] F. von Hayek, *Law, Legislation and Liberty vol.1—Rules and Order* (1976).

expansive notion of political society as a general domain of relatively free-floating relationships without prior specification of common ends, while the *universitas* or teleocracy stands for a more specific form of cooperation animated by some set collective purpose.

We need to be careful how far and in which direction we pursue this distinction. The broader political philosophical orientation of both Oakeshott and von Hayek[34] suggests that it might be used to justify a strictly limited role for the state as a pure *societas*—as a pact whose collective bonds are restricted to those necessary to allow individual interests maximum scope to flourish in a framework of voluntary relations. As Oakeshott himself insists, however, that would be a caricature. Within the category of states there are no perfect cases of *societas*, or, indeed, of *universitas*, only hybrids variously placed along a continuum.[35] Yet, once we concede this more spectral understanding, we can see that the state remains a more encompassing, *societas*-type association than any other type of entity. It speaks to the settled framework for the organization of a common form of life within a particular political society viewed as a whole, whether and to what extent that settlement be articulated in 'thin' voluntarist terms or in terms of a 'thicker' sense of common commitments. In so doing it differs markedly from the EU which, at least in earlier incarnations, supplied a bespoke tool for the pursuit of particular shared ends, notably the economic prosperity that would flow from the establishment of a common market.

The same purpose-based distinction can be developed, and its limits more fully drawn, by reference to different uses of the language of 'publicness'. On the one hand, the state claims in principle to embody and to pursue the general *public good* of a political community that recognizes itself as such; *as* a single and distinct public, and so as possessing the requisite level of affinity and mutual sympathy to put and hold matters in common and to evaluate its achievements by reference to the collective as a whole. On the other hand, the EU was from the outset a vehicle for the pursuit of discrete jointly generated *public goods* by parties bonded for those specific and limited objectives.[36] Yet, in practice, matters become more mixed. On

[34] Both being members of Perry Anderson's so-called 'intransigent Right'. See P. Anderson, 'The Intransigent Right: Michael Oakeshott, Leo Strauss, Carl Schmitt, Friedrich von Hayek', in his *Spectrum: From Right to Left in the World of Ideas* (2005) 3.

[35] For Oakeshott, a state, *in nuce*, 'may . . . be understood as an unresolved tension between the two irreconcilable dispositions represented by the words *societas* and *universitas*': Oakeshott (n. 32) 200–201.

[36] I do not mean to restrict 'public goods' to those so defined in the classical economic sense. Public goods under that narrow definition are socially assured or generated goods characterized, first and foremost, by non-excludability of access to their enjoyment—just as public 'bads' may be said to suffer from non-excludability of vulnerability to harm—and, secondly, by non-rivalry of consumption. See e.g. M. Olsen, *The Logic of Collective Action* (1971). The term 'public goods' in the broader sense (sometimes also called collective, communal, common, shared, or social goods) refers to particular products, resources, or conditions that are of value to individuals and are more effectively realized or better enjoyed on a collective basis. Ranging beyond the material objects and conditions covered by the classic definition, such as a bridge, a railway network, or clean air, this would embrace more general institutions or forms of social organization such as democracy or the rule of law, or even more abstract states, such as conviviality or solidarity. Unlike the singular sense of the public good, the identification of public goods,

the one hand, all states, both in reliance upon and in 'thickening' their claim to embody an already integrated sense of the general public good, come to pursue particular public goods to a greater or lesser extent. On the other hand, certain visions of the EU, particularly of the federalist and neo-functionalist variety, see the unprecedented (for a non-state polity) intensity and scope of its aggregate pursuit of particular public goods as a means to generate a general and integrated sense of the supranational public good. That more ambitious sense of supranational publicness was an aspiration present in some quarters from the outset, but is becoming (for its supporters) more pressing as the Union's institutional means and policy remit gradually extend, and its growing influence is a factor to which we shall return. Nevertheless, the founding *public goods/public good* distinction remains an important one for our understanding of the basic structural properties of the EU.

The more limited standing of the EU in terms of capacity, in turn, has implications for its spatiality; that is, for how it relates to other polities implicated in the same territorial and jurisdictional space. The only *self*-limiting state polity treats other law-sites either as its (mutually exclusive) fully sovereign counterparts, or, in the case of non-state sites, as entities to whom certain limited powers are delegated or that perform strictly demarcated functions. Indeed, the EU itself, for all its unprecedented capacity as a non-state polity, was traditionally viewed in such dependent or subsidiary terms by many who adopted a state-centred perspective.[37] The spatial features of the only partial EU polity perforce look quite different from those of the comprehensive state model. We may summarize this by saying that the sovereign state has a self-contained framework of authority, and its web of exchanges with other polities, however dense in today's world, are a product of its own political agency, whereas the EU has a constitutively relational quality. It was born of other (state) polities and its relational properties have been intrinsic to its structural evolution. First, it is a polity whose jurisdiction and capacity is only partial; thus inevitably in the pursuit of its public policy objectives these overlap the boundaries of other polities and their jurisdictions. Secondly, and as a deeper implication of its relational character, the EU can be understood to represent the 'crowded space' at the point of intersection of various different polities. These two aspects of its situation—'inside-out' boundary overlap and 'outside-in' interlocking—indicate four further distinguishing features of the EU as a structurally complex constitutional polity.

whether narrowly or widely defined, is prior to and indifferent to their sponsorship by any particular public. See further, Walker, 'The European Public Good and European Public Goods' Edinburgh School of Law Research Paper Series, 2020/20; available at: https://papers.ssrn.com/sol3/papers.cfm?abstract_id=3712265.

[37] See e.g. P. Lindseth, *Power and Legitimacy: Reconciling Europe and the Nation State* (2010). For evidence of more expansive views of the role and standing of the EU, see e.g. C. Sternberg, *The Struggle for EU Legitimacy: Public Contestation, 1950–2005* (2013).

The first 'inside-out' perspective accounts for two contending features of the EU's open and overlapping boundaries. Here, it should be noted, there applies with particular force the caveat that the EU itself has contributed to the transformation of the state in ways that soften its 'ideal typical' contrast with the EU, including the state's orientation towards the EU as a merely dependent or subsidiary polity.[38] In order to sharpen our conceptual tools, however, we should temporarily set aside that caveat. What, then, are the two distinctive features of the EU? On the one hand, as a limited polity in terms of scope and capacity, the EU's orientation towards its Member States is not that of the modern state classically understood as the comprehensive and *exclusive* source of final authority, but instead often that of a collaborative and *complementary* polity. It seeks through various inter-systemic normative 'bridging mechanisms'[39]—from the preliminary reference procedure to the use of the Open Method of Co-ordination[40]—to coordinate its objectives and its means for realizing its objectives with these other polities. On the other hand, the shift from self-reference to external reference also has a less ordered connotation, and again the contrast with the system of high modern states, at least as conventionally understood, is marked. The exclusively empowered and self-sufficient state in the ideal typical modern image tends to treat its domain of authority, and the domain of authority of other exclusively empowered and self-sufficient states, in *monopolistic* terms—any grant of authority to others is within its retractable gift. The polity of the EU has extensive and unavoidable jurisdictional overlap with other polities—not only with Member State polities but also with non-Member States and other international organizations. Alongside and in some tension with its collaborative approach to these other polities, the EU as a policy entrepreneur in matters as diverse as carbon emissions, food safety, and peace-brokering, can also find itself in a rivalrous and *competitive* relationship with these same polities over their respective domains of authority.[41]

The situation is further complicated by the third and fourth 'outside-in' relational dimensions of the EU polity. Here the logic of polity interpenetration extends a stage further. The environment of polity diversity is understood not just to affect the margins—the sometimes cooperative and sometimes contested boundaries—of the EU polity, but to shape its internal composition. Whereas the comprehensively and exclusively authorized state polity, grounded in the unitary collective agency

[38] The quite voluminous literature on constitutional pluralism in the EU, for example, is predicated on the gradual development of a more equal and cooperative form of communication and normative exchange between national and supranational legal orders (and their apex courts), neither of which understands itself as the sole legal authority within its sphere of competence; see G. Davies and M. Avbelj, *Research Handbook on Legal Pluralism and EU Law* (2018).

[39] S. Weatherill, *Law and Integration in the European Union* (1995) chs 4–5.

[40] See e.g. G. de Burca and J. Scott (eds), *Law and New Governance in the EU and the US* (2006).

[41] For discussion of a range of complementary and competitive techniques in the EU's external relations, see Scott, 'Extraterritoriality and Territorial Extension in EU Law', 62 *American Journal of Comparative Law* (2013) 87.

of the 'people' or 'nation', possesses a *simple* form of structural integrity—one in which all institutional parts contribute to and are resolved in terms of one and the same polity whole with its own integrated sense of the public good—the EU may instead be viewed as a *composite* entity. It is a hybrid—a 'mixed'[42] or 'compound'[43] structure—which through its different institutions with their different normative emphases reflects and interlocks its different polity-sourced parts. Whereas the Council and the European Council are primarily seen as the 'intergovernmental' vehicle of the Member States, and the Commission and—more controversially—the Court of Justice are viewed as the conduit of the 'supranational' interest, the European Parliament is often understood as the 'federal' representative of the European *demos* conceived of as a self-standing popular force in a manner more analogous to the constituent power of independent statehood.[44]

As a further consequence of its unitary source, the state polity also possesses a basic *singularity* of normative design. It is based on a set of common commitments in which norms are either generally applicable across the polity as a whole; or where a measure of diversity is allowed to different territorial, ethnic, or functional parts, that diversity is the product of a single, multilaterally negotiated, collectively endorsed, and largely symmetrical design. In contrast, the EU, reflected in and encouraged by five waves of Enlargement, has increasingly come to permit a more *differentiated* normative arrangement where the separate national parts engage in bilateral negotiation with the supranational polity in pursuit of optimal arrangements. The most prominent cases are Economic and Monetary Union, with membership of the Eurozone gradually increasing from 11 to 19 states, and the Schengen Agreement on open borders, signed by 5 out of the then 10 members 30 years ago, and today comprising 26 parties, only 22 of them EU members. Yet this is the tip of the iceberg, with as many as 50 types of differentiation provided under the treaties.[45] Moreover, as in the abortive pre-Brexit agreement to exclude the UK from the *telos* of 'ever closer Union', discussions of the future of the EU increasingly place a more differentiated architecture centre-stage.[46]

Alongside these four spatial features of the constitutional particularity of the EU there are two distinguishing features of its *temporality*. Although their resilience is highly variable[47] and their sequence of development differs markedly,[48] we

[42] See e.g. Majone, 'Delegation of Regulatory Powers in a Mixed Polity', 8 *European Law Journal* (2002) 319; MacCormick (n. 1) ch. 9.

[43] S. Fabbrini, *Compound Democracies: Why the United States and Europe are becoming similar* (2007).

[44] See e.g. J. Weiler, *The Constitution of Europe* (1999) ch. 8.

[45] See e.g. D. Leuffen, B. Rittberger, and F. Schimmelfennig, *Differentiated Integration: Explaining Variation in the European Union* (2013).

[46] European Council—Conclusions (18–19 February 2016), available at https://www.consilium.europa.eu/media/21787/0216-euco-conclusions.pdf (accessed 11 November 2020).

[47] See e.g. Z. Elkins, T. Ginsburg, and J. Melton, *The Endurance of National Constitutions* (2009) chs 2 and 4.

[48] See e.g. M. Rosenfeld, *The Identity of the Constitutional Subject: Selfhood, Citizenship, Culture and Community* (2010) chs 5–7.

encounter the vast majority of enduring state constitutions and associated systems of public law as achieved states of affairs. We typically confront them as always/already 'thickly' *accomplished* projects whose dynamic is one of consolidation or adaptation of that which has already been constructed. In contrast, the EU today, even though it has already survived longer than the constitutional orders of many state polities,[49] remains a constitutional work in progress—an *incipient* structure still self-consciously under construction rather than a fully realized form. Moreover, the EU's unfinished condition is not just empirical but also conceptual. Whereas the completeness of the state constitutional model presupposes a recognizable template for its mature form, and so a *determinacy* and finality of conception, the incompleteness of the EU and its irreducibility to these state-centred terms suggests the absence of any such settled model of its mature form—an *indeterminacy* and open-endedness of conception that remains subject to contestation in terms of different general polity visions. Where any particular state refers back to a received paradigm of statehood, the EU looks forward as it continues to fashion its own bespoke model.

A final distinctive characteristic of EU constitutionalism flows from—indeed, summarizes—all previous features. The state constitutional polity is a *settled* political form. Its embeddedness, self-sufficiency, self-containment, and structural unity, and its typical manifestation as an already accomplished state and conformity to a familiar template, mean that neither its basic eligibility as a constitutional polity nor the general terms on which that eligibility depends are the subject of serious contestation. That does not mean that its basic status *qua* constitutional state will not be challenged. The very identity of the state or, more commonly, its satisfaction of basic constitutional standards, may be contested, both externally and internally. But however sharply engaged, the contest is about specific cases rather than the general type. The EU is instead a constitutionally unsettled and disputable polity. In light of its limited jurisdiction, its secondary form of political identity and agency, its open and unsettled relationship with states and other polities, its hybrid structure, and its still emergent status and provisional conception, both its basic eligibility as a constitutional polity and the terms on which that eligibility rest are subject to continuing uncertainty and contestation.

In a nutshell, as set out earlier in Table 2.1, whereas the state, at least in its dominant high modern form, has generally been considered as a comprehensive, elementary, prior, nomocratic, exclusive, monopolistic, relatively simple, singular, accomplished, determinate and settled political form and constitutional polity, the EU remains a partial, derivative, accessory, teleocratic, complementary, competitive, composite, differentiated, incipient, indeterminate, and unsettled political form and constitutional polity.

[49] According to Elkins *et al.*, the average life expectancy of a modern state constitution is 19 years: Elkins, Ginsburg, and Melton (n. 47) 2.

4. The Challenge to EU Legal Theory

A. The Weakness of Familiar Supports

When we come to explain and evaluate the role of law and legal actors in the EU in light of these structural features we face a basic conundrum. On the one hand, EU law appears to lack many of the supportive conditions we are familiar with in the state context. On the other hand, that weakness notwithstanding, law appears even more central to the operation of the EU polity than to the national polity. Only by looking closely at how the deep assumptions associated with the different candidate schools of legal theory may apply differently in the case of the EU, with its distinctive structural features, can we unlock this conundrum.

What of the absent supportive conditions? Jürgen Habermas has recently revived and reinforced a line of thinking that holds the EU legal order to be novel in its mode of articulation of the political order since, unlike the state, it is effectively underpinned neither by a sovereign political will, nor by *sittlichkeit* (the idea of a prior common ethical framework).[50] These features often hang together in the state context—democratic foundations reflecting and reinforcing the existence of elements of a common societal culture, and law providing a medium to channel and express both. EU law, in contrast, cannot rely heavily on the claims of legal efficacy associated either with a clearly institutionalized common will or with a strong cultural affinity, and so cannot draw unreservedly on the resources either of the positivist or the culturalist tradition of legal theory.

With regard to the positivist tradition, the problem has become more marked over time. Simply put, the EU today has no clear line of democratic 'input legitimacy'[51] and so no clear dividend for a positivist tracing of sources to unearth and declare. Unlike the state, there is no single undisputed political *voluntas*, whether—to name the main rival candidates[52]—that be the undifferentiated European citizenry, the European states or 'peoples' in perpetual combination, each national sovereign people considered separately, or some combination of the above. Yet in the earlier phase of European integration, as we have already noted, there is a case for arguing that, in pedigree terms, there was a default answer; that the EU was merely a special form of delegate of each of the national sovereignties considered separately, with their continuing mandate supplied by a rolling programme of international agreements. It was a delegated authority possessed of an unusually extensive but still clearly demarcated jurisdiction—fundamentally more

[50] Habermas, 'Plea for a Constitutionalization of International Law', 40 *Philosophy and Social Criticism* (2014) 5–11.

[51] F. Scharpf, *Governing in Europe: Effective and Democratic?* (1999) ch. 1.

[52] For discussion of options, see Patberg, 'Challenging the Masters of the Treaties: Emerging Narratives of Constituent Power in the European Union', 7 *Global Constitutionalism* (2018) 263.

concerned with the administrative implementation of prior Treaty objectives than the articulation of its own agenda.[53]

Writing in the early 1980s, Joseph Weiler had teased out the implications of this by drawing attention to the 'dual character of supranationalism'.[54] At that point, developed legal supranationalism in the internal market—framed by the Court of Justice's gradual assertion of the vigorous formal properties of the EU as an autonomous legal system with a distinct Treaty pedigree, complete with supremacy over national law in matters within its jurisdiction, direct effect, pre-emptive authority, and independent standards of rights protection—stood in contrast to a modestly conceived political supranationalism. Yet the two were symbiotically related. The early prominence of legal supranationalism, and its self-assertion as superordinate to the national legal orders of the Member States, was encouraged or acquiesced in precisely *because* political supranationalism remained so modest, with a relatively limited jurisdiction and the Member States retaining a veto power in most areas of European policy-making within that jurisdiction.

This element of input legitimacy was important not only in its own terms—as an assertion of an authoritative source—but also because it provided particularly strong support for some of the 'output' benefits associated with positivism. The virtues of a coherent framework of legislative planning for the world's largest single market, and of certainty and predictability for those operating within the market, flowed more easily from a positivist baseline. That baseline also provided a platform for the emergence of a prominent supranational judiciary; a cadre largely drawn from the civilian jurisdictions of Europe with their strong tradition of legal formalism. Their confidently legalistic mindset and self-presentation was facilitated by a stable consensus over the clearly delineated sources of EU law, as well as by the emphasis within the first generation of EU law of a philosophy of individual economic right-centred 'negative integration'[55] with which the tradition of legal formalism had long been familiar. They were able to populate their newly autonomous legal order with rules and concepts that could themselves be treated as the autonomous product of that new order, and therefore apparently insulated from the controversies of everyday politics and disputed long-term objectives.[56]

But the conditions which allowed the EU's legislative product to be treated as an attenuated form of national sovereignty of each Member State in aggregate did not last. From the Single European Act onwards, expansion of legislative jurisdiction beyond the positive-sum market-making core towards areas of security, economic, and social policy that were more transparently controversial or involved an uneven distribution of winners and losers across national boundaries, as well as the

[53] See e.g. Lindseth (n. 37).
[54] Weiler, 'The Community System: The Dual Character of Supranationalism', *Yearbook of European Law* (1981) 267.
[55] Scharpf (n. 51) ch. 2.
[56] See e.g. Weiler (n. 44) ch. 5.

gradual development of Qualified Majority Voting in the Council and the greater involvement of the European Parliament in the legislative process in response to this extended jurisdiction, tended towards a more multi-polar balance of power. The pedigree question thus became more contentious—with the intensification of clashes between the Court of Justice and national apex courts about the division of competence in increasingly overlapping policy domains being the most obvious manifestation of this.[57] The legitimacy dividend of law's connection to a nationally democratic source of authority became depleted without being adequately compensated for by the European Parliament's relatively weak new pan-European claim. In a nutshell, while many of the 'output legitimacy' benefits associated with the EU legal order's positive foundations remained relatively robust, this was no longer matched to and complemented by a strong element of 'input legitimacy'.

If we turn to the culturalist tradition, we see a similar picture of an increasingly challenged vein of legitimacy. There have been persistent claims linking the EU to a common continental cultural heritage, but these have always been of limited strength and carried some unwanted connotations. The idea of a European *Rechtsgemeinschaft* (roughly translatable as 'Community of the Rule of Law') was championed by Walter Hallstein, the first President of the EEC, and was influential in the early understanding of integration in key supranational circles.[58] We have already noted how the work of the Court of Justice in securing an autonomous and effective supranational legal order owed much to the firm positivist foundations of the Treaties and to the way in which these supported a method of legal formalism familiar from various national traditions. Yet it would be wrong to see support for integration as a mere legalistic reflex and as entirely empty of pro-European cultural content. Instead, alongside the ingrained habits of formalism, we see the gathering of an attitude that, acknowledging the absence of a deeper common culture and *sittlichkeit* to underpin the new community, would take Hallstein's cue to favour and fashion a more focused legal-cultural project at the European centre.[59] As well as supporting various elements of a vertical discipline (direct effect, supremacy, etc.), in seeking to refine and impose a specifically law-themed regime of integration, this approach would also draw upon and cultivate certain horizontal vectors of connection. For example, a narrative of 'common constitutional traditions' became woven through the EU's attachment to fundamental rights, both in its case-law[60] and, subsequently, its Treaty sources.[61] Additionally, many so-called general

[57] See e.g. Walker, 'Constitutional Pluralism Revisited', 23 *European Law Journal* (2016) 333–355.

[58] For his mature reflections, see W. Hallstein, *Europe in the Making* (1972).

[59] See Stein, 'Lawyers, Judges, and the Making of a Transnational Constitution', 75 *American Journal of International Law* (1981) 1.

[60] *Internationale Handelsgesellschaft* (11/70 [1970]) ('*Solange I*').

[61] Treaty on European Union, Art. 6; see further, the 'Common Constitutional Traditions in Europe Project' (2018–21) initiated by the European Law Institute in Vienna, available at https://www.europeanlawinstitute.eu/projects-publications/current-projects-feasibility-studies-and-other-activities/current-projects/common-constitutional-traditions-in-europe/ (accessed 11 November 2020).

principles of EU law, such as proportionality, subsidiarity, legal certainty, and the protection of fundamental rights, present both as the consolidation of strands of a transnationally shared legal culture and as the platform for new forms of mutual learning and convergence. The elevation of the 'Rule of Law' itself to the status of a foundational value of the Union in the 1998 Treaty of Amsterdam, together with the introduction of a sanctioning procedure for Member States in breach of core values,[62] and, more recently, the rolling out of a broader Commission-led Rule of Law monitoring framework, reinforces the sense of the centrality of law and of high legal officialdom to a cultural project of integration.[63]

The affirmation and projection of elements of a common legal heritage along these lines should not be discounted and, as we shall see later, it is a current that also flows into the more focused pragmatic argument for the legitimacy of European law. Yet these initiatives are selective in focus, of variable impact, and in some cases carry, or may seem to carry, imperialistic pretentions—conveying a sense of the innate superiority of the European legal cultural tradition.[64] More precisely, they convey the sense of the superiority of *one specific* European legal cultural tradition, for their tendency to promote 'one best way' also runs against the grain of successive Enlargements and the adoption of the motto of 'unity in diversity'.[65] At the level of performative politics, the dangers of this have been exposed in the long-running, ideologically charged dispute with the strongly nationalistic governments of Hungary and Poland over the legitimacy of reforms affecting the constitutional independence of their state judiciaries. The leaders of the two post-Central and Eastern European Enlargement states have been quick to dismiss criticism of their populist assaults on the domestic constitutional order on the pretext that this represents the difference-blind imposition of a certain type of liberal-constitutional orthodoxy at the European centre.[66]

More soberly, in their 'top-down' generation and selective attention, these cultural initiatives can also be criticized as elitist—their manifestation more indicative of a common judicial and administrative and diplomatic culture rather than a shared *popular* European culture.[67] The German-inspired idea of a *europäischer*

[62] Treaty on European Union, Art. 7.

[63] For a recent Commission initiative to reconsider the 2014 Rule of Law monitoring framework, see 'The Commission opens a debate to strengthen the rule of law in the EU', Brussels, 3 April 2019, available at https://europa.eu/rapid/press-release_IP-19-1912_en.pdf (accessed 11 November 2020).

[64] As in the reference to a 'Special area of human hope' in the Preamble to the 2004 Draft Constitutional Treaty. (2004/C 310); see also von Bogdandy, 'The European Constitution and European Identity: Text and Subtext of the Treaty establishing a Constitution for Europe', 3 *International Journal of Constitutional Law* (2005) 473.

[65] Which became the EU's motto in 2000.

[66] See e.g. W. Sadurski, *Poland's Constitutional Breakdown* (2019) esp. chs 8 and 9; Scheppele, 'Autocratic Legalism', 85 *University of Chicago Law Review* (2018) 545–583.

[67] The notion of a European *Rechtsgemeinschaft* sponsored by Hallstein has been criticized as increasingly divorced from national legal-cultural concerns and sensibilities; seevon Bogdandy, 'Beyond the Rechtsgemeinschaft, with Trust—Reframing the Concept of European Rule of Law', Max Planck Institute for Comparative Public Law & International Law (MPIL) Research Paper No. 2018-02,

Verfassungsgerichtsverbund ('A European Club of Constitutional Courts'[68]) may, in the Hallstein tradition, speak to the development of a common judicial vernacular amongst national constitutional courts and the Court of Justice that can deflect or moderate conflict arising from an ever denser interlocking of national and supranational jurisdictions. But the very idea of 'club government' projects a sense of a closed circle of privilege—a contemplative arena distant from the material conditions and sentiments of ordinary Europeans.

While the imperialist and elitist tendency should not be overstated, it is subtly reinforced if we look to the relevance of the broader idealist tradition of legal theory in the development of EU law. In the grand claims made for EU law in the Preambles and common provisions of the key Treaties, the emphasis upon universal morality is at least as strong as the emphasis on continental cultural distinctiveness. This may reflect an awareness of the 'thinness' of any claim to shared cultural distinctiveness. It may also reflect a complacent assumption that the two are convergent—that the universalism of values is proof of their European-ness and, equally, the European-ness of values is proof of their universal warrant.[69] In turn, this 'particular universalism'[70] finds an amplifying presence, but also a strong anti-imperial reaction, in the ways in which the EU has sought to export its ethical standards and aspects of its legal *acquis* in the context of its external relations, whether through its Enlargement policy, its Neighbourhood policy, or more broadly.[71]

30 January 2018, available at SSRN: https://ssrn.com/abstract=3103691 or http://dx.doi.org/10.2139/ssrn.3103691 (accessed 11 November 2020). On the foundational influence of European legal elites more generally, see A. Vauchez, *Brokering Europe: Euro-Lawyers and the Making of a Transnational Policy* (2015).

[68] See e.g. Steinbas, 'Piercing the Hull', *Verfassungsblog* (12 January 2019), available at https://verfassungsblog.de/piercing-the-hull/ (accessed 11 November 2020).

[69] See e.g. the blend of universalism and distinctiveness of origins evident in the Preamble to the 2004 Draft Constitutional Treaty, later reproduced in the Preamble to the Treaty on European Union (as amended by the Treaty of Lisbon (2007/C 306/01): 'Drawing inspiration from the cultural, religious and humanist inheritance of Europe, from which have developed the universal values of the inviolable and inalienable rights of the human person, freedom, democracy, equality and the rule of law . . .'

[70] See e.g. Walker, 'The Place of European Law', in G. De Burca and J. Weiler (eds), *The Worlds of EU Constitutionalism* (2012) 57.

[71] For example, Art. 3(1) of the Treaty on European Union (TEU) states that the Union's aim 'is to promote peace, its values and the well-being of its peoples'; these aims are reproduced in Art. 3(5) (international promotion) and Art. 49 (accession). For analysis, see e.g. Manners, 'Normative Power Europe: A Contradiction in Terms?', 40 *Journal of Common Market Studies* (2002) 235–258; Johansson-Nogués, 'The (Non-)Normative Power EU and the European Neighbourhood Policy: An Exceptional Policy for an Exceptional Actor', 7 *European Journal of Political Economy* (2007) 181–194; Kleinfeld and Nicolaidis, 'Can a Post-Colonial Power Export the Rule of Law? Elements of a General Framework', in G. Palombella and N. Walker (eds), *Relocating the Rule of Law* (2008) 139–169.

B. The Virtue of Necessity

If EU law today represents neither a strong instrumental good securely supported by the political will of a clear democratic voice, nor a strong symbolic good tied to and reflecting and reinforcing a particular cultural way of life, how might this apparent weakness underscore rather than undermine its functioning? The answer involves distilling virtue from necessity. The key lies in understanding EU law's *less supported* situation, compared to state law, as also one of *lesser dependence*, and so as also somehow requiring and enabling a more robustly autonomous role.

Renaud Dehousse and Joseph Weiler once alluded to something like this in describing EU law as the 'agent and object of integration';[72] in other words, as both the means and end of the European project, each element supporting the other.[73] We may put it more boldly. We may assert that EU law has established itself as the *principal* 'agent and object of integration' in the supranational context. The core technique of integration could not be to offer law as an instrument of political will backed by force, thereby treating law as a *secondary* and derivative agent of political accomplishment—as in the positivist understanding of the state tradition. Nor could the object of integration be to sustain a thick political community, of which law would be a trace and expression, so treating law as a *secondary* and derivative object of integration—as in the context of the state and national culture. Rather, EU law was conceived as a new type of *primary* agent and object—means and end—a division and combination of legal labour that recalls and recasts the duality of law's normative and expressive functions. And, crucially, in pursuing this double track EU law was bound to draw heavily upon the assets of legal pragmatism.

As regards the question of agency, EU law is not an instrument for channelling a prior general political authority and its integrated sense of the public good; rather it is a primary means for stabilizing mutual commitments to achieve various complex public goods under a new transnational political authority. The lack of clear prior underpinnings of democratic authority together with other structural features of the EU—the emphasis on a plural, shifting, and incomplete *telos*, the need to find optimal ways of interfacing with and adding value to other polities, and the complexities of managing internal differentiation and of resolving the tensions within a composite institutional structure oriented towards different constituencies—combine to place a premium on the twin pragmatic virtues; both the *security* and the *versatility* of legal technique. Law matters so much precisely because of its capacity to 'get things done' where other steering mechanisms cannot. This capacity is also associated with the 'output' side of legal positivism but in the

[72] Dehousse and Weiler, 'The Legal Dimension', in W. Wallace (ed.), *The Dynamics of European Integration* (1990) 234, 242.

[73] See further, Augenstein and Dawson, 'What Law for What Polity? "Integration Through Law" in the European Union Revisited' in D. Augenstein (ed.), *'Integration through Law' Revisited: The Making of the European Polity* (2012).

case of pragmatism, importantly, the focus is more on its dependable contextual adaptability and less on its steady generality and uniformity of coverage.

On the one hand, as we see from the earliest polity-defining cases of *Van Gend en Loos*[74] and *Costa*,[75] the clarity and certainty that law can deliver secures against free-riding in a context of highly provisional trust where other underpinnings of commonality may be absent. This is so especially as regards the 'four freedoms', with their emphasis upon the kinds of individual rights and obligations that law is particularly effective at registering and protecting. In an environment of market-making where the temptation for each national member of the continental trade-liberalizing cartel to engage in protectionism while exploiting the general opening of the markets of other national members posed a significant collective action problem, law performed a vital disciplining function. The reliable application and enforcement of the rules of the game by independent legal institutions, with the Court of Justice at the apex of the system, was crucial in rendering common commitments more credible.[76]

On the other hand, the increasing need to track a shifting horizon of policy goals and to do so in a crowded regulatory space and in a context of multi-polar governance with high levels of internal plurality and polity overlap, has meant that law's versatility is repeatedly called upon. Throughout the history of EU law we see successive new waves of legally innovative methods of governance—from the basic form of directives, to the New Approach to Harmonization, to mutual recognition,[77] to Comitology, to the Open Method of Co-ordination,[78] and to ever more complex forms of differentiated integration and ever more diverse methods of conditionality in external relations.[79] Where a different and changing legal eco-system has required ever-altering methods, law's flexibility as a tool has been at a premium.

As regards EU law as an object of integration, again virtue has been a function of necessity. In the absence—or only flickering presence—of other 'sacred' objects on which it can reflect—whether a clear affirmation of continental popular will, a popular European culture, or a universal good—law *itself* has often been projected as a prominent mark and symbol of (pragmatically adaptive) community at the EU level. The Customs Union, the Single Market, the '1992' Project, the Area of Freedom, Security and Justice, the Eurozone, EMU, the euro itself, European

[74] Case 26/62, *Van Gend en Loos v. Nederlandse Administratie der Belastingen* (EU:C:1963:1).

[75] Case 6/64, *Flaminio Costa v. ENEL* (EU:C:1964:66).

[76] See e.g. Shapiro, 'The European Court of Justice', in P. Craig and G. de Búrca, *The Evolution of EU Law* (1st ed., 1999) 321.

[77] Case 120/78, *Rewe-Zentral AG v. Bundesmonopolverwaltung für Branntwein ('Cassis de Dijon')* (EU:C:1979:42).

[78] See De Burca and Scott (n. 40); see also Scott and Trubek, 'Mind the Gap: Law and New Approaches to Governance in the European Union', 8 *European Law Journal* (2002) 1–18; E. Psychogiopoulou, 'Policy Co-ordination in the EU: Taking Stock of the Open Method of Co-ordination', 3 *European Papers* (2018) 203.

[79] See Scott (n. 41).

citizenship, the Central and Eastern European Enlargement, and perhaps most vividly (but also, as we shall see, problematically)[80] of all, the Constitutional Treaty project of 2003–2005,[81] are amongst the key artefacts that have been presented as strongly legally coded measures of community. A similar point about the prominent legal registering of the EU's achievements can be made about its bespoke legal institutions, in particular the Court of Justice, its assiduous cultivation of a posture of formal legal rectitude, and its investment in a house culture of integration-through-law[82] feeding into a public reputation as the dignified expression of the incremental progress of the law-centred polity.

Separately and in combination these events, processes, and institutional achievements are cast widely as cultural objects—manifestations of a shared world of meaning and accomplishment—that are legible and primarily expressible in legal form. They have become prominent *self-signifiers*, pointing to the significance of their own achievement, rather than being merely or mainly of secondary and derivative import in signifying other and prior cultural features of the polity, as is often the case with polity-evocative legal symbols in the national context.[83]

It is worth reiterating, in summary, how the contribution of legal pragmatism in the EU context in some measure relies upon yet is also quite separate from and significantly additional to the relatively modest offerings of legal positivism and of culturalism (and also of culturalism's idealist cousin). The emphasis on legal form and design in securing a flexible delivery capacity builds on the residual positivist pedigree, and the integrationist orientation of a narrow legal-cultural elite helped put and keep law at the front of the supranational project. Yet legal pragmatism brings a range of additional attributes well suited to the distinctive supranational context, adding value both as a technique of governance and as a symbolic good. The pragmatic method's output-oriented focus and openness to institutional versatility—as much an acquired habit and cumulative pattern of adjustment to and innovation before fluid environmental demands as a conscious orientation—is well attuned to a polity of shifting objectives, changing conditions, and requirements of institutional delivery, and a still provisional sense of its definitive structure. And the legacy of that sustained pattern of legally coded adjustment and

80 See Section 5.B.

81 For a retrospective, see Walker, 'Europe's Constitutional Overture', in N. W. Barber, M. Cahill, and R. Ekins (eds), *The Rise and Fall of the European Constitution* (2018) 177–196; see also Maduro, 'The Importance of Being Called a Constitution: Constitutional Authority and the Authority of Constitutionalism', 3 *International Journal of Constitutional Law* (2005) 332–356.

82 See e.g. Weiler (n. 44) ch. 5; Stone Sweet, 'The European Court of Justice' in P. Craig and G. de Búrca (eds), *The Evolution of EU Law* (2nd ed., 2011) 121; Shapiro (n. 76).

83 As noted earlier, in Section 1, law always performs expressive functions alongside its instrumental functions, but it is unusual for it to have such a prominent self-signifying function as in the EU case. The partial exception is as regards written Constitutions. Even in the state context, constitutions, particularly those of long duration, can become key tokens of community in their own right. At the same time, however, more so than in the case of the legal symbols of the EU they remain powerful ways of projecting other aspects and accomplishments of common culture.

innovation is present in a series of events and institutions, themselves framed in legal terms, that express these pragmatic strengths of the supranational construction before a wider audience.

5. Conclusion: Theorizing the Future

A. The Limits of Pragmatism

Just how resourceful is the pragmatic strain in EU law, and how sustainable is an orientation that relies so much on that strain to legitimate a polity in which the idea of legal authority figures so prominently? It was the lack of strong democratic and cultural supports that led to a greater emphasis on a pragmatic approach to EU law in the first place and that only encourages its continued expansion, yet that expansion both exposes certain inherent weaknesses in the pragmatic approach and reveals growing tensions in its relationship with these other supporting legal narratives. We may present these difficulties synoptically in terms of four paradoxes.

First, and most generally, there is the *paradox of support*. The more we lack the society-specific political and cultural underpinnings familiar from state law, the more we are bound to rely on EU law to achieve progressive 'outputs' *without the support of* these underpinnings. Law has to do more pragmatic work just as it increasingly lacks the independent democratic and cultural foundations that bolster legal pragmatism's virtue of security of delivery, and the more it strives to do so the more distant it becomes from these foundational supports. Examples include the raft of responses to actual or anticipated resistance to the lack of democratic undergirding in the supply of post-2009 financial crisis relief measures that, in the name of providing more agile and issue-tailored solutions, have involved shifting power further from popular and parliamentary sources. In particular, this has led to the centralizing of executive authority in elite entities such as the European Central Bank, the Ecofin Council, and the European Stability Mechanism (ESM).[84] This has been summarized as the problem of 'post-democratic executive federalism'.[85]

Secondly, and closely related, there is the *paradox of deformalization*. The more we rely on law to achieve progressive results with unstable democratic and cultural underpinnings, the more we depart from certain key virtues of legal formality that also underpin legal certainty and security. Examples include, again in the context of the financial crisis, the exploitation of the 'liminal' legal space of the intergovernmental (rather than full EU) treaty option for the ESM Treaty, discretionary financial sanctions for deficit management failures, and the use of discretionary forms

[84] See e.g. Chalmers, 'The Retransformation of Europe', in D. Chalmers, M. Jachtenfuchs, and C. Joerges (eds), *The End of the Eurocrats' Dream: Adjusting to European Diversity* (2016) 1–28.
[85] See J. Habermas, *The Crisis of the European Union: A Response* (2012).

of conditionality for bail-outs—here including 'memoranda of understanding' only loosely related to legal competences and rights.[86] In other words, the security aspect of the post-foundational pragmatic justification of law may be further compromised by anti-formalist pressure in the teleocratic order demanding greater innovation and a departure from general norms.

Thirdly, there is the *paradox of blocked progress*. Given the struggle to develop new policy agendas in a framework of partial competence, EU law confronts situations of blocked progress where it is exposed by its 'halfway house' jurisdiction, which in turn constrains and compromises legal pragmatism's other great virtue—its flexible capacity to deliver workable solutions. Recent examples include the crab-like development of citizenship law, where free movement rights are not consistently complemented by economically supported residence rights;[87] and, even more vividly, in the context of the Eurozone the absence of instruments of fiscal competence necessary to stabilize monetary policy.[88] In short, the lack of 'joined-up' competence can deprive EU law of the context-specific dexterity and room for manoeuvre on which its pragmatic credentials depend.

Fourthly, there is the *paradox of differentiation*. In a broader constitutional horizon, we can view the many-faceted post-Maastricht trend towards greater differentiation as a strategy of accommodation designed to safeguard the underlying integrity of the whole.[89] It speaks to a greater emphasis on optimal sector-specific outputs, and the pragmatic flexibility required for this, and lays less stress on the core and always precarious idea of a singular jurisdictional foundation for the EU as whole. We see the intensification of this approach in recent moves to revive the idea of multi-speed Europe, and similar models of flexible integration.[90] But as the Brexit process indicates, the idea of bespoke membership not only undermines the residual sense of a common cultural foundation, but also the very sense of a basic unity of transnational discipline whose preservation is the ultimate strategic purpose of differentiation. And so we observe the endangering of an idea of generality and equality of treatment *across* sectors to match the endangering of the idea of generality and equality of treatment *within* sectors produced by the paradox of deformalization. The corrosive effects of this danger can be seen both in the increasing indifference of Eurosceptic voices, both Brexiteer and more generally, to the very idea of a common project, and in the defensive reaction of an EU

[86] See e.g. Markakis and Dermine, 'Bailouts, the Legal Status of Memoranda of Understanding and the Scope of Application of the EU Charter: *Florescu*', 55 *Common Market Law Review* (2018) 643–671.

[87] See in particular, Case C-333/13, *Dano v. Jobcenter Leipzig* (EU:C:2014:2358); see further McCrea, 'Forward or Back: The Future of European Integration and the Impossibility of the Status Quo', 23 *European Law Journal* (2017) 66–93.

[88] See McCrea (n. 87); see also A. Hinarejos, *The Euro Area Crisis in Constitutional Perspective* (2015).

[89] See Leuffen, Rittberger, and Schimmelfennig (n. 45).

[90] See e.g. European Commission, *White Paper on the Future of Europe* COM(2017)2025 of 1 March 2017, available at https://ec.europa.eu/commission/sites/beta-political/files/white_paper_on_the_future_of_europe_en.pdf (accessed 11 November 2020).

establishment concerned at the possible spread of a culture of disinvestment in the legal order.[91]

B. Law as Frame

Law's pragmatic role, *in nuce*, depends on certain positive underpinnings and formal credentials, a task-sensitive flexibility of design, and a residual sense of a common cultural investment in a single project, all of which come under increasing strain because of the very tendencies which made pragmatism such an attractive approach in the first place. Given this, what other theoretical resources, if any, might EU law draw on to justify itself and to further its contribution to the legitimacy of the EU project?

The various candidate conceptions of law we have considered so far and the theoretical traditions to which they speak, namely positivism, idealism, culturalism, and pragmatism, involve quite different background assumptions about the place of law in the generation and maintenance of a polity. Yet when applied to the EU rather than to the modern state, what they all have in common is that they are somehow compromised by certain inherent structural features of the polity in question. Recall that rather than unlimited authority, original agency, and primary political identity, the EU historically has boasted only a partial authority, a derivative agency, and a secondary and accessory form of political identity. In the case of positivism the state-derivative nature of the EU's agency calls into question the strength of its legal pedigree. In the case of culturalism the accessory quality of its political identity weakens the ethical sense of EU law as 'our' law; a weakness likely to be exposed as much as it is redressed by the invocation of a universal strain of ideal morality to replace or supplement that identity. And pragmatism, like idealism though more prominently, seeks to offset the shortcomings of the other strains of justification, but is faced with various paradoxes whereby the more it is required to do because of those shortcomings the more it undermines its own capacity to succeed.

We can say, concisely, that when applied to the EU these different legal conceptions and traditions either *reflect* certain vulnerabilities peculiar to supranational political community or are prone to *overcompensate* for these structural vulnerabilities. But what of a conception of law that instead addresses these vulnerabilities head-on and seeks to *overcome* them? Such a conception we may associate with a proceduralist paradigm of law.[92] According to this paradigm, law is justified

[91] See e.g. Hix and Sitter, 'Svexit or Huxit? How another country could follow the UK out of the EU', *Politico* (30 January 2018), available at https://blogs.lse.ac.uk/brexit/2018/01/30/svexit-or-huxit-how-another-country-could-follow-the-uk-out-of-the-eu/ (accessed 11 November 2020).

[92] Within legal theory, proceduralism as a general polity-level theory (as opposed to an approach to particular legal policy questions) is most closely associated today with the communicative ethics of Habermas, and in particular his *magnum opus*, *Between Facts and Norms: Contribution to a Discourse*

by its articulation of the procedural norms that supply the enabling frame *of* and *for* a political community.

This may at first glance sound like just another variation on the tendency to overburden law and to emphasize too much its primacy in the justification of the EU political community. Does it not both grant too much influence and attribute too great a responsibility to law—and to the law-givers—to envisage the basic shaping of political community as something that takes place in legal terms and through legal means? To address this challenge requires a fuller exposition of what is involved in the proceduralist paradigm in terms of both its operational dynamics and its epistemic assumptions.

To begin with the operational dynamics, the proceduralist approach would not see law as somehow prior to political commitment and to cultural recognition in the making of political community. Rather, it would view these various factors as *co-constitutive* and mutually reinforcing. Recall our use of multiple prepositions. Law should be understood both as the frame *of* and as the frame *for* political community; and so as both *framed* and *framing*. More concretely, the argument for proceduralism at the macro-level of the polity[93] is one that typically sees the process of the making of a written Constitution and of establishing its key decision-making procedures as the key catalyst through which the relationship between the legal and the socio-political is forged and energized. According to Habermas, as the best known contemporary exponent of the proceduralist paradigm and someone who has also taken a sustained interest in the European construction, through the 'power of symbolic crystallization which only a political act of foundation can give',[94] a constitution-making process could connect with and reinforce the three features—transnational civil society, European public sphere, and common political culture—whose circular relationship would provide the wellsprings of the European polity. The outward-looking and inclusive activities of a Constitutional Convention would encourage social movements with aspirations beyond national boundaries. The publicity generated in constitutional debate, especially its simultaneous and interlinked occurrence in various national media and associational contexts, would help to irrigate a European public sphere. And the

Theory of Law and Democracy (Willam Rehg trans., 1992). On the complex roots of this theoretical approach and its close connection with other recent strains of legal and political theory, including deliberative and reflexive approaches, see M. Rosenfeld and A. Arato (eds), *Habermas on Law and Democracy: Critical Exchanges* (1998).

93 At the micro-level of particular legal projects, democratic experimentalism, which we have categorized under the general umbrella of legal pragmatism, and which finds an outlet in the EU through new governance forms such as the Open Method of Co-ordination (n. 78), is one example of an approach that is also firmly wedded to a proceduralist methodology. See references at n. 22. More generally, there are close links between proceduralism and pragmatism, each opposed to general *a priori* solutions to questions of legal and political morality. On Habermas's own complex links to the pragmatic tradition in philosophy, see M. Aboulafia, M. Bookman, and C. Kemp (eds), *Habermas and Pragmatism* (2002).

94 Habermas, Why Europe Needs a Constitution', 11 *New Left Review* (2001) 5, at 6.

debate over constitutional values and purposes would ground deliberation over what a common European political culture might mean. Gradually, in response to the prompts of the self-consciously constitutional debate, the relationship between these three community-generating features would develop its own momentum and transcend the confines of the original constitutional event.

In elaborating this scheme, Habermas remained true to his proceduralist conviction, also present in his analysis of the civic nation as an earlier product of active exchange between citizens and amongst their democratically mandated institutions rather than as a 'community of fate shaped by common descent, language and history'.[95] According to this view, political community can, in the manner of a 'self-fulfilling prophecy',[96] emerge voluntarily at any and all levels through the iterative force of procedurally governed political dialogue.

But what underpins belief in the transferability across quite different polity types and levels of a constitution-centred dynamic logic of proceduralism? Habermas's own answer, and the approach of proceduralism more generally, involves an abstraction from the particular context of political exchange in search of a common underlying orientation. He employs his epistemic method of rational reconstruction to identify within established and emergent social or political practices alike certain normative strands that all participants in the practice could in principle agree to; which shared normativity would then provide a basis for the reworking of that practice among all parties under procedural conditions of free and undistorted exchange.[97] Rational reconstruction, then, involves a mechanism through which the implicit is rendered explicit, the practice reshaped by the ideal latent within it. And importantly, the formal legal process and framework of constitutional democracy itself had long supplied a key 'hinge' concept for Habermas in this regard.[98] For it is nothing other than the implicitly shared normative assumption—*at all political or proto-political sites*—that we are free and equal persons who should govern ourselves through law that provides the germ of an ideal of collective self-legislation which, in turn, finds its best practical form as the outcome of a constitution-making process in which all participants would argue with each other and reach agreement under conditions of freedom and equality.

Yet can the evidence justify such proceduralist faith? On one view the failure of the 2003–2005 Convention on the Future of Europe, which Habermas both anticipated and studied closely,[99] to deliver a ratified constitutional settlement exposed

[95] Ibid. 15.

[96] Ibid. 17.

[97] See e.g. Habermas, 'Democracy in Europe, Why the Development of the EU into a Transnational Democracy is Necessary and How it is Possible', 21 *European Law Journal* (2015) 546; see also Patberg, 'A Systematic Justification for the EU's *pouvoir constituant mixte*: Principles of Constitutional Politics in Supranational Polities', 23 *European Law Journal* (2017) 441.

[98] As fully developed in *Between Facts and Norms* (n. 92).

[99] On his shifting views on the topic of a European Constitution, see Walker, 'Habermas's European Constitution: Catalyst, Reconstruction, Refounding', 25 *European Law Journal* (2019).

the fallacy of this gambit. For even if one accepts the relevance of a proceduralist constructivism to the process of political nation building in some places and times—and some would say that this underestimates the strength of prior common culture in providing traction for the national constitutional project—is it not a step too far, even a 'category error',[100] to assume the validity of the epistemic assumption that this can be replicated at a level above the nation state's political community at a point in time where the state itself remains a robust centre of democratic will formation? The ties of national political culture are arguably just too strong and its claims of political authority too encompassing to allow the kind of ambitiously multi-centred articulation of political belonging envisaged by the strong version of EU constitutionalism.

To that sceptical view, however, one could respond that the failure of this particular convention proves nothing. Perhaps the time was not ripe, the absence of immediate 'situations of crisis'[101] meaning that the energy and focus of the proto-constitutional moment was insufficient to spark the circular process of demos construction. Perhaps, too, the process simply lacked conviction and direction. After all, the unratified text was only an 'accidental constitution',[102] the product of a power grab by a Convention set up for other and lesser purposes, and confined to a process that, for all its improvement on a narrowly state-centred intergovernmental conference, did not engage the European 'people' with the singularity or depth necessary to foster new forms of Union-wide 'we-feeling' or provide a counterpoint to the fears and concerns of various state-level constituencies. On this view, the draft constitution that emerged and was subsequently aborted was largely a rhetorical accomplishment, modest in its reform ambitions and received—indeed, by some of its authors *intended*[103]—as a naked naming exercise involving the projection of a new 'object' or mark of community onto what was mainly the consolidation of 'old' text. It was a legal event that, as has become familiar within the pragmatist narrative, assumed the role of self-signifier, but in this case indicating nothing significantly novel or transformative beyond its own formal production.

Perhaps, then, the proceduralist gambit, rather than lost, is still to be properly put to the test. The cumulative crises of recent years—fiscal, migration, security, and the broader Brexit-accompanying challenge of national populism—have suggested to a number of European constituencies that the time for root and branch reform is no longer unripe. From Macron to Varoufakis, there are today more constitutional stirrings, more public narratives of constituent power being rethought and rehearsed, than at any time since the failed Constitution of 2003–2005.[104]

[100] Moravcsik, 'Europe without Illusions: A Category Error', *Prospect* (July) (2005).
[101] Habermas (n. 94) 8.
[102] P. Norman, *The Accidental Constitution* (2003).
[103] See e.g. Walker, 'Europe's Constitutional Momentum and the Search for Polity Legitimacy', 3 *International Journal of Constitutional Law* (2005) 211–231.
[104] See Patberg (n. 52); Walker (n. 81 and n. 99).

Unlike its predecessor, for any such project to succeed it should not be seen as a symbolic end in itself. Rather, it should supply a frame to reflect and project something more substantively polity-generative, which, perhaps through giving greater emphasis to the legitimizing pedigree of the undifferentiated European citizenry alongside the traditional national constituencies,[105] would help to irrigate the democratic and cultural supports of which the EU has always—and more apparently in recent years—been in short supply.

Can the EU juridical order both continue to pursue an approach that explores a rich but increasingly challenged pragmatic seam of legitimacy and, at the same time, frame the very procedural foundations that law has traditionally both relied on and reinforced in the context of 'thicker' polities?[106] A vital contemporary question for political practice, as much as for legal theory.

[105] On the idea of a dual or mixed constituent power, see Habermas, 'Citizen and State Equality in a Supranational Political Community; Degressive Proportionality and the *pouvoir constituant mixte*', 55 *Journal of Common Market Studies* (2017) 171; see also Patberg (n. 97).

[106] On synergies between pragmatism and proceduralism, see n. 93.

3

Challenges to EU Legality in the Field of Asylum and Migration Law

*Evelien Brouwer**

1. Introduction

With the adoption of the Tampere conclusions in 1999, the heads of state of the then 15 Member States of the EU provided the basis for the legislative framework for a common EU asylum and migration policy.[1] Since then, immigration law, traditionally perceived as belonging to the legislative area in which Member States retained their sovereignty, has been extensively 'Europeanized' whether it concerns asylum and refugee law, freedom of movement of migrant workers, family reunification, or return and detention of third-country nationals. As highlighted by Groenendijk, among others, there are few decisions related to migration law which are not covered by EU law.[2] Even nationality law, one of the preserved fields of national sovereignty, is 'touched' by general principles of EU law, as we know since the famous *Rottmann* and *Tjebbes* cases on the protection of the fundamental right of EU citizenship.[3] Due to this Europeanization or application of 'EU legality', general principles of EU law, including effectiveness, proportionality, and the right to effective judicial protection, have been incorporated in asylum and migration laws. Even where these EU rules offer Member States much leeway for a restrictive application, in its case-law the Court of Justice of the European Union (CJEU) has limited this discretionary power by treating EU immigration and asylum as 'normal EU laws'. This case-law, as will be dealt with in Section 2, has often resulted in a stronger legal protection for third-country nationals.

More recently, this 'strengthening effect' of EU legality for third-country nationals is being challenged by several developments in the EU. First, especially since the influx of asylum seekers in 2015–2016, we have seen that Member States

* The author thanks in particular Joanne Scott and Claire Kilpatrick for their useful comments during the EUI seminar organized to discuss drafts of this publication, February 2019. Of course, any errors remain my own.

[1] Presidency Conclusions European Council, Tampere, 15–16 October 1999.

[2] Groenendijk, 'Introduction: Migration and Law in Europe', in E. Guild and P. Minderhoud, *The First Decade in EU Migration and Asylum Law* (2011) 1–22.

[3] Case C-135/08, *Rottmann* (EU:C:2010:104); Case C-221/17, *Tjebbes* (EU:C:2019:189).

Evelien Brouwer, *Challenges to EU Legality in the Field of Asylum and Migration Law*. In: *Contemporary Challenges to EU Legality*. First edition. Edited by: Claire Kilpatrick and Joanne Scott, Oxford University Press (2021). © Evelien Brouwer.
DOI: 10.1093/oso/9780192898050.003.0003

are able to deviate from shared obligations and responsibilities due to the lack of political will of the Commission and other Member States to combat this, but also due to the lack of effective EU tools to enforce the implementation of EU laws. An important exception in this regard has been the actions by the Commission against Hungary, the Czech Republic, and Poland. This resulted in the judgments in April 2020 in which the CJEU found that the three countries failed to fulfil their obligations from Decisions 2015/1523 and 2015/1601, which were adopted during the asylum crisis in order to relocate people from Greece and Italy to the other Member States.[4] Whereas the Common European Asylum System (CEAS) provides harmonized rules on asylum reception, procedures, and qualification for international protection, it is clear that EU Member States have failed to offer an effective and shared approach to migration.[5] Aside from the adoption in 2015 of emergency measures, providing for the relocation of asylum seekers from the overburdened countries Greece and Italy, EU policies have been increasingly focused on the strengthening of external border controls, including the use of technologies, joint maritime operations, and cooperation with third states. On the 'inside', Member States persist with the continuation of the 'Dublin system', a mechanism to determine the responsible Member State for an asylum application, which in practice results in lengthy procedures, costly decision-making, and only in relatively few cases leads to actual Dublin transfers; this approach is also reflected in the New Pact on Migration and Asylum, presented by the European Commission in September 2020.[6] Here we see that 'EU legality' fails because of, on the one hand, the insistence of Member States on applying the rather bureaucratic rules of the Dublin Regulation and, on the other hand, the lack of means to ensure the implementation of the underlying goals of Dublin and CEAS. These goals are swift determination of asylum claims and offering protection to those in need of international protection.

Another challenge to EU legality is related to one of the underlying principles of EU cooperation: the principle of mutual trust. Within the Area of Freedom, Security and Justice (AFSJ) several instruments, including the European Arrest Warrant (EAW), the Dublin Regulation, and the Schengen border and visa policy,

[4] Joined cases C-718/17, C-719/17, and C-715/17, *Commission v. Hungary, Czech Republic, and Poland* (EU:C:2020:257).

[5] See, in more detail, M. Garlick, 'Solidarity Under Strain: Solidarity and Fair Sharing of the Responsibility for the International Protection of Refugees in the European Union' (2016) (PhD thesis on file at Radboud University Nijmegen); Thym and Tsourdi, 'Searching for Solidarity in the EU Asylum and Border Policies: Constitutional and Operational Dimensions', 24(5) *Maastricht Journal of European and Comparative Law* (2017) 605–621.

[6] The Dublin III Regulation 604/2013 provides that only one Member State is responsible for the examination of asylum applications. This responsibility is determined based on a hierarchy of criteria included in the Regulation. See for criticism on the Dublin system, among others Mouzourakis, 'We Need to Talk about Dublin. Responsibility under the Dublin System as a Blockage to Asylum Burden-sharing in the European Union', University of Oxford, Refugee Studies Centre, Working Paper Series No. 105, 2014. COM (2020) 609 final, Brussels, 23.09.2020.

are based on mutual trust. In these cases, national authorities, and to an even greater extent national courts, are confronted with a difficult balancing act between the implementation of mutual trust and the protection of fundamental rights. In its case-law, the CJEU has defined conditions and criteria where trust may be 'rebutted', especially in cases dealing with the EAW and the Dublin Regulation. Despite this case-law, achieving a balance between mutual trust and fundamental rights remains a complicated task for national courts. Furthermore, there are other, less documented, areas of law in which the mutual recognition of national decisions, connected with the wide discretionary power of national authorities, may result in the violation of fundamental rights. This concerns, in particular, decision-making with regard to the refusal of entry and residence of third-country nationals based on public order and security grounds. As will be dealt with in Section 3.A, the combination of national sovereignty with regard to the definition of 'inadmissible aliens' and the obligation of mutual enforcement of national entry bans and public order considerations, affects the right of effective judicial protection of third-country nationals.[7]

A third development challenging 'EU legality' concerns the externalization of border and immigration control and the deliberate choices of Member States and EU institutions to exclude migration and asylum measures from the applicability of EU law.[8] This externalization is, of course, most visible in the bilateral agreements between the EU and third states on border control and the interception of irregular immigrants by third states, such as the EU-Turkey Statement of 2016. As we will see later (in Section 3.C.1), by denying the status of this bilateral agreement as an EU act, the CJEU legitimized the exemption of Member States' responsibility under EU law. Another example of a formal and narrow interpretation of EU law concerns a judgment of 2017, in which the CJEU concluded that the issuing of a humanitarian visa would not fall within the scope of the Visa Code. The goal of this contribution is to illustrate that 'EU legality' is a double-edged sword. The first part of this chapter describes how the CJEU, by the mere application of general principles of EU law, offered in its case-law important tools or criteria strengthening rights, and legal protection for third-country nationals. The second part focuses on developments and examples of case-law by the CJEU, with regard to mutual trust and the use of public order criteria in immigration law and the externalization of EU measures. In this more recent case-law, the CJEU seems to take a more restrictive role with regard to the interpretation and meaning of EU values and principles in immigration law cases. I will argue that this approach further challenges

[7] Brouwer, 'Schengen's Undesirable Aliens', in P. Minderhoud, S. Mantu, and K. Zwaan (eds), *Caught in between Borders: Citizens, Migrants, Humans: Liber Amicorum in honour of Prof. Dr Elspeth Guild* (2019).

[8] V. Moreno-Lax, *Accessing Asylum in Europe: Extraterritorial Border Controls and Refugee Rights under EU Law* (2017).

the applicability of general principles of EU legality, including the right to effective judicial protection for third-country nationals.[9]

2. EU Legality as a Challenge to Migration Law

A. Principles of Fundamental Rights, Effectiveness, and Proportionality

European Parliament v. the Council concerns one of the first judgments in which the CJEU confronted Member States with the extent of obligations included by the EU legislator itself, and thus the consequences of 'EU legality' in EU migration law.[10] In this case, the CJEU dealt with the claim of the European Parliament that Directive 2003/86 on the right to family reunification for third-country nationals legally residing in the EU[11] (the Family Reunification Directive (FRD)) was to be annulled because of violation of fundamental rights and the obligation to protect the rights of the child. Although the CJEU rejected this claim by concluding that the Directive was not unlawful, this judgment provided important considerations, limiting the powers of Member States to adopt or apply a restricted family reunification policy. First, the CJEU held that as the FRD includes precise positive obligations with corresponding and clearly defined individual rights, Member States are obliged to protect the right to family reunification in determined cases, without being left a margin of appreciation.[12] Second, the CJEU underlined the obligation of Member States to respect the principles included in the Directive, such as the principle of proportionality and the obligation to decide in the best interest of the child.[13] In a later judgment, *O, S, and L*, the CJEU referred directly to the right to family life as protected in Article 7 of the Charter on Fundamental Rights (CFR) and the right of the child, protected in Article 24 CFR, thus stressing the obligation of Member States to apply the FRD in accordance with fundamental rights.[14]

In *Chakroun*, the CJEU further applied the principle of effectiveness to the FRD.[15] In this judgment, the CJEU declared that the FRD precluded the (at that time) Dutch use of a reference level of income (120 per cent of national minimum income) as the sole means of proving the 'stable and regular resources' of the person living within the EU, necessary to allow that person's family reunification

[9] For an extended analysis of 155 judgments of the CJEU in the field of asylum and immigration law, see Thym, 'A Bird's Eye View on ECJ Judgments on Immigration, Asylum and Border Control Cases', 21 *European Journal of Migration and Law* (2019) 166–193.

[10] Case C-540/03, *European Parliament v. Council* (EU:C:2006:429).

[11] OJ 2003 L 251/12.

[12] Ibid. para. 60.

[13] Ibid. paras 66, 73.

[14] Joined Cases C-356/11 and C-357/11, *O, S, and L* (EU:C:2012:776).

[15] Case C-578/08, *Chakroun* (EU:C:2010:117).

with a third-country national from outside the EU. The CJEU, quoting its decision in *European Parliament v. Council*, emphasized that the EU Directive includes 'precise positive obligations' while respecting Article 8 of the European Convention on Human Rights (ECHR). According to the CJEU, where authorization of family reunification is the general rule, on the basis of the FRD, the margin for manoeuvre left for Member States may not undermine the objective of the Directive and its effectiveness.[16]

The effectiveness test was also applied by the CJEU in *K and A*, which dealt with the Dutch requirement for third-country nationals to pass an integration test abroad before being allowed family reunification.[17] The CJEU was asked whether this requirement was compatible with Article 7(2) FRD, which allows Member States to require third-country nationals to comply with 'integration measures in accordance with national laws'. As the content of 'integration measures' was not further defined by the EU legislator, the aim of this provision was not clear. On the one hand, it was interpreted (among others by the Dutch government) as a legal basis allowing further restrictions to family reunification. On the other hand, it was argued that this implied a duty for the state to take a more active role in supporting the integration of third-country nationals. The CJEU held that as such the Dutch requirement was not in violation of Article 7(2) FRD and thus allowed the requirement to pass the integration test as a condition for the exercise of the right to family reunification. However, it did so by underlining the principle of proportionality as one of the general principles of EU law. This principle implies that the conditions imposed on applicants for such requirements of integration should not exceed what is necessary to achieve its aims. Therefore, national authorities must take into account the individual circumstances of the cases, including age, level of education, or health of the applicants, while respecting the objective of the FRD, which is to promote family life.[18] According to the CJEU, this condition is supported by the obligation in Article 17 FRD to examine applications for family reunification on a case-by-case basis.[19]

Within the framework of the Citizenship Directive 2004/38,[20] the CJEU dealt in *Coman* with the refusal of a residence right to a third-country national spouse of an EU citizen because of the non-recognition of same-sex marriages in a Member State.[21] In this case, the CJEU addressed in particular the tension between public policy and the national identity of individual Member States on the one hand, and the goals of Article 4(2) of the Treaty on European Union (TEU) and Article 21 of the Treaty on the Functioning of the European Union (TFEU), on the right to

16 Ibid. paras 41 and 43.
17 Case C-153/14, *K. and A.* (EU:C:2015:453).
18 Ibid. paras 51, 56.
19 Ibid. paras 58–60.
20 OJ 2004 L 158/77.
21 C-673/16, *Coman* (EU:C:2018:385).

free movement, on the other. According to the CJEU, 'spouses' in Articles 2(2)(a) and 7 of the Citizens Directive would also cover spouses in same-sex marriages lawfully conducted in another Member State. Therefore, within the scope of this Directive, residence rights of family members of EU citizens who want to return to the Member States of their nationality cannot be made subject to the stricter conditions of that latter state. The CJEU underlined that Member States' discretion to define the scope of the freedom of movement is limited by fundamental principles of EU law, including the fundamental right to private life and family life, and the principle of effectiveness.[22]

B. The Right to Effective Judicial Protection

Of even more ground-breaking importance for national migration laws, has been the case-law of the CJEU underlining the right to effective judicial remedies of third-country nationals when assessing national decisions or measures within the field of migration and asylum policies.

Dealing with EU legislation in general, the close connection between effective implementation of EU rules and the individual right of access to legal protection in order to safeguard that implementation, was emphasized at an early stage by both the EU legislator and the CJEU. The EU legislator provided in the first place for a 'judicial dialogue' between national courts and the CJEU, by the instrument of preliminary procedures in (now) Article 267 TFEU to ensure a coherent and equivalent implementation of EU law in cooperation with the CJEU. Article 19 TEU, on the role of the CJEU, obliges individual Member States to ensure in their national legal systems the availability of remedies 'to ensure effective legal protection law in fields covered by EU law'.[23] Already in 1986, in *Johnston* the CJEU had held that this 'requirement of effective judicial control reflects general principles of law', referring to constitutional traditions of the Member States and Articles 6 and 13 ECHR.[24]

With the inclusion of Article 47 on the right to effective judicial protection in the CFR, which became binding in 2009, the EU legislator explicitly chose to combine the guarantees of the right to fair trial in Article 6 ECHR with the right to effective

22 Ibid. paras 48–53.

23 See e.g. Case 64/16, *Associação Sindical dos Juízes Portugueses* (EU:C:2018:117): 'The principle of the effective judicial protection of individuals' rights under EU law, referred to in the second subparagraph of Article 19(1) TEU, is a general principle of EU law stemming from the constitutional traditions common to the Member States, which has been enshrined in Articles 6 and 13 of the European Convention for the Protection of Human Rights and Fundamental Freedoms, signed in Rome on 4 November 1950, and which is now reaffirmed by Article 47 of the Charter' (para. 35) and 'the very existence of effective judicial review designed to ensure compliance with EU law is of the essence of the rule of law' (para. 36).

24 Case C-222/84, *Johnston* (EU:C:1986:206) paras 18–21.

remedies, as protected in Article 13 ECHR. In *Maaouia*, the European Court of Human Rights (ECtHR) had explicitly excluded immigration law decision-making from the scope of Article 6 ECHR.[25] Therefore, the inclusion of Article 47 in the CFR was a major development for immigration law procedures covered by EU law, the practical effect of which became clear in several judgments of the CJEU. Important judgments in this area dealt with, for example, the Dublin Regulation and the Visa Code. Both concern EU instruments of which the Member States had generally assumed that, even if the EU legislator included 'a right to appeal' in the text itself, Member States retained the discretionary power to decide upon the scope and content of these remedies. In *Ghezelbash*, the CJEU underlined the importance of a legal remedy for the asylum seeker against the incorrect application of Dublin criteria when dealing with a decision that the asylum seeker was to be transferred to another 'Dublin state'.[26] In this case, the CJEU deviated from its earlier *Abdullahi* judgment.[27] In *Abdullahi*, dealing with the interpretation of the former Dublin II Regulation, the CJEU had denied the right of appeal against transfer decisions based on the application of Dublin criteria. The CJEU explains this deviation in *Ghezelbash* by referring to the fact that, in contrast to the former Dublin II Regulation, Article 27 of the Dublin III Regulation 604/2013[28] explicitly provides the right to have an effective remedy, and that Dublin III provides 'various rights and mechanisms guaranteeing the involvement of asylum seekers in the process for determining the Member State responsible', such as the right to obtain information or to have a personal interview.[29] In a later judgment, the CJEU also affirmed the right of asylum applicants to obtain legal remedies against transfer decisions which are based on the expiry of the Dublin time limits.[30]

In the *El Hassani* case, the CJEU was asked to provide an explanation of the right to legal remedy against a (short-term) visa refusal or, with other words, the scope and content of Article 32(3) of the Visa Code,[31] according to which 'Applicants who have been refused a visa shall have the right to appeal'.[32] The CJEU held that, contrary to the perception prevailing at that time, this provision does not entail a discretionary power for Member States, by explicitly underlining the close relationship between Article 32 Visa Code and Article 47 CFR.[33] According to the CJEU, even if it is for the national legal order of each Member State to establish procedural rules for actions intended to safeguard the rights of individuals, this

[25] ECtHR, *Maaouia v. France*, Appl. no. 39652/98, 5 October 2000.
[26] Case C-63/15, *Ghezelbash v. Netherlands/Karim v. Sweden* (EU:C:2016:409).
[27] Case C-4/11, *Bundesrepublik Deutschland v. Kaveh Puid* (EU:C:2013:740) and Case C-394/12, *Abdullahi v. Bundesasylamt* (EU:C:2013:813).
[28] OJ 2013 L 180/31.
[29] Case C-63/15, *Ghezelbash v. Netherlands/Karim v. Sweden* (EU:C:2016:409) paras 34 and 46–49.
[30] Case C-201/16, *Shiri* (EU:C:2017:805).
[31] Regulation 810/2009, OJ 2009 L 243/1.
[32] Case C-403/16, *El Hassani* (EU:C:2017:960).
[33] Ibid. paras 33–42.

is based on the condition 'that those rules are not less favourable than those governing similar domestic situations (principle of equivalence) and that they do not make it excessively difficult or impossible in practice to exercise the rights conferred by EU law (principle of effectiveness)'.[34] Where 'in examining a visa application the national authorities have a broad discretion as regards the conditions for applying the grounds of refusal laid down by the Visa Code and the evaluation of the relevant facts, the fact remains that such discretion has no influence on the fact that the authorities directly apply a provision of EU law'.[35] This means that the CFR applies, including the right to effective judicial protection in Article 47 CFR. Therefore, Article 32(3) of the Visa Code, read in the light of Article 47 of the Charter, must be interpreted as meaning that it requires Member States 'to provide for an appeal procedure against decisions refusing visas, the procedural rules for which are a matter for the legal order of each Member State in accordance with the principles of equivalence and effectiveness'.[36]

These repeated references by the CJEU to the application of Article 47 CFR in EU immigration law, and thus to the effects of 'EU legality', obliged Member States to change their national laws and procedures to safeguard the right to effective judicial protection of third-country nationals.

3. Challenges to EU Legality: Mutual Trust and National Sovereignty and Externalization

In the preceding sections I described the importance of EU law as a legality constraint and the role of the CJEU as ensuring that immigration rules are implemented in accordance with general principles of EU law. The following sections deal with different mechanisms within the EU by which Member States evade their responsibilities under EU law, challenging the principle of EU legality on the basis of the principle of mutual trust. Section 3.C describes the effect of the externalization of migration control.

Cases dealing with the mutual recognition of immigration law or judicial decisions, establish the tension between the EU principle of mutual trust, on the one hand, and other general principles of EU law, including the right to effective judicial protection. In their landmark judgments in 2011 dealing with the Dublin Regulation, both the ECtHR and the CJEU have underlined that mutual trust cannot be considered irrebuttable.[37] National authorities and courts have the duty to assess whether exceptions to mutual trust are necessary to safeguard the

[34] Ibid. para. 26.
[35] Ibid. para. 36.
[36] Ibid. para. 42.
[37] Case C-411/10, *N.S. v. SSHD* (EU:C:2011:865); ECtHR, *M.S.S. v. Belgium and Greece*, Appl. no. 30696/09.

absolute right in Article 3 ECHR and Article 4 CFR, on the protection against inhuman or degrading treatment. In later judgments, this exception to mutual trust was further defined with regard to specifically vulnerable persons, such as individuals with health problems and children. Nevertheless, the criteria and conditions under which Member States must refrain from 'mutual trust', also outside the scope of the Dublin Regulation, remain difficult for national courts to assess and apply.[38] The next sections (Sections 3.A and 3.B) focus on two examples of mutual trust in immigration law not related to the Dublin Regulation: the interpretation of public order grounds in immigration law decisions and visa refusals based on bilateral representation agreements within the scope of the Visa Code. I will argue that the application of mutual trust combined with a lack of harmonization of laws or uniform interpretation of definitions within the aforementioned fields, may affect the effective judicial protection of third-country nationals.

A. The Use of the 'Public Order' Criterion in EU Migration Laws

1. Borders, Entry Bans, and the 'Public Order' Criterion

The rules on entry conditions at the external borders of the EU are included in Article 6 of the Schengen Borders Code (SBC).[39] One of these criteria entails that third-country nationals should not be reported for the purpose of refusal of entry in the Schengen Information System (SIS), as provided in Regulation 1987/2006.[40] Although the relationship between the different rules applying is not clear, SIS alerts for the purpose of refusal can be based on two grounds mentioned in Article 24(1)(a) and (b): either an 'entry ban' which follows a return decision on the basis of the Return Directive 2008/115,[41] or a national decision based on public order or national or public security grounds. This second category of public order and security grounds can be based on either a conviction by a Member State of an offence, punishable by a term of imprisonment of at least one year, or when there are serious grounds for believing that the individual 'has committed serious criminal offences or concerning whom there are clear indications of an intention to commit such offences on the territory of a Member State'. These grounds, already included in the Schengen Convention of 1990, have been criticized for providing a wide and disproportional basis for refusal of entry and expulsion. For example, a conviction

[38] Brouwer, 'Mutual Trust and Human Rights in the AFSJ: In Search of Guidelines for National Courts', 11(3) *European Papers* (2016) 893–920.

[39] Regulation (EU) 2016/399, OJ 2016 L 77/1.

[40] Regulation 1987/2006, OJ 2006 L 381/4. This Regulation has been recently amended by SIS II Regulation (EU) 2018/1861, OJ L 312/14, adding a new category for SIS alerts, namely for third-country nationals who circumvented or attempted to circumvent EU or national laws on entry or stay, and adding the criterion that a SIS alert will take effect in SIS as soon the third-country national has left the territory of the Member States.

[41] OJ 2008 L 348/98.

for a minor crime in one of the Schengen States may result in a long-term banishment from the whole Schengen territory. Furthermore, the public order and security grounds provide states a wide margin of appreciation of not only who is to be considered as a risk in terms of committing a serious crime, but also what is to be considered a serious crime.

The power of states to issue a SIS alert is restricted by two conditions, added in the SIS II Regulation of 2006. First, before issuing a SIS alert for the purpose of refusal, Member States must determine whether the case is 'adequate, relevant, and important enough' (Article 21 SIS II Regulation) and, second, a SIS alert ban based on Article 24(1)(a) (public order and security grounds) must be based on an individual assessment. Therefore, any decision to report a person as 'inadmissible' into the SIS is bound by the purpose of the SIS (to 'ensure a high level of security within the area of freedom, security and justice of the European Union, including the maintenance of public security and public policy and the safeguarding of security in the territories of the Member States') and the principle of proportionality.

A more recent instrument, which involves the recording of national criminal convictions and which may be used for immigration control, concerns the ECRIS-TCN.[42] The ECRIS-TCN Regulation 2019/816, adopted in April 2019, provides for a centralized system containing information on third-country nationals following national decisions related to criminal convictions or prosecutions. This may include criminal convictions of third-country nationals based on violations of national immigration laws. Following Article 7 of the Regulation, information in ECRIS-TCN can be requested for criminal proceedings or 'for any of the other purposes mentioned in this provision, if provided by national law'. These 'other purposes', as described in the Regulation, may include security clearances, vetting for voluntary activities involving contacts with children or vulnerable persons, and also 'visa, acquisition of citizenship and migration procedures, including asylum procedures'. This means that national immigration and asylum authorities may, if provided by national law, check ECRIS-TCN and may decide to use information on criminal records from other Member States in their immigration law decision-making.

In my view, this use of SIS and ECRIS-TCN is an example of 'liminal legality' within the scope of EU law, meaning that the identity of acts or actors are insufficiently clear. EU law requires Member States to report third-country nationals issued with an entry ban into SIS, or to store information on criminal convictions of third-country nationals into ECRIS-TCN, without harmonizing the specific grounds for such an entry ban or conviction. With regard to the entry bans in SIS, this results in a compulsory refusal of entry or stay for the Schengen territory, whereas information in ECRIS-TCN may be used for immigration law purposes.

[42] OJ 2019 L 135/1. See also press release available at http://europa.eu/rapid/press-release_IP-19-2018_en.htm (accessed 11 November 2020).

This use of ECRIS-TCN reinforces national sovereignty at two levels: with regard to the reporting of individuals in ECRIS-TCN and with regard to the use of this large-scale database. This brings me to the necessity of a uniform interpretation of 'public order grounds' in EU immigration law and the interpretation by the CJEU in its case-law, including the more recent judgments of 12 December 2019.

2. Interpretation of 'Public Order' in CJEU Case-law

In different EU immigration laws, entry or residence permits of third-country nationals can be rejected or withdrawn on the basis of public order and security grounds. Whereas the EU Citizenship Directive 2004/38,[43] following previous case-law by the CJEU, includes the more detailed criterion that the freedom of movement and residence of EU citizens and their family members may only be restricted if the personal conduct of the individual represents 'a genuine, present, and sufficiently serious threat to public policy', there is a lack of clarity about the scope and content of public order criteria with regard to third-country nationals who fall outside the scope of this Directive. Initially, this problem seemed partially solved by the judgment *Zh. and O.*, in which the CJEU addressed the 'public order criterion' when dealing with an entry ban following a return decision on the basis of the Return Directive.[44] On the basis of the Return Directive 2008/115, when a return decision is issued to an irregular migrant, normally a period is granted for voluntary return, except if there is a risk of absconding or 'risk for public policy', in accordance with Article 7(4) of the Return Directive. If no voluntary period for return is granted, the return decision will be followed by an entry ban to be reported into SIS II. For the assessment of the decision whether or not a third-country national should be granted a voluntary period of return, the CJEU has been asked by national courts for an interpretation of 'the risk for public policy'. In *Zh. and O.*, the CJEU applied the same criteria as with regard to EU citizens on the basis of the Citizenship Directive, stating that the 'risk to public policy' must be assessed on a case-by-case basis in order to ascertain whether the personal conduct of the third-country national concerned poses 'a genuine and present risk to public policy'. The CJEU held that while 'Member States essentially retain the freedom to determine the requirements of public policy in accordance with their national needs, which can vary from one Member State to another and from one era to another', these requirements must be interpreted strictly 'to ensure that the fundamental rights of third-country nationals are respected when they are removed from the European Union'.[45] Furthermore, according to the CJEU, the evaluation of a public order risk requires the same individual assessment as provided in the Citizenship Directive. Following this judgment, Member States are required to assess, on a case-by-case

[43] OJ 2004 L 158/77.
[44] Case C-554/13, *Zh. and O.* (EU:C:2015:377).
[45] Ibid. paras 50, 59–60.

basis, whether the personal conduct of the third-country national concerned poses a genuine, present, and sufficiently serious threat to public policy.[46] Finally, the CJEU made clear that this decision must be based on an individual examination of the case concerned and respect the principle of proportionality.[47]

In the *Zh. and O.* judgment, the CJEU did not explicitly state that 'public order' must be treated as an autonomous concept, to be applied in the same way within all EU immigration laws. As such, it was not clear whether the criteria based on the Citizens Directive should also be applied to other EU instruments dealing with third-country nationals. It was only with regard to the scope of 'public security', in the *Fahimian* case of 2017, that the CJEU held that Member States when dealing with applications for student visas have a wider discretionary power than that based on the Citizenship Directive.[48] This lack of clarity was one of the reasons why, in 2018, the Dutch highest administrative court submitted preliminary questions dealing with the interpretation of 'public order' in decisions based on the FRD and the SBC.

In its judgments of 12 December 2019, the CJEU decided that both with regard to the FRD and the SBC the concept of 'threat to public policy' does not 'necessarily have to be understood as referring exclusively to individual conduct representing a genuine, present and sufficiently serious threat affecting one of the fundamental interests of the society of the Member States concerned'.[49] Therefore, according to the CJEU, the public order criterion on the basis of the FRD and the SBC should not necessarily be the same as that applied on the basis of the Citizenship Directive. The CJEU takes a formal approach, referring on the one hand to the legal texts of the FRD, and on the other, in the case of border controls, to the wide discretion of the national authorities to determine whether a third-country national is a threat to public policy within the meaning of Article 6(1) SBC.[50] It seems disappointing that the CJEU did not use this opportunity to ensure a uniform interpretation of 'public order grounds' in EU migration law. It is arguable that when the protection of public order within the EU is at stake, and it is necessary to assess the nature and scope of the threat the presence of an individual on the territory would involve, the nationality or status of this person is irrelevant. With regard to the implementation

[46] In Case 240/17, *E.* (EU:C:2018:8). Furthermore, in para. 49, the CJEU repeated the criteria with regard to the scope and definition of 'public order' as developed in *Zh. and O.*

[47] Case C-554/13, *Zh. and O.* (EU:C:2015:377) paras 50, 69. See also Terlouw, 'Voluntary Departure of Irregular Migrants and the Exception of Public Orders: The Case of *Z.ZH. & I.O. v Staatssecretaris voor Veiligheid en Justitie*', 18 *European Journal of Migration and Law* (2016) 126–137.

[48] Case C-544/15, *Fahimian* (EU:C:2017:255) paras 40–43. On the interpretation of 'public security' in immigration procedures, see further Stehlík, 'Discretion of Member States vis-à-vis Public Security: Unveiling the Labyrinth of EU Migration Rules', 17(2) *International and Comparative Law Review* (2017) 127–142.

[49] Joined cases C-381/18 and C-382/18, *G.S. and V.G.* (EU:C:2019:1072) para. 54, dealing with the FRD and Case C-380/18, *E.P.* (EU:C:2019:1071) paras 28–29, dealing with the SBC.

[50] Respectively, Joined cases C-381/18 and C-382/18, *G.S. and V.G.* (EU:C:2019:1072) paras 56–58 and Case C-380/18, *E.P.* (EU:C:2019:1071) para. 37.

of the FRD, the objective of which is the protection of the right to family reunification, one may also question why the CJEU did not use the same reasoning as in the *Zh. and O.* case. As we have seen, in this case the CJEU argued that because of the involvement of fundamental rights when the expulsion of third-country nationals is at stake, the same public order criterion must be applied as in the Citizenship Directive. But the justification in the case of border controls is also disputable. The SBC explicitly states that border control is in the interest of all the states which have abolished internal border control and to prevent any threat to the internal security, public policy, public health, and international relations of all these Member States.[51] Considering this goal, it is illogical that national authorities should be able to apply their own interpretation of threats to public order or security.

With regard to both the FDR and the SBC, the CJEU did, however, stress the obligation for both authorities and courts of a more individual examination. Referring to the EU principle of proportionality, the CJEU held that the application of public order grounds cannot go beyond what is necessary to ensure that public policy is safeguarded. According to the CJEU dealing with the rejection of an application for family reunification on the basis of FRD this means that national authorities cannot 'automatically take the view that a third-country national is a threat to public policy . . . merely because he or she has been convicted of some or other criminal offence'.[52] This means, according to the CJEU, that taking into account Article 17 FRD, there must be an individual assessment 'taking due account of the nature and solidity of that person's family relationships, of the duration of his or her residence in the Member State and of the existence of family, cultural and social ties with his or her country of origin'. With regard to the refusal of entry based on the SBC in the absence of a conviction, the CJEU held that, based on the principle of proportionality, 'the infringement which the third-country national at issue is suspected of having committed must be sufficiently serious, in the light of its nature and of the punishment which may be imposed, to justify that national's stay on the territory of the Member States being brought to an immediate end'.[53] Furthermore, national authorities may only invoke a threat to public policy if there is a 'consistent, objective and specific evidence that provides grounds for suspecting that that third-country national has committed such an offence'. This criterion adds to the one the CJEU formulated in the aforementioned *Fahimian* case dealing with the notion of public security. In this case, the CJEU underlined that Member States in order to determine whether an applicant for a student visa 'represents a threat, if only potential, to public security', should 'perform an overall assessment of all the elements of that person's situation'. According to the CJEU, such 'evaluations involve predicting the foreseeable conduct of the applicant for the visa,

[51] Preamble 6 and Art. 6(1)(e) SBC.
[52] Joined cases C-381/18 and C-382/18, *G.S. and V.G.* (EU:C:2019:1072) paras 65–70.
[53] Case C-380/18, *E.P.* (EU:C:2019:1071) paras 47–49.

and must be based inter alia on an extensive knowledge of his country of residence and on the analysis of the various documents and of the applicant's statements'.[54]

Therefore, even if aforementioned case-law does not provide clear rules on the content and the conditions for further substantiation of the public order grounds in immigration law decisions, it underlines the requirement of case-by-case decision-making and the necessity to comply with the principle of proportionality. For third-country nationals, it nevertheless remains difficult to challenge the wide discretionary powers with regard to the application of public order grounds, especially when—as seen in the previous sections on the use of SIS and ECRIS-TCN—such decisions are based on public order grounds from other Member States.

B. Visa Representation in the Visa Code and Access to Legal Remedies

Another example of how mutual trust may challenge fundamental rights of third-country nationals, concerns the cooperation of Member States based on the Visa Code. In July 2019, the CJEU published a judgment dealing with the right to effective judicial remedies in the case of visa representation.[55] The Visa Code allows Member States, on the basis of bilateral agreements, to decide that visa applications for one state can be submitted to and be decided by another state. This means, in practice, that if in a third country a Member State is represented by another Member State, visa applications for the former state must be submitted in the latter state. Based on Article 8(4) of the current Visa Code, the Member State may even agree that the latter state may reject a visa application. For years, there has been a discussion on whether a visa applicant in the case of a rejection by the representing state has the right of appeal in the represented state (or state of destination) or whether the applicant should lodge an appeal in the representing state.[56] Article 32(3) only provides that appeals must 'be conducted against the Member State that has taken the final decision on the application and in accordance with the national law of that Member State'. The European Commission and several Member States have argued that the representing state is the state taking the final decision. However, in practice, this interpretation causes problems for an applicant whose visa for the Member State of destination has been refused by the embassy representing that Member State: as the applicant must lodge an appeal in the second state, there may be problems with regard to language, higher fees, role sponsors,

[54] Case C-544/15, *Fahimian* (EU:C:2017:255) paras 40–43.

[55] Case C-680/17, *Vethanayagam* (EU:C:2019:627).

[56] In 2019, the Visa Code was amended by Regulation 2019/1155 of 20 June 2019, OJ 2019 L 188/25. Following this amendment, visa representation, including refusals on behalf of the represented state, becomes the more general rule.

access to legal aid, etc.[57] Therefore it has been submitted that the state of destination, or the state on whose behalf the visa application has been rejected, should be considered to be the state taking the final decision. In several reports it was documented that the right to effective judicial protection was affected by the obligation to start procedures in another EU state, especially where applicants already have contacts or representatives in the state of destination. In 2017, a Dutch court submitted preliminary questions to the CJEU in the *Vethanayagam* case, concerning the visa application of a national from Sri Lanka. The case was especially interesting because the visa refusal was taken by the Swiss embassy in Colombo on behalf of the Dutch authorities, based on an agreement between the Netherlands and a non-EU state. In its preliminary questions, the Dutch court submitted the question whether the Visa Code allows a sponsor to bring an appeal in its own name against a visa refusal (which in the Netherlands is allowed and is used by lawyers, for example, and also by employers of the applicants). Furthermore, the national court requested from the CJEU an interpretation of 'final decision' in Article 8(4) of the Visa Code and asked whether a reading of Article 32(3), on the basis of which an appeal can only be lodged in the representing state, would be in accordance with the right to effective judicial protection. Finally, the court requested that the fact that Switzerland, as a non-EU state, is not bound by the same standards as other EU Member States should be taken into account when answering the questions related to the right to appeal. In the judgment, the CJEU took a formal approach, deviating in all answers from the opinion of Advocate-General Sharpston.[58] First, the CJEU decided that, despite the procedural autonomy of Member States (to which the Advocate-General referred in her opinion), the Visa Code would not allow sponsors to bring an appeal in their own names. Second, the CJEU found that where there is a bilateral representation arrangement providing that the consular authorities of the representing Member State are entitled to take decisions refusing visas, 'it is for the competent authorities of that Member State to decide on appeals brought against a decision refusing a visa'. And, third, a combined interpretation of Article 8(4)(d) and Article 32(3) of the Visa Code according to which an appeal against a decision refusing a visa must be conducted against the representing state, is compatible with the fundamental right to effective judicial protection.

Addressing the question related to Switzerland as a non-EU state, the CJEU referred to the fact that Switzerland is bound by the ECHR and to the text of the Preamble to the EU Swiss Association Agreement which states that the Schengen cooperation is based on principles of freedom, democracy, rule of law, and

[57] For an extended analysis of this topic, see the expert opinion submitted during the proceedings in this case, Migration Law Clinic, *Access to Legal Remedies under the Visa Code in the Case of Representation Agreements*, Vrije Universiteit Amsterdam: March 2018, available at https://migrationlawclinic.files.wordpress.com/2018/06/2018-03-29-expert-opinion-mlc.pdf (accessed 11 November 2020).

[58] Case C-680/17, *Vethanayagam*, Opinion of Advocate General Sharpston (EU:C:2019:278), 28 March 2019.

respect for fundamental rights. Accordingly, the CJEU found that the interpretation of the Visa Code, on the basis of which one must lodge an appeal against the representing state (including a non-EU state such as Switzerland), is consistent with the fundamental right of effective judicial protection.[59] The CJEU did not mention any of the points submitted by the Advocate-General related to the fact that Switzerland as a non-EU state is not bound by general principles of EU law such as effectiveness and proportionality and the right in Article 47 CFR. Therefore, the CJEU did not take into account that, as stated earlier, Article 13 ECHR does not provide the same scope of protection as Article 47 CFR and Article 6 is not applicable in immigration law procedures. Furthermore, the CJEU did not address the point raised by the Advocate-General that Swiss courts cannot submit preliminary questions to the CJEU.[60] That this non-observance of EU principles is not a theoretical problem was illustrated in the underlying case where the applicant had to pay a preliminary sum for the costs of the proceedings on the basis of Swiss law and at the same time was refused any financial aid to cover these costs. As has been ruled by the CJEU in *DEB*, such denial of financial aid may result in a breach of the right to effective judicial protection in Article 47 CFR.[61] Taking into account the conclusions in *El Hassani*, where the CJEU affirmed the importance of effective judicial protection in accordance with Article 47 CFR, the *Vethanayagam* judgment seems to be a deviation from the CJEU's own previous case-law.

In this regard, it is relevant to refer to a comparable problem on the basis of the Visa Code, which concerns the consultation procedure. According to Article 22, Member States may submit a list of third countries to the European Commission and require that if nationals from one of these countries apply for a visa for another Member State, the visa authorities of the issuing state must consult the authorities from the former state first. If the consulted state subsequently objects against the issuing of a visa, the consulting state must refuse the short-term visa even if the applicant does not intend to visit the objecting state. This cooperation is based on interstate trust. In practice, it means that the consulting state may refuse a visa on public order or public security grounds without knowing the grounds of objection of the objecting state. In March 2018, the Dutch District Court submitted preliminary questions to the CJEU in two cases in which the Dutch visa authorities had refused a short-term visa to third-country nationals following objections from other Member States (Hungary and Germany, respectively).[62] In these cases,

59 Case C-680/17, *Vethanayagam* (EU:C:2019:627) para. 88.

60 See Opinion of Advocate General Sharpston, at para. 82. I referred to this problem when dealing with mutual trust and the issue of 'variable geometry' in EU law: Brouwer, 'Mutual Trust and Judicial Control in the Area of Freedom, Security, and Justice: an Anatomy of Trust', in E. Brouwer and D. Gerard (eds), *Mapping Mutual Trust, Understanding and Framing the Role of Mutual Trust in the EU*, Florence/Fiesole: EUI Working Papers MWP 2016/3, at 65.

61 Case C-279/09, *DEB v. Germany* (EU:C:2010:811) paras 59–63.

62 C-225/19 and C-226/19 based on the preliminary questions of the District Court Den Haag zp Haarlem, 31 July 2018, AWB 17/15895 and AWB 18/7781.

the Dutch authorities did not provide information on the reasons for refusal and claimed they had no discretion to issue a visa in the face of the objection of another state. Furthermore, the applicants were referred to the objecting states with regard to their right to appeal under Article 32 of the Visa Code, despite the fact that due to the absence of a formal decision, it was difficult if not impossible for the applicants to lodge legal proceedings in the respective states. In its judgment of 24 November 2020, answering these preliminary questions, the CJEU emphasized that to ensure that the right to judicial protection is effective, the person concerned must be able to ascertain the reasons upon which the decision taken in relation to him or her is based, either by reading the decision itself, or by requesting and obtaining notification of those reasons.[63] With regard to the role of the courts, the CJEU made a distinction between on the one hand the review by courts of the Member State which adopted the final decision of refusing a visa, which concerns the examination of the legality of that decision, and on the other hand the review of the merits of the objection to the issuing of a visa raised by another Member State. The CJEU emphasized the obligation of the Member State refusing a visa, to ensure that the rights of defence and the right to a remedy of the visa applicant are guaranteed. This includes the obligation to indicate in the visa refusal decision, the identity of the Member State which raised that objection, the specific ground for refusal on the basis of that objection, and, 'where appropriate', the essence of the reasons for that objection. According to the CJEU, the courts of the Member State adopting the final decision, cannot examine the substantive legality of the objection raised by another Member State to the issuing of the visa. However, to enable the visa applicant to exercise in accordance with Article 47 CFR, his or her right to challenge such an objection, the Member State which adopted the final decision refusing a visa, should provide information on the authority the applicant may contact in order 'to ascertain the remedies available in that other Member State'.

C. Externalization: Keeping EU Measures Outside the Scope of EU Law

1. Ceci n'est pas une Acte d'EU: The EU-Turkey Statement

In the decision on the EU-Turkey Statement of 18 March 2016, the General Court dismissed an action for annulment of this bilateral agreement.[64] The annulment claim was submitted by a Pakistani asylum seeker who had entered Greece by boat from Turkey on 19 March 2016 and applied for asylum in Greece on 11 April 2016. On the basis of the EU-Turkey statement, which provided for the return of irregular migrants to Turkey, he faced expulsion to this third country. The General

[63] Joined Cases C-225/19 and C-226/19, *R.N.N.S. and K.A.* (EU:C:2020:951) paras. 43–56.

[64] Case T-192/16, *NF v. European Council* (EU:T:2017:128), Order of 28 February 2017.

Court's dismissal was based on the ground of lack of jurisdiction, following the European Council's argumentation that the 'Statement' was adopted by the heads of states of the EU Member States, and not by the European Council on behalf of the EU.[65] The General Court reached this conclusion despite the numerous references to the EU as 'co-author' of the agreement, not only in the statement itself, but also in several EU reports dealing with the alleged 'success' of this cooperation with Turkey for the closure of the EU's external borders.[66] According to the General Court, the statement would not involve an EU act but an 'intergovernmental act' by heads of states during a session parallel to the summit of the European Council.[67] Furthermore, according to the General Court, the expression 'Members of the European Council' and the term 'EU', contained in the EU-Turkey statement as published in Press Release No 144/16, must be understood as references to the Heads of State or Government of the EU.[68] In September 2018, the CJEU rejected the appeals against the decisions of the General Court as manifestly unfounded.[69]

The approach by the European Council and its legitimization by the General Court has been criticized by different organizations and commentators.[70] First, because the framing of the agreement as a non-EU act creates a legal limbo by which EU Member States cannot be held responsible under EU law. Furthermore, by adopting this measure, EU Member States agreed to cooperate with a non-EU state for the effectuation of their external border policies, whereas Turkey is not bound by the same EU and international standards of refugee protection. Various reports have shown that Turkey has violated the human rights of refugees and asylum seekers, including by detaining them and forcibly returning them to the country of origin.[71] The refusal of the General Court to recognize this agreement as an act of the EU means, in practice, that third-country nationals are denied the possibility to challenge—under EU law—human rights violations on the basis of this cooperation.

[65] Ibid. para. 75.

[66] See the text of the EU-Turkey Statement, available at https://www.consilium.europa.eu/en/press/press-releases/2016/03/18/eu-turkey-statement/pdf (accessed 11 November 2020) and the fourth report on the progress made in the implementation of the EU-Turkey statement of the European Commission, COM (2016) 792.

[67] Case T-192/16, *N.F. v. European Council* (EU:T:2017:128), Order of 28 February 2017, paras 62–64.

[68] Ibid. para. 69.

[69] Case C-208/17, C-209/17, and C-210/17 Order of 12 September 2018 (EU:C:2018:705).

[70] For example, Leino and Wyatt, 'No Public Interest in Whether the EU-Turkey Refugee Deal Respects EU Treaties and International Human Rights?', *Europeanlawblog* (28 February 2018), available at https://europeanlawblog.eu/2018/02/28/no-public-interest-in-whether-the-eu-turkey-refugee-deal-respects-eu-treaties-and-international-human-rights/ (accessed 11 November 2020) and Peers and Roman, 'The EU, Turkey and the Refugee Crisis: What Could Possibly Go Wrong?', *EU Law Analysis* 2016, available at http://eulawanalysis.blogspot.nl/2016/02/the-eu-turkey-and-refugee-crisis-what.html (accessed 11 November 2020).

[71] For a description of the situation of migrants and refugees readmitted to Turkey, see Ulusoy and Battjes, 'Situation of Readmitted Migrants and Refugees from Greece to Turkey under the EU-Turkey Statement', VU Migration Law Working Paper Series No. 15, 2017.

This brings me to a second example of externalization and the consequences of the limited interpretation of the Visa Code by the CJEU in *X and X v Belgium* in 2017.

2. ... And this is not the Visa Code: The Issuing of Humanitarian Visas

The case of *X and X v Belgium* concerned preliminary questions from the Belgian court dealing with the interpretation of Article 25(1)(a) of the Visa Code.[72] This provision allows Member States to issue a Schengen visa with 'territorial limited validity' if one or more of the conditions for a short-term visa are not fulfilled, if this is considered 'necessary on humanitarian grounds, for reasons of national interest, or because of international obligations'. In the submitted case, a visa application by a Syrian family was rejected by the Belgian embassy in Lebanon. In its preliminary questions, the Belgian court asked the CJEU whether the Visa Code requires a Member State to issue a visa with limited territorial validity applied for 'where a risk of infringement of Article 4 and/or Article 18 of the Charter or another international obligation by which it is bound is established'. The CJEU did not answer this question, but instead focused on the scope of competence of EU law, stating that the Visa Code is based on Article 62(2)(a) and (b) of the former EC Treaty. According to the CJEU, no legislation has been adopted on the basis of Article 79(2)(a) TFEU with regard to the issuing of long-term visas and residence permits to third-country nationals on humanitarian grounds.[73] The CJEU reasoned that the particular situation of the Syrian family, applying for visas with a limited territorial validity to be able to apply for asylum in Belgium, would not be covered by EU law. As the purpose of this visa application was to apply for asylum in Belgium, and therefore differed from a short-term visa application, the Visa Code did not apply.[74] Therefore, the provisions of the Charter did not apply to the situation at stake. According to the CJEU, the issuing of humanitarian visas is a matter of national sovereignty 'as European law currently stands'.[75]

With this conclusion, the CJEU explicitly excluded the issuing of humanitarian visas from the scope of EU law and provided a narrow and, in my view, incorrect interpretation of Article 25 of the Visa Code. This provision does offer a legal basis to issue visas not only on humanitarian grounds, but also 'because of international obligations'. These obligations include the principle of *non-refoulement*, protected in Article 4 of the Charter, Article 3 ECHR, and the Refugee Convention. In practice, as has been submitted before the CJEU, different EU Member States did issue Schengen visas with limited territorial validity on the basis of the Visa Code, with the purpose of granting them international protection within their territory.[76] But

[72] Case C-638/16 PPU, *X and X v. Belgium* (EU:C:2017:173).
[73] Ibid. paras 40 and 44.
[74] Ibid. paras 43 and 47.
[75] Ibid. para. 45.
[76] See U. I. Jensen, 'Humanitarian Visas: Option or Obligation?' Study for the European Parliament (Policy Department for Citizens' Rights and Constitutional Affairs) September 2016, 43 ff, available

also with regard to other purposes of long-term residence, such as family reunification, Article 22 has been used by Member States to grant a territorial limited visa, to allow the applicants to apply for these residence permits within the territory of that state. The decision of the CJEU could also be contested on the basis that as a territorial limited visa has been 'formally submitted' on the basis of Article 25 of the Visa Code, from that moment the Visa Code—and thus EU law—applies. Furthermore, the CJEU failed to take into account the general principles of EU law included in Articles 2 and 3 TEU with regard to the protection of fundamental rights and international obligations, and in Article 78(1) TFEU describing the goal of 'offering appropriate status to any third-country national requiring international protection and ensuring compliance with the principle of non-refoulement' in accordance with the Geneva Convention. Instead, the CJEU pointed to the fact that the Procedure Directive (Directive 2013/32) and the Dublin Regulation (Regulation 604/2013) explicitly exclude asylum applications at embassies and consulates abroad, in order to substantiate its conclusion that in this case EU law does not apply.[77] However, the current case did not question the applicability of the Procedure Directive or the Dublin Regulation. The question, as submitted by the Belgian court, dealt with the obligation of Member States under Articles 4 and 18 of the Charter when dealing with applications based on Article 25 of the Visa Code. Even if Article 25 offers Member States a wide margin of appreciation to decide whether or not to issue a humanitarian visa, under specific circumstances this discretionary power may turn into a positive obligation when the absolute right of *non-refoulement* is at risk.[78] It was precisely because of these circumstances that the Belgian court asked for clarification of the meaning of the words 'international obligations' in Article 25, and why the Advocate General found that Member States do have an obligation to issue humanitarian visas.

Interestingly, one month earlier, the CJEU had found that the fact that EU law leaves Member States the sovereign power of whether or not to provide protection did not mean that this power did not fall within the scope of EU law. This was underlined by the CJEU when dealing with the sovereignty clause in Article 17(1) of the Dublin Regulation in *C.K. v. Slovenia*.[79] The CJEU ruled that the application of the sovereignty clause is part of EU law and therefore involves an interpretation of EU law within the meaning of Article 267 TFEU. The discretion allowed to Member States by this sovereignty clause is 'an integral part of the system for

at http://www.europarl.europa.eu/RegData/etudes/STUD/2014/509986/IPOL_STU(2014)509986_EN.pdf (accessed 11 November 2020), where she describes the different policies in the EU Member States and the unclear provisions of the current Visa Code.

[77] Case C-638/16 PPU, *X and X v. Belgium* (EU:C:2017:173) para. 49.

[78] Brouwer, 'AG Mengozzi's Conclusion in X and X v. Belgium on the Positive Obligation to Issue Humanitarian Visa. A Legitimate Plea to Ensure Safe Journeys for Refugees', *CEPS Policy Insights* No. 2017/09, March 2017.

[79] Case C-578/16 PPU, *C.K. and Others v. Slovenia* (EU:C:2017:127) para. 53.

determining the Member State responsible developed by the EU legislature ("the Dublin system")'. Therefore, according to the CJEU, a Member State also implements EU law, within the meaning of Article 51(1) of the Charter, when it makes use of that clause. In my view, in *X and X v. Belgium*, the CJEU could have reasoned, along the same lines, that the decision to issue or not to issue a limited territorial visa or humanitarian visa, as applied for under the Visa Code, always falls within the scope of EU law. Dealing with the question of the availability of legal remedies and the sovereignty clause in the Dublin Regulation, the CJEU applied a comparable line of reasoning in *MA v. UK*.[80] In this judgment of 2019, the CJEU emphasized the 'absolute discretion' and 'prerogative' of Member States to decide to examine an application for asylum for which it is not responsible under the applicable criteria of the Dublin Regulation. This means, that where in this case, UK, was 'designated' as the responsible Member State for the asylum claim on the basis of these criteria, but notified its intention to withdraw from the EU, the determining Member State is not obliged to use the discretionary clause as provided in the Dublin regulation, and to examine the asylum application itself. Therefore, the CJEU held that the right to an effective remedy in Article 27(1) of the Dublin III Regulation does not require Member States to make a legal remedy available against the decision not to use the sovereignty clause in Article 17(1).[81]

4. Conclusion

The 'Europeanization' of immigration and asylum laws has generally resulted in the strengthening of the legal position of third-country nationals. Although this effect of 'EU legality' was not foreseen by the EU legislator while drafting different instruments of immigration law, the CJEU repeatedly made it clear that these laws should be implemented in accordance with general principles of EU law. This active approach of the CJEU resulted in a continuing line of jurisprudence, stressing the principle of effectiveness and proportionality in EU immigration law decision-making, for example when dealing with the right to family reunification. Furthermore, the CJEU clarified the content of vague provisions dealing with the right to legal remedies in, for example, the Dublin Regulation or the Visa Code, underlining that these provisions must be interpreted in accordance with the guarantees of the right to effective judicial protection in Article 47 CFR.

Aside from this strengthening effect for the legal position of third-country nationals, in this chapter different, and more recent, challenges to 'EU legality' and the protection of fundamental rights have been identified. Current EU laws offer Member States leeway to exclude their responsibility with regard to the legal

[80] Case C-661/17, *M.A. v. UK* (EU:C:2019:53) paras 58–61.
[81] Ibid. para. 86.

protection of third-country nationals, either by the externalization of immigration policies or by the mutual enforcement of national immigration decisions. This exclusion of EU legality, either by 're-nationalization' or externalization, as such affects the effectiveness of the protection of fundamental rights and principles under EU law. By withdrawing national or EU acts from the scope of EU law, it becomes difficult, if not impossible, to hold individual Member States responsible for non-implementation of EU standards, including the protection of the human rights of migrants. This is illustrated by the example of entry bans and the use of information systems. Whereas EU law obliges Member States to report entry bans or to exclude immigrants from the EU territory, the definition of 'inadmissible aliens' and the use of ECRIS-TCN almost fully remains within the sovereignty of the national state. Another example concerns the obligation of consultation in short-term visa procedures. According to the Visa Code, national authorities have retained the power to block, on the basis of national and often non-transparent grounds, third-country nationals from entry to and residence in the whole Schengen area.

These aforementioned challenges to EU legality became visible in more recent judgments of the CJEU. In contrast to its former decisions, underlining the obligations of Member States under general principles of EU law, the CJEU seems to have taken a more restrictive approach. Member States are given further discretionary power to exclude their responsibility under EU law by formal and narrow readings of the applicable laws. With its judgment on the EU-Turkey agreement and on the non-applicability of the Visa Code on the issuing of humanitarian visas, the CJEU established a less rigorous scrutiny at the cost of general principles of EU law within the field of externalized EU migration and asylum policies. The conclusions of the CJEU with regard to visa representation and, more recently, the visa consultation system, illustrate the limitations to third-country nationals' access to effective judicial protection in practice. Furthermore, in response to questions from national courts on the concept of 'public order' in EU migration laws, the CJEU did not really provide any more clarity, but focused instead on procedural guarantees; this may be to the benefit of the discretionary power of national authorities, but to the cost of the legal protection of third-country nationals.

Nevertheless, to conclude, one could argue that it is a matter of a glass which is half full or half empty. As we have seen, the CJEU's case-law provides important standards by referring continuously to the application of general principles of EU law. Based on principles of effectiveness and proportionality, this means that in national immigration law procedures, national authorities remain obliged to make balanced decisions, on a case-by-case basis, and taking into account the objectives of the EU laws involved. Access to legal remedies may be hampered by choices of the EU legislator or national authorities; however, the right to effective judicial protection as a general principle of EU law to be protected in immigration law procedures remains undisputed. Hopefully, in future, the CJEU will continue to safeguard the objectives and coherence of EU law by underlining the obligations of EU

Member States in respecting the fundamental rights and legal protection of third-country nationals. Regardless of which approach the CJEU chooses, it is clear that national courts will continue to have an important role in protecting EU principles and the right to effective judicial protection within the field of asylum and immigration law.

4

Legality in EU Common Foreign and Security Policy

The Choice of the Appropriate Legal Basis

*Ramses A. Wessel**

1. Introduction

To some it may not be self-evident to discuss questions of legality in the context of the EU's Common Foreign and Security Policy (CFSP). In early studies in particular, CFSP was perceived and presented as 'political' rather than 'legal'.[1] Even today, the Treaties indicate that any review of the legality of CFSP decisions is limited to 'certain decisions' (Article 24(1) of the Treaty on European Union (TEU)). Any general review of legality on the basis of Article 263 of the Treaty on the Functioning of the European Union (TFEU) thus seems to have been excluded for CFSP.[2]

Limitations to the enforcement of legality in the area of CFSP, however, do not allow for the conclusion that legality, as such, should be measured or approached differently in CFSP than in other parts of the Union's legal order. The 'normalization' of CFSP has been analysed quite extensively over the past few years,[3] and has pointed to a shift away from intergovernmentalism, even in a sensitive policy domain such as the Common Security and Defence Policy (CSDP).[4] Its further

* The author is indebted to Dr Graham Butler for his very helpful comments on an earlier draft of this contribution as well as to the Editors of this volume for their guidance. The usual disclaimer applies.

[1] For references, see R. A. Wessel, *The European Union's Foreign and Security Policy: A Legal Institutional Perspective* (1999).

[2] Yet, see further Section 2.B on the role of the Court of Justice.

[3] See Wessel, 'Integration and Constitutionalisation in EU Foreign and Security Policy', in R. Schütze (ed.), *Governance and Globalization: International and European Perspectives* (2018) 339; 'Editorial Comments', 55 *Common Market Law Review* (2018) 1; Sánchez-Taberno, 'The Choice of Legal Basis and the Principle of Consistency in the Procedure for Conclusion of International Agreements in CFSP Contexts: Parliament v. Council (Pirate-Transfer Agreement with Tanzania)', 54 *Common Market Law Review* (2017) 899; Van Elsuwege, 'EU External Action after the Collapse of the Pillar Structure: In Search of a New Balance between Delimitation and Consistency', 47 *Common Market Law Review* (2010) 987; Eckes, 'Common Foreign and Security Policy: The Consequences of the Court's Extended Jurisdiction', 22 *European Law Journal* (2016) 492.

[4] Cf. J. Strikwerda, 'Integration in the European Union's Field of Defence and Security' (2019) (PhD thesis at the University of Oslo), available at http://urn.nb.no/URN:NBN:no-69552 (accessed 11 November 2020).

Ramses A. Wessel, *Legality in EU Common Foreign and Security Policy: The Choice of the Appropriate Legal Basis.* In: *Contemporary Challenges to EU Legality.* First edition. Edited by: Claire Kilpatrick and Joanne Scott, Oxford University Press (2021). © Ramses A. Wessel. DOI: 10.1093/oso/9780192898050.003.0004

integration into the Union's legal order has brought about new questions related to the legality of the acts adopted under CFSP as well as to their legal basis. These analyses highlighted the consolidation of EU foreign policy, its constitutionalization as part of the Union's legal order,[5] as well as institutional adaptations.[6] These changes have put the distinction between CFSP and other external Union policy areas into perspective.[7]

Hence, in the present era, it is more and more accepted that CFSP is 'a policy producing norms just as any other EU public policy does'.[8] As will be shown later, this statement is supported by recent case-law of the Court of Justice of the European Union, revealing a principled effort 'to further embed the CFSP into the EU legal order'.[9] The main consequence of the further 'legalization' of CFSP is that questions of legality have become more prominent in that area, keeping in mind the Court's famous statement in *Les Verts*, that 'the Treat[ies] established a complete system of legal remedies and procedures designed to permit the Court of Justice to review the legality of measures adopted by the institutions'.[10] This has been apparent both before and after the entering into force of the Treaty of Lisbon in 2009. After the

[5] Art. 21(3) TEU; see later. See also G. Butler, *Constitutional Law of the EU's Common Foreign and Security Policy: Competence and Institutions in External Relations* (2019); Lonardo, 'Common Foreign and Security Policy and the EU's External Action Objectives: An Analysis of Article 21 of the Treaty on the European Union', 14 *European Constitutional Law Review* (2018) 584. As argued by Larik: 'The Lisbon Treaty has both expanded and streamlined the Union's global objectives. [W]e can see that the EU Treaties codify a range of global objectives both in terms of substance but also specifically harnessing law ... Together, these elements coincide with the idea of the Union as a "transformative power", changing not only fundamentally the relations among its members but also of the world around it.' Larik, 'Entrenching Global Governance: The EU's Constitutional Objectives Caught Between a Sanguine World View and a Daunting Reality', in B. Van Vooren, S. Blockmans, and J. Wouters (eds), *The EU's Role in Global Governance: The Legal Dimension* (2013) 7, at 10–11.

[6] Such as the introduction of the European External Action Service and the combination of the High Representative for CFSP and the Commission for external relations. For instance, see M. Gatti, *European External Action Service: Promoting Coherence through Autonomy and Coordination* (2017); and De Baere and Wessel, 'EU Law and the EEAS: Of Complex Competences and Constitutional Consequences', in J. Bátora and D. Spence (eds), *The European External Action Service: European Diplomacy Post-Westphalia* (2015) 175. On the High Representative, see in the latter volume Helwig, 'The High Representative of the Union: The Quest for Leadership in EU Foreign Policy', 87.

[7] Yet, Cardwell pointed out the difficulty in changing the 'tradition of otherness' in analyses of CFSP, which made it awkward to fully value the (post-Lisbon) changes. Cardwell, 'On "Ring-Fencing" the Common Foreign and Security Policy in the Legal Order of the European Union', 64 *Northern Ireland Legal Quarterly* (2015) 443. See further Broberg, 'EU Development Cooperation and the CFSP: Mutual Encroachment?', in S. Blockmans and P. Koutrakos (eds), *Research Handbook on the EU's Common Foreign and Security Policy* (2018) 254; and in the same volume: Koutrakos, 'The Nexus between CFSP/CSDP and the Area of Freedom, Security and Justice', 296; Ott and Van der Loo, 'The Nexus between the CCP and the CFSP: Achieving Foreign Policy Goals through Trade Restrictions and Market Access', 230.

[8] Saurugger and Terpan, 'Studying Resistance to EU Norms in Foreign and Security Policy', 2(1) *European Foreign Affairs Review* (2015) 1.

[9] T. Verellen, 'Pirates of the Gulf of Aden: The Sequel, or How the CJEU Further Embeds the CFSP into the EU Legal Order', *European Law Blog*, 23 August 2016, available at https://europeanlawblog.eu/2016/08/23/pirates-of-the-gulf-of-aden-the-sequel-or-how-the-cjeu-further-embeds-the-cfsp-into-the-eu-legal-order/ (accessed 11 November 2020).

[10] Case C-294/83, *Parti écologiste 'Les Verts' v. European Parliament* (EU:C:1986:166) para. 23. See on the relevance of this notion for CFSP Butler, 'Implementing a Complete System of Legal Remedies in EU Foreign Affairs Law', 24 *Columbia Journal of European Law* (2018) 637.

Kadi cases in particular, legality review of CFSP measures has received abundant attention;[11] an attention that has intensified following recent cases in which the Court was confronted with CFSP questions.[12] These cases underline the importance of two elements. First of all, questions of legality make sense only in the context of legal acts. This chapter will therefore briefly revisit the nature of CFSP acts as well as their consequences in the light of the 'normalization' of CFSP. Secondly, legal bases matter. Hence, questions of legality will be assessed in relation to the legal basis of CFSP acts and, in particular, the choice of legal basis and the possibility of combining CFSP and other legal bases for acts covering both CFSP and other external policies.

This focus on questions regarding legal basis does not aim to deny the broader scope of the concept of legality. The choice of legal basis is essential for a number of principles that are usually seen as being connected to legality of function, such as the structural principles (including proportionality and conferral), or principles of the rule of law and good administration (including the right to an effective judicial remedy, transparency, and the protection of legitimate expectations).[13] Furthermore, the analysis in this chapter is informed by the emphasis on the principle of consistent interpretation in the current treaty regime, in particular, to establish a legal connection between all external objectives.[14] Thus, Article 21(3) TEU provides:

> The Union shall respect the principles and pursue the objectives ... in the development and implementation of the different areas of the Union's external action covered by this Title and by Part Five of the Treaty on the Functioning of the European Union, and of the external aspects of its other policies.
>
> The Union shall ensure consistency between the different areas of its external action and between these and its other policies. The Council and the Commission, assisted by the High Representative of the Union for Foreign Affairs and Security Policy, shall ensure that consistency and shall cooperate to that effect.

Specifically, through the case-law of the Court of Justice, this consistency obligation has become directly connected to the objective of 'ensur[ing] the coherence

[11] See on the review of the sanctions regimes, for instance C. Eckes, *EU Counter-Terrorist Policies and Fundamental Rights: The Case of Individual Sanctions* (2009).

[12] See on the more recent role of the Court in relation to CFSP Hillion and Wessel, 'The Good, the Bad and the Ugly: Three Levels of Judicial Control over the CFSP', in S. Blockmans and P. Koutrakos (eds), *Research Handbook on the EU's Common Foreign and Security Policy* (2018) 65; P. Koutrakos, 'Judicial Review in the EU's Common Foreign and Security Policy', 67 *International and Comparative Law Quarterly* (2018) 1; and Butler (n. 10).

[13] Cf. C. Barnard and S. Peers, *European Union Law* (2014) 203. More generally, see M. Cremona (ed.), *Structural Principles in EU External Relations* (2018).

[14] See further on the many aspects of the consistency requirement and its use by the Treaties R. A. Wessel and J. Larik (eds), *EU External Relations Law: Text, Cases and Materials* (2020) chs 1 and 2.

and consistency of the action and its [the Union's] international representation'.[15] In other words, the principle of consistency underlines the need to assess questions of legality in CFSP in the context of the overall legal order of the EU where legal bases choices have to be made.[16] Whereas 'consistency' calls for the exclusion of discrepancies and the absence of conflicting policies, 'coherence' is a less binary notion, demanding that different Union policies are taken into account.[17]

In addressing questions of legality in relation to CFSP, this chapter will first of all briefly revisit the legal nature of this policy area (Section 2). As well as defining the binding nature of CFSP acts, this section will also examine the Court's approach in assessing the legality of CFSP norms. Section 3 will follow up by investigating the rules guiding the choice of the correct legal basis. As the possibilities for a review of legality largely depend on the legal basis that was used to adopt a certain act, this forms a crucial aspect when establishing the Court's role. The same holds true where a CFSP legal basis is combined with one in the TFEU (Section 4). The unity of the Union's legal order, the integrated external objectives, and the principle of consistency all point to a holistic perspective. Yet the question remains to what extent and in which situations problems related to legality review in CFSP may be solved by combining acts across different policy fields. Finally, Section 5 will draw some conclusions and set out some aims to answer the question to what extent the legal nature of CFSP is reflected in possibilities to review the legality of the Union's acts in that area.

2. Does Legality Even Matter? The Legal Nature of CFSP Acts

A. The Binding Nature of CFSP Acts

Given the traditional image of CFSP as an area that is dominated by politics rather than legal rules, the first question in relation to the legality of CFSP acts is whether these acts are legal at all. This is an old question, which has been addressed many times over the past decades by both legal scholars, and political scientists. The main legal arguments will be summarized here.[18] Given my legal theoretical preference, the question is—admittedly—approached from a formalistic, positivist perspective.[19] The issue originates from Article 24(1) TEU, which provides

[15] Case C-266/03, *Commission v. Luxembourg* (EU:C:2005:341) para. 60, and Case C-476/98, *Commission v. Germany* (EU:C:2002:631) para. 66.

[16] Cf. also Sánchez-Taberno (n. 3).

[17] See quite extensively on consistency and coherence in EU external relations, Gatti (n. 6) ch. 1.

[18] See for a more extensive analysis and further references to earlier literature, Wessel, 'Resisting Legal Facts: Are CFSP Norms as Soft as They Seem?', 20 *European Foreign Affairs Review* (2015) 123. This section partly draws from that publication.

[19] Cf. the distinction made by Walker between *positivism, idealism, culturalism, and pragmatism* in Chapter 2 of this work.

that CFSP is formed on the basis of 'specific rules and procedures' and that the use of 'legislative acts' is excluded. The reference to 'specific rules and procedures' has largely been interpreted as a reason to set CFSP apart from the 'general' rules—what has become known as the 'Community method' that would form the basis to enact legal rules in the Union's other policy areas. The exclusion of 'legislative acts' would, however, deny the legal nature of CFSP acts if this were to be taken at mere face value. Both provisions largely relate to decision-making *procedures* and tell us less about the legal *nature* of the acts. The fact that no 'legislative acts' can be concluded is mainly intended to exclude the use of the 'legislative procedure', which leads to the regular EU types of decisions: Regulations, Directives, and Decisions, and other forms of legal acts emanating from Article 288 TFEU.[20] The exclusion of the legislative procedure (as the regular decision-making procedure for other Union policies), the requirement of unanimity rather than qualified majority voting (QMV) as the default voting rule, the 'specific role of the European Parliament and of the Commission', and the fact that 'the Court of Justice of the European Union shall not have jurisdiction' with respect to a number of specific CFSP provisions, may leave the reader with an initial view on how the 'legality' of CFSP acts is perceived in this chapter—that it may not be so legal at all. At the same time, however, the Treaties are quite clear about the legal (and binding) nature of CFSP treaty provisions and acts.[21] CFSP decisions are to be found under 'legal acts' in the EurLex databases and are published in the L-series of the Official Journal. It thus goes without saying that both the procedural norms in the Treaties as well as the decisions taken under CFSP are 'legal', in the sense that they form part of the Union's legal order and 'must be implemented into the national legal orders when applicable'.[22] They form part of the overall institutional structure of the EU, which will take the specific legal effects of instruments into account in the choice of legal basis. Or, as clearly argued by Butler:

> Despite seeming to be the contrary, CFSP matters are a legalised field. For lawyers, everything in EU external relations begins with a discussion on the legal basis for supporting actions. As the Union strives for more coordination, consistency and cooperation, the choice of legal basis is of profound importance. The law is only one element of EU external relations, but it is an integral component that caters for the execution of external action. This is even more so in CFSP matters where strict conditions for the procedural issues are set down in the treaties. This is not only in EU external relations law, but for all EU acts or measures, which must have a legal basis.[23]

[20] See on EU legal acts also an earlier volume in the Academy's series M. Cremona and C. Kilpatrick (eds), *EU Legal Acts: Challenges and Transformations* (2018).

[21] Cf. Butler (n. 5) 47.

[22] Ibid. 68.

[23] Ibid. 5.

Article 26(2) TEU entails a general competence for the Council to 'frame the common foreign and security policy and take the decisions necessary for defining and implementing it on the basis of the general guidelines and strategic lines defined by the European Council'. A combination of this provision and the more specific key legal bases in Articles 28 (actions), 29 (positions), 33 (appointment of special representatives), 37 (international agreements), 42/43 (military and civilian missions), and 46 (permanent structured cooperation) allows for the Council to adopt different CFSP legal and political instruments. Article 25 TEU lists them as follows: *general guidelines* (a specific task for the European Council); *decisions* (entailing both actions and positions as well as arrangements for the implementation of the decisions); and *systematic cooperation* between Member States. This chapter will focus on the 'decisions' and leave the more informal instruments (including 'declarations' or Council minutes that are the result of the systematic cooperation) aside. In comparison to the many legal acts that are adopted under the TFEU on a daily basis, the adoption of CFSP legal acts is a relatively rare phenomenon. In many instances, the minutes of the Foreign Affairs Council meetings contain the decisions of the Council, without these being adopted as formal CFSP Decisions at a later stage. Most CFSP Decisions are related to restrictive measures or to the CSDP (see further Section 2.B).

It remains noteworthy that the Treaties are quite clear about the binding nature of these CFSP acts. The mandatory force of CFSP Decisions can clearly be derived from Article 28(2) TEU: 'Decisions referred to in paragraph 1 shall commit the Member States in the positions they adopt and in the conduct of their activity.' Hence, CFSP Decisions, once adopted, limit the freedom of Member States in their individual policies. Member States are not allowed to adopt positions or otherwise to act contrary to the Decisions. They have committed themselves to adapting their national policies to the agreed Decisions.[24]

Overall, the system is based on a duty of good faith, which is clearly laid down in Article 24 TEU: 'The member states shall support the common foreign and security policy actively and unreservedly in a spirit of loyalty and mutual solidarity and shall comply with the Union's action in this area.' CFSP acts are concrete norms of conduct, demanding a certain unconditional behaviour from the Member States, which is underlined by the strict limits on the ways in which exceptions are permitted.[25]

The above findings reveal the legal nature of CFSP acts. At the same time, they divulge the challenges in applying the principle of legality to these acts and allowing

[24] It is even tempting to make comparisons with EU Regulations, which also demand the unconditional obedience of Member States once they are adopted. The notion that CFSP acts restrain the EU Member States is, of course, far from new. See already Hillion and Wessel, 'Restraining External Competences of EU Member States under CFSP', in M. Cremona and B. De Witte (eds), *EU Foreign Relations Law: Constitutional Fundamentals* (2008) 79.

[25] See on the exceptions Wessel (n. 18).

the 'complete system of legal remedies'[26] to function in this area, despite the fact that general principles of EU law are equally valid in a CFSP context. As I have argued elsewhere, this holds true for all key EU principles, including the principle of cooperation; the principles of conferral, subsidiarity, and proportionality; and more substantive principles; as well as some general principles of international law referred to in the Treaties.[27]

B. The Court's Approach to the Legality of CFSP Norms

Pre-Lisbon, the Court clearly struggled with its lack of jurisdiction to review the legality of CFSP acts. In the 2006 *OMPI* case it noted its own limitations when confronted with a CFSP decision related to terrorism, while acknowledging the jurisdictional gap:

> In the Community legal system founded on the principle of conferred powers, as embodied in Article 5 EC, the absence of an effective legal remedy as claimed by the applicant cannot in itself confer independent Community jurisdiction in relation to an act adopted in a related yet distinct legal system, namely that deriving from Titles V [CFSP] and VI of the EU Treaty.[28]

At the same time, the Court acknowledged the committing nature of CFSP norms and the need to assess them in the context of the overall EU legal order. A statement in that regard was made a year later in the *Segi* case in 2007, when the Court for the first time confirmed the binding nature of Common Positions (currently CFSP Decisions based on Article 29 TEU):

> A common position requires the compliance of the Member States by virtue of the principle of the duty to cooperate in good faith, which means in particular that Member States are to take all appropriate measures, whether general or particular, to ensure fulfilment of their obligations under European Union law.[29]

[26] Case C-294/83, *Parti écologiste 'Les Verts' v. European Parliament.*

[27] See Wessel, 'General Principles in CFSP Law', in V. Morena-Lax, P. Neuvonen, and K. Ziegler (eds), *Research Handbook on General Principles of EU Law* (2021).

[28] Case T-228/02, *Organisation des Modjahedines du peuple d'Iran v. Council and UK ('OMPI')* (EU:T:2006:384) para. 54. See on this case Eckes, 'Case T-228/02, Organisation des Modjahedines du peuple d'Iran v. Council and UK (OMPI)', 44 *Common Market Law Review* (2007) 1117.

[29] Case C-355/04 P, *Segi and Others v. Council* (EU:C:2007:116) para. 52. While the case primarily concerned the (former) area of police and judicial cooperation in criminal matters (PJCCM), a transposition to CFSP seems legitimate as the Common Position in question could also be regarded a CFSP decision since it was equally based on both PJCCM and CFSP.

The early case-law already made clear that in certain constitutional areas the Court opted for a Union-wide application of certain fundamental rules and principles. Thus, the Court made clear that wherever access to information is concerned, no distinction is made on the basis of the content of the requested document.[30] Similarly, the Court argued that judicial protection was to be applied Union-wide. It referred to Article 6 TEU and concluded:

> the Union is founded on the principle of the rule of law and it respects fundamental rights as general principles ... It follows that the institutions are subject to review of the conformity of their acts with the treaties and the general principles of law, just like the Member States when they implement the law of the Union.[31]

On the basis of Article 275 TFEU the Court now furthermore enjoys the competence to rule on proceedings brought in accordance with the conditions laid down in the fourth paragraph of Article 263 TFEU, reviewing the legality of decisions providing for restrictive measures against natural or legal persons. This provision, which gives the Court the possibility to *directly* scrutinize a CFSP measure, is the result of the proliferation of sanctions targeted at individuals in the (global) fight against terrorism. The implication is that, even in a case where restrictive measures are only laid down in CFSP measures (and not followed up through a Regulation), the Court has jurisdiction once the plaintiff is directly and individually concerned.

More recent case-law confirms the notion that the exclusion of the Court's jurisdiction in relation to CFSP which could be derived from Articles 24(1) TEU and 275 TFEU[32] is not absolute.[33] The case-law that has developed since the entry into force of these provisions displays the Court's broader conception of its CFSP-related jurisdiction. Thus, in the fundamental *Mauritius* judgment, the Court held:

> the final sentence of the second subparagraph of Article 24(1) TEU and the first paragraph of Article 275 TFEU introduce a *derogation* from the rule of the general jurisdiction which Article 19 TEU confers on the Court to ensure that in the

[30] Case T-174/95, *Svenska Journalistförbundet v. Council* (EU:T:1998:127). More implicitly this was already accepted by the Court in Case T-194/94, *Carvel and Guardian Newspapers v. Council* (EU:C:1996:172). See further Butler (n. 5) 237 and 249.

[31] Case C-355/04 P, *Segi and Others v. Council* (EU:C:2007:116) para. 51.

[32] Art. 24(1) TEU provides: '... The Court of Justice of the European Union shall not have jurisdiction with respect to these provisions, with the exception of its jurisdiction to monitor compliance with Article 40 of this Treaty and to review the legality of certain decisions as provided for by the second paragraph of Article 275 of the Treaty on the Functioning of the European Union. ...' Article 275 TFEU adds: 'The Court of Justice of the European Union shall not have jurisdiction with respect to the provisions relating to the common foreign and security policy nor with respect to acts adopted on the basis of those provisions.'

[33] Hillion and Wessel (n. 12). Parts of this section draw from that publication.

> interpretation and application of the Treaties the law is observed, and they must, therefore, be interpreted narrowly.[34]

Thus, legality control over CFSP restrictive measures is not limited to the annulment proceedings envisaged in Article 263(4) TFEU, but includes the possibility for the Court to give a preliminary ruling on their validity. In *Rosneft*, the Court considered CFSP acts to be fit to be the subject of a preliminary question, albeit in relation to restrictive measures only where the Court also enjoys the competence to review sanctions in direct actions:

> Since the purpose of the procedure that enables the Court to give preliminary rulings is to ensure that in the interpretation and application of the Treaties the law is observed, in accordance with the duty assigned to the Court under Article 19(1) TEU, it would be contrary to the objectives of that provision and to the principle of effective judicial protection to adopt a strict interpretation of the jurisdiction conferred on the Court by the second paragraph of Article 275 TFEU, to which reference is made by Article 24(1) TEU …
>
> In those circumstances, provided that the Court has, under Article 24(1) TEU and the second paragraph of Article 275 TFEU, jurisdiction *ex ratione materiae* to rule on the validity of European Union acts, that is, in particular, where such acts relate to restrictive measures against natural or legal persons, it would be inconsistent with the system of effective judicial protection established by the Treaties to interpret the latter provision as excluding the possibility that the courts and tribunals of Member States may refer questions to the Court on the validity of Council decisions prescribing the adoption of such measures.[35]

Recent case-law thus points to a notable development, keeping in mind the distinctive nature of CFSP: the Court's legality control over *certain* CFSP acts is the same as the control it exercises over other EU acts. It is an expression of its general mandate as established in Article 19 TEU; it is governed by the same principles—in particular, the principle of effective judicial remedies enshrined in Article 47 of the Charter of Fundamental Rights and, even more generally, the rule of law.[36] This development is further illustrated by a number of cases with a clear CFSP dimension. First—in the *Mauritius* and *Tanzania* judgments[37]—the Court has made clear that international agreements in the area of CFSP are concluded on the basis

[34] Case C-658/11, *European Parliament v. Council* ('*Mauritius*') (EU:C:2014:2025) para. 70 (emphasis added). See also Case C-439/13 P, *Elitaliana* (EU:C:2015:753) para. 41; Case C-455/14 P, *H v. Council* (EU:C:2016:569) para. 40.

[35] Case C-72/15, *Rosneft* (EU:C:2017:236).

[36] Cf. Van Elsuwege, 'Upholding the Rule of Law in the Common Foreign and Security Policy: H v. Council', 54 *Common Market Law Review* (2017) 841.

[37] Case C-658/11, *European Parliament v. Council* ('*Mauritius*') (EU:C:2014:2025); and Case C-263/14, *European Parliament v. Council ('Tanzania')* (EU:C:2016:435).

of the general provisions of Article 218 TFEU, albeit subject to some specific arrangements. Thus, the Court would exercise judicial control to ensure compliance with the terms of that procedure. Second, and in the same vein, the Court has considered that it would have jurisdiction to control the legality of a decision which, despite its CFSP context, relates to a more general or different issue, such as awarding a public service contract in the context of an EU CSDP Mission[38] or staff issues.[39] One of the latter situations formed the background of *H. v. Council and Commission*—a case brought by a staff member of the EU Police Mission in Bosnia and Herzegovina (EUPM), established under the CFSP:

> the scope of the limitation, by way of derogation, on the Court's jurisdiction ... cannot be considered to be so extensive as to exclude the jurisdiction of the EU judicature to review acts of staff management relating to staff members seconded by the Member States the purpose of which is to meet the needs of that mission at theatre level, when the EU judicature has, in any event, jurisdiction to review such acts where they concern staff members seconded by the EU institutions.[40]

These rulings underline that the Court of Justice considers the CFSP as part-and-parcel of the Union's constitutional set-up, and that it sees CFSP acts as legal acts that can be subject to legal scrutiny.[41] Yet, the Court's legality review remains limited in the sense that it cannot yet provide 'full review',[42] and so a systemic gap in the EU system of legality review remains. While one option would be to simply grant the Court full judicial oversight over the CFSP, and thus suppress the current derogatory provisions of Articles 24(1) TEU and 275 TFEU,[43] this is unlikely to happen soon. We are therefore stuck in a situation where, in the Court's own

[38] Case C-439/13 P, *Elitaliana* (EU:C:2015:753) para. 49.

[39] Case C-455/14 P, *H v. Council* (EU:C:2016:569); Case T-286/15, *KF v. SatCen* (EU:T:2018:718). See Butler (n. 5) 189–90.

[40] Case C-455/14 P, *H v. Council* (EU:C:2016:569). More recently, the Court also confirmed its jurisdiction in relation to the non-contractual liability of the Union in relation to CFSP acts, plugging another gap in the judicial review of these acts (see Case C-134/19 P, *Bank Refah Kargaran* (EU:C:2020:396)).

[41] Hillion and Wessel (n. 12).

[42] As famously phrased in *Kadi I*: 'the Community judicature must ... ensure the review, in principle the full review, of the lawfulness of all Community acts in the light of the fundamental rights forming an integral part of the general principles of Community law, including review of Community measures which, like the contested regulation, are designed to give effect to the resolutions adopted by the Security Council under Chapter VII of the Charter of the United Nations'. Joined Cases C-402/05 P and C-415/05 P, *Yassin Abdullah Kadi and Al Barakaat International Foundation v. Council and Commission ('Kadi I')* (EU:C:2008:461) para. 327.

[43] In this respect, see the intervention of President of the CJEU Lenaerts at the ICON-S Conference 2016, Day 3, Plenary Session 3: 'Judicial Interview and Dialogue', available at https://www.youtube.com/watch?v=_Vrjbte9Yfg (accessed 11 November 2020).

words, 'certain acts, actions or omissions performed in the context of the CFSP fall outside the ambit of judicial review by the Court of Justice'.[44] While this statement still leaves us in the dark to some extent, this probably concerns acts *within* the CFSP legal order (related to foreign policy obligations laid down in the Treaty or adopted by the Council), and particularly elements in these decisions that do not concern general restrictive measures. The Treaty clearly places the monitoring and enforcement of the compliance with CFSP acts in the hands of the Council and the High Representative (Article 24(3) TEU). With regard to issues related to civilian and military missions launched in the context of the CSDP, the Court's jurisdiction also seems difficult to establish. Obviously, this has consequences for accountability or responsibility claims arising from military activities abroad. Any legality review of action in the context of CFSP missions legality is not only hampered by the Treaty rules, but also by the quite extensive immunities granted to EU missions abroad.[45] At the same time it remains clear that fundamental values need to be applied Union-wide, even in a CSDP context. In view of the Court's recent case-law, a review by the Court of certain acts or activities by military or civilian missions in relation to general rules and principles of EU law is not excluded.

3. The Choice of Legal Basis

Given the integration of CFSP into the EU's legal order and the consolidation of external relations objectives, the question is to what extent the choice of legal basis can be helpful in correcting a number of flaws in the legality review of CFSP acts. After all, the choice of legal basis in this area is key, and largely defines the possibilities for the Court to review the legality of adopted acts.[46] Indeed, as held by the Court, 'the choice of the appropriate legal basis has constitutional significance'.[47] This section addresses this issue from two perspectives: the general rule to choose either a CFSP or a TFEU legal basis; and the more specific rules on how to make that choice.

[44] Opinion 2/13 ('EU Accession to the ECHR') (EU:C:2014:2454) para. 252.

[45] See more extensively on these questions (with further references): Sari and Wessel, 'International Responsibility for EU Military Operations: Finding the EU's Place in the Global Accountability Regime', in B. Van Vooren, S. Blockmans, and J. Wouters (eds), *The EU's Role in Global Governance: The Legal Dimension* (2013) 126; as well as Wessel, 'Immunities of the European Union', 11 *International Organizations Law Review* (2014) 395.

[46] Cf. Butler (n. 5) 58: 'The objective of an action in deciding the legality of the legal basis is a key determinant that is used by the practitioner which, for CFSP matters, is the Council. The importance of the legal basis cannot be understated.'

[47] Opinion 2/00 ('Cartagena Protocol') (EU:C:2001:664) para. 5, and recited later in CFSP case-law, including Case C-244/17, *Commission v. Council ('PCA Kazakhstan')* (EU:C:2018:662).

A. Article 40 TEU and its Current Value

Obviously, the choice of legal basis is closely related to the effects of the different legal instruments, the applicable procedures, and the possibilities for a review of legality. As the Court noted in *Tanzania*:

> The choice of the appropriate legal basis of a European Union act has constitutional significance, since to proceed on an incorrect legal basis is liable to invalidate such an act, particularly where the appropriate legal basis lays down a procedure for adopting acts that is different from that which has in fact been followed.[48]

In different legal and political contexts, institutions may prefer to influence the procedure and their own involvement as well as the preferred effects of measures by opting for a specific legal basis.[49] The Treaties allow the Court to annul a measure if the choice for a certain legal basis was not made correctly. As discussed earlier, CFSP acts form part of the Union's legal order and they should be assessed and interpreted in the context of the overall EU legal order (see also the rules on consistency referred to earlier, in Section 2). Yet, apart from the example of restrictive measures, which has a CFSP Decision as the foundation for subsequent action in that area (see later), no automatic hierarchy exists. In the pre-Lisbon version of the TEU, choices for the correct legal basis were to be made according to (former) Article 47 TEU. The main purpose of this so-called 'non-affect clause' was to 'protect' the *acquis communautaire* from incursion by the special CFSP method, and provided that 'nothing in [the TEU] shall affect the Treaties establishing the European Communities or the subsequent Treaties and Acts modifying and supplementing them'. The landmark case at that time was *ECOWAS* (or *Small Arms and Light Weapons*). The result of the *ECOWAS* case was that the Council's CFSP Decision was annulled because it also included aspects of development

[48] Case C-263/14, *European Parliament v. Council ('Tanzania')* (EU:C:2016:435). Dashwood has formulated the legal basis rule ('Rule (i)') as follows: '[T]he choice of the legal basis for a European Union measure, including the measure adopted for the purpose of concluding an international agreement, must rest on objective factors amenable to judicial review, which include the aim and content of that measure.' Dashwood, 'EU Acts and Member State Acts in the Negotiation, Conclusion, and Implementation of International Agreements', in M. Cremona and C. Kilpatrick (eds), *EU Legal Acts: Challenges and Transformations* (2018) 189, at 210.

[49] See extensively on these choices, A. Engel, *The Choice of Legal Basis for Acts of the European Union* (2018). Cf. also Kuijper, 'The Case Law of the Court of Justice of the EU and the Allocation of External Relations Powers: Whither the Traditional Role of the Executive in EU Foreign Relations', in M. Cremona and A. Thies (eds), *The European Court of Justice and External Relations Law: Constitutional Challenges* (2013) 95, at 102 on the somewhat mundane nature of the legal basis quarrels: 'as a consequence of the "multi-power character" of some institutions, litigation on so-called "separation of power issues" often takes the character of ultra vires claims in respect of the powers allocated to individual institutions and seems closer to questions of the constitutional attribution of precise powers to these institutions than to questions related to broad constitutional principles ...'

cooperation, an area that was not covered by the CFSP legal basis.[50] Post-Lisbon, the pillars no longer exist, and Article 47 has been replaced by what is now Article 40 TEU. The current provision reflects the current focus on coherent EU external relations, and is therefore more balanced between the TFEU policy fields and CFSP. As also confirmed in a subsequent case—*Philippines Border Management*[51]—in substantive terms, it essentially reflects the method whereby the correct legal basis is found through establishing the 'centre of gravity' of the decision at stake (see further later).

Article 40 TEU provides:

> The implementation of the common foreign and security policy shall not affect the application of the procedures and the extent of the powers of the institutions laid down by the Treaties for the exercise of the Union competences referred to in Articles 3 to 6 of the Treaty on the Functioning of the European Union.
>
> Similarly, the implementation of the policies listed in those Articles shall not affect the application of the procedures and the extent of the powers of the institutions laid down by the Treaties for the exercise of the Union competences under this Chapter.

In other words, in adopting CFSP decisions the Council should be aware of the external policies in the TFEU, *and vice versa*. Despite its 'balanced' approach, Article 40 TEU implies that foreign policy measures are excluded once they would affect powers of the Union related to, for instance, the area of Common Commercial Policy. This could thus limit the freedom of the Member States in, for instance, the area of restrictive measures or the export of 'dual goods' (commodities which can also have a military application).[52] Yet, Article 40 TEU forces the Court to adopt a holistic view on the relationship between CFSP and other areas of external action. No longer should an automatic preference be given to a non-CFSP legal basis whenever this is possible. It could be argued that Article 40 TEU is a confirmation of the principle of consistency, now that it no longer establishes a hierarchy between

[50] See for details and further references, Hillion and Wessel, 'Competence Distribution in EU External Relations after *ECOWAS*: Clarification or Continued Fuzziness?', 46 *Common Market Law Review* (2009) 551.

[51] Case C-403/05, *Parliament v. Commission* (EU:C:2007:624). See also Klamert, 'Conflicts of Legal Basis: No Legality and No Basis but a Bright Future under the Lisbon Treaty?', 35 *European Law Review* (2010) 497.

[52] Council Regulation 1334/2000/EC setting up a Community regime for the control of exports of dual-use items and technology, OJ 2000 L 159/1; in the meantime replaced by Council Regulation 428/2009/EC setting up a Community regime for the control of exports, transfer, brokering and transit of dual-use items, OJ 2009 L 134/1. Exception was only made for certain services considered not to come under the CCP competence. For these services (again) a CFSP measure was adopted: Council Joint Action 2000/401/CFSP concerning the control of technical assistance related to certain military end-uses, OJ 2000 L 159/216.

CFSP and other policies.[53] Be that as it may, Article 40 underlines the competence of the Court to assess the legality of both CFSP and other external relations acts from a perspective of their interconnectedness.

B. The 'Centre of Gravity' and 'Lex Specialis' Tests

The next question is which methods the Court has at its disposal to check whether decisions on external action are based on the correct legal basis. While practice continues to pose problems, the rules on the correct choice of legal basis are quite clear and—as argued here—equally apply to instruments partly dealing with CFSP issues.[54] It is well known that in *Titanium Dioxide* the Court started to develop the 'centre of gravity' test, which included 'in particular the aim and content of the measure' as the decisive criterion.[55] Defining the centre of gravity was necessary in order to avoid having to use incompatible procedures. The test was further developed in subsequent case-law, in which the Court also held that a mere incidental effect was not decisive for the choice of legal basis.[56]

The latter point was confirmed in a CFSP context in the *Kazakhstan* case,[57] where the Court was given a chance to clarify how to deal with the legal basis questions for decisions or agreements that cover both CFSP and other policy areas. The 'Enhanced Partnership and Cooperation Agreement' is a bilateral mixed

[53] Pre-Lisbon, Art. 47 TEU contained the clear rule that 'nothing in the TEU shall affect the EC Treaty'. See also Case C-91/05, *Commission v. Council (Small Arms/ECOWAS)* (EU:C:2008:288). See further Hillion and Wessel (n. 50). At the same time, it has been argued that the fact that Article 40 does not really add anything to the treaty regime may be interpreted as confirming a separate status of CFSP, which again underlines what has been termed the 'integration-delimitation paradox' that from the outset has characterized the position of CFSP in the Treaties. See H. Merket, *The European Union and the Security-Development Nexus: Bridging the Legal Divide* (2016).

[54] See also Naert, 'The Use of the CFSP Legal Basis for EU International Agreements in Combination with Other Legal Bases', in J. Czuczai and F. Naert (eds), *The EU as a Global Actor—Bridging Legal Theory and Practice: Liber Amicorum in honour of Ricardo Gosalbo Bono* (2017) 394, at 402: '[The *Mauritius* and *Tanzania*] cases clarify that the CJEU applies its traditional jurisprudence on the choice of legal bases also where the choice is between a CFSP and a non-CFSP legal basis.' See, however, some critical remarks by Van Elsuwege, who wonders 'whether a traditional centre of gravity test is appropriate to distinguish between CFSP and non-CFSP competences'. Van Elsuwege, 'Old Habits Die Hard: Questions of Facultative Mixity in Relation to the Common Foreign and Security Policy', in M. Chamon and I. Govaere (eds), *EU External Relations Post-Lisbon: The Law and Practice of Facultative Mixity* (2020) 169, at 173.

[55] Case C-300/89, *Commission v. Council ('Titanium Dioxide')* (EU:C:1991:244) para. 10. Cf. also 'Rule (ii)' formulated by Dashwood (n. 48) 211 on the basis of the case-law: 'If examination of a European Union measure reveals that it pursues a twofold purpose or that it has a twofold component and if one of those is identifiable as the main or predominant purpose or component, whereas the other is merely incidental, the measure must be founded on a single legal basis, namely that required by the main or predominant purpose or component.'

[56] Case C-70/88, *European Parliament v. Council* (EU:C:1991:373) para. 12; Case C-42/97, *European Parliament v. Council* (EU:C:1999:81); Case C-36/98, *Spain v. Council* (EU:C:2001:64); Case C-301/06, *Ireland v. European Parliament and Council* (EU:C:2009:68).

[57] Case C-244/17, *Commission v. Council ('PCA Kazakhstan')* (EU:C:2018:662).

agreement between the EU and its Member States of the one part and the Republic of Kazakhstan of the other part. It was based on both CFSP (Articles 31(1) and 37 TEU) and TFEU provisions (Articles 91 and 100(2) (transport) and Articles 207 and 209 (trade and development cooperation)). The case was about the correct legal basis for the adoption of an EU position in the Cooperation Council that was established under the Agreement. Article 37 TEU was added as the legal basis for the conclusion of CFSP agreements, but the Council felt that Article 31(1) TEU (on the CFSP voting requirements) should also be included as a legal basis of the decision, as it had also been included in the decision approving the provisional application of the Agreement with Kazakhstan. The Court thus had to apply the 'centre of gravity test' to decide whether it was indeed necessary for the Decision to be adopted unanimously, and whether the inclusion of a CFSP legal basis was at all necessary.[58] As the judgment may form the basis for answering similar questions in the future, it is important to quote some paragraphs in full (emphasis added):

> 42. It is true that, as the Advocate General has noted in points 64 to 68 of her Opinion, the Partnership Agreement *displays certain links with the CFSP*. Thus, Article 6 of that agreement, in Title II headed 'Political dialogue, cooperation in the field of foreign and security policy', is specifically devoted to that policy, the first paragraph of Article 6 providing that the parties are to intensify their dialogue and cooperation in the area of foreign and security policy and are to address, in particular, issues of conflict prevention and crisis management, regional stability, non-proliferation, disarmament and arms control, nuclear security and export control of arms and dual-use goods. Furthermore, Articles 9 to 12 of the Partnership Agreement, which define the framework of the cooperation between the parties regarding conflict prevention and crisis management, regional stability, countering the proliferation of weapons of mass destruction and the fight against illicit trade in small arms and light weapons, may also be linked with the CFSP.
>
> 43. However, it is clear that, as the Advocate General has observed in essence in point 69 of her Opinion, those links between the Partnership Agreement and the CFSP are not sufficient for it to be held that the legal basis of the decision on the signing of that agreement, on behalf of the European Union, and its provisional application had to include Article 37 TEU.
>
> 44. First, *most of the provisions* of the Partnership Agreement, which contains 287 articles, fall within the common commercial policy of the European Union or its development cooperation policy.

[58] See also Kuijper, 'Case C-244/17—Commission v Council: The Centre of Gravity Test Revisited in the Context of Article 218 (9) TFEU', *European Law Blog*, 26 November 2018, available at http://europeanlawblog.eu/2018/11/26/case-c-244-17-commission-v-council-the-centre-of-gravity-test-revisited-in-the-context-of-article-218-9-tfeu/ (accessed 11 November 2020).

> 45. Second, *the provisions of the Partnership Agreement displaying a link with the CFSP* and cited in paragraph 42 of the present judgment, apart from being few in number in comparison with the agreement's provisions as a whole, are limited to declarations of the contracting parties on the aims that their cooperation must pursue and the subjects to which that cooperation will have to relate, and *do not determine in concrete terms the manner in which the cooperation will be implemented* (see, by analogy, judgment of 11 June 2014, *Commission* v *Council*, C-377/12, EU:C:2014:1903, paragraph 56).
>
> 46. *Those provisions*, which fall fully within the objective of the Partnership Agreement, set out in Article 2(2) thereof, of contributing to international and regional peace and stability and to economic development, *are not therefore of a scope enabling them to be regarded as a distinct component* of that agreement. On the contrary, *they are incidental to that agreement's two components* constituted by the common commercial policy and development cooperation.
>
> 47. Therefore, in the light of all those considerations, *the Council was wrong to include Article 31(1) TEU in the legal basis of the contested decision* and that decision was wrongly adopted under the voting rule requiring unanimity.

It is striking that the Court's ruling in the *Kazakhstan* case was done without any particular reliance upon Article 40 TEU; Article 40 TEU is only mentioned with respect to the pleadings of the parties, not anywhere in the 'Findings of the Court' part.[59] Also, the judgment did not rule out future situations where a decision or agreement could use both a CFSP and non-CFSP legal basis.[60] The point the Court does make is that, although there is a clear CFSP dimension in the decision and the agreement, it is 'incidental to that agreement's two components constituted by the common commercial policy and development cooperation'. In other words: it is not necessary to include a CFSP basis merely because there are CFSP elements in a certain agreement or decision. This line of reasoning is consistent with views earlier held by the Court in judgments relating to the agreements bringing Somali pirates before courts in *Mauritius* and *Tanzania* (the Pirates cases; see also later, in Section 4.A).[61] And, for the purpose of the present contribution it is important to note that leaving out the CFSP legal basis in acts or agreements that partly cover CFSP issues, implies that any restrictions on the Court's jurisdiction are no longer applicable.

At the same time, earlier case-law has revealed that the 'gravity test' is not the only test used by the Court in deciding on the correct legal basis. The Court has also made clear that a more specific provision will prevail over the use of generic

[59] See also Butler (n. 5) 127.

[60] Ibid.

[61] See respectively Case C-658/11, *European Parliament v. Council* (*'Mauritius'*) (EU:C:2014:2025); and Case C-263/14, *European Parliament v. Council ('Tanzania')* (EU:C:2016:435).

legal bases.[62] Engel has summarized the distinction between the two tests as follows:

> while under the 'centre of gravity' theory two different provisions with two different aims are at stake; the *lex specialis derogatat legi generali* principle concerns two different provisions, both of which have the same aim, but one being more specific than the other.[63]

The rules on the correct choice of legal basis have particularly proven their value in internal market cases,[64] but there are no reasons not to apply them in CFSP-related cases as well. This has to be done on a case-by-case basis. Thus, the 'centre of gravity' test would define whether an instrument falls more in the area of CFSP than, for instance, development cooperation or the Area of Freedom, Security and Justice (AFSJ). The *lex specialis* test could favour a CFSP legal basis in for instance decisions on security and defence policy (CSDP), but it could also lead to a TFEU legal basis when for instance specific financial individual sanctions are issued for which a *lex specialis* exists (Article 75 TFEU). Yet practice reveals that outcomes are difficult to predict. In *European Parliament v. Council (Smart Sanctions)*, the Court was given a first chance to develop an approach towards the function of Article 40.[65] Being confronted with the question of the appropriate legal basis for 'restrictive measures directed against certain persons and entities associated with Usama bin Laden, the Al-Qaeda network and the Taliban',[66] the Court held that Article 215 TFEU (following a previous CFSP decision) rather than Article 75 TFEU (in the AFSJ) was the correct choice. As in the later *Mauritius* case, the *context* of peace and security proved to be decisive for the Court's conclusion rather than the specific *content* of the decision.[67] These cases also revealed that the limited role of the European Parliament in the CFSP procedures was not decisive.[68]

In general, it has been argued that, while a 'CFSP context' may be relatively easy to establish in view of its broad scope (CFSP 'shall cover *all areas* of foreign policy and *all questions* relating to the Union's security'),[69] the same would not hold for

[62] The *lex specialis derogat legi generali principle*; Case C-48/14, *European Parliament v. Council (Euratom)* (EU:C:2015:91).

[63] Engel (n. 49) 19.

[64] Ibid. 20–27.

[65] Case C-130/10, *Parliament v. Council* (EU:C:2012:472).

[66] Council Regulation (EU) 1286/2009 of 22 December 2009 amending Regulation (EC) 881/2002 imposing certain specific restrictive measures directed against certain persons and entities associated with Usama bin Laden, the Al-Qaeda network and the Taliban, OJ 2010 L 346/42.

[67] See Matera and Wessel, 'Context or Content? A CFSP or AFSJ Legal Basis for EU International Agreements—Case C-658/11, European Parliament v Council (Mauritius Agreement)', 18 *Revista de Derecho Comunitario Europeo* (2014) 1047.

[68] Despite the fact that this element was part of the Court's reasoning in Case C-300/89, *Commission v. Council ('Titanium Dioxide')* (EU:C:1991:244).

[69] Cf. also the Court's remark that there is 'broad scope of the aims and objectives of … CFSP [matters], as expressed in Articles 3(5) TEU and 21 TEU'; C-220/14 P, *Ahmed Abdelaziz Ezz and Others v. Council* (EU:C:2015:147) para. 46.

the *lex specialis* nature of a CFSP provision, due to that same broad general description.[70] At the same time, this argument could be used the other way around as this provision seems to point to a CFSP legal basis as the default starting point whenever issues of foreign policy or security are at stake. Overall, any choice between either a CFSP or a non-CFSP legal basis will be subject to the legal limitations imposed by the Treaties and the jurisprudence of the Court as this choice has a clear impact on the role of the Institutions during the decision-making process and, in particular, on the possibility for the Court to engage in any review of legality after the decision has been adopted.

4. Combinations of CFSP and other Legal Bases

Given the requirement of consistency in EU external relations, a final question is to what extent gaps in the legality review by the Court of CFSP acts can be plugged by combining legal bases in acts containing both CFSP and other external relations elements. The argument for these combinations would be that it would allow for a more comprehensive review of the acts. The binary question (CFSP or not CFSP) does not seem to do justice to the full and complete review that can be seen as the ambition of both the Treaties and the Court, nor to the post-Lisbon consolidation of EU external relations objectives. The present section approaches the possibility of combinations of legal bases from a problematic (procedural) perspective and a pragmatic (international agreements) perspective. While combining different legal bases seems difficult in the EU's internal relations, it does seem to work much better in its external relations.

A. Problematic Procedural Combinations

As indicated previously, it has become increasingly difficult to clearly separate CFSP from other external action or to link external objectives to certain specific EU competences.[71] The need to combine CFSP and other issues in single decisions or international agreements has become more apparent.[72] The earlier analysis on the 'normalization' of CFSP implies that the general rules, largely based on the

[70] Engel (n. 49) 122; referring to Art. 24(1) TEU.

[71] As argued by Merket on the basis of a study on the relationship between development (TFEU) and security policy (TEU): 'Objectives of conflict prevention, crisis management, reconciliation and post-conflict reconstruction cannot be assigned to one or the other EU competence, forging an indissoluble link between development cooperation and the CFSP.' Merket (n. 53) ch. 3.

[72] Cf. 'Rule (iii)' formulated by Dashwood (n. 48) 211 on the basis of the relevant case-law: 'By way of exception, if it is established that the measure pursues several objectives which are inseparably linked without one being secondary or indirect in relation to the other, the measure must be founded on the various corresponding legal bases.'

Titanium Dioxide case-law, continue to apply in this area. Yet, the different procedures to adopt CFSP and other EU acts make it difficult to combine legal bases.[73] Combinations are, however, certainly not impossible, and, as already discussed, they were not ruled out by the Court in the *Kazakhstan* case. In relation to the conclusion of international agreements, Advocate Kokott in her Opinion in the *Tanzania* case argued that 'the Court has certainly not thus far rejected the possibility of such a dual legal basis in a case like the present one' (on CFSP and AFSJ). She concluded:

> It is by no means impossible to rely on legal bases other than the CFSP for the Union's external action as the Parliament and the Commission argue. For example, it is expressly recognised in Article 21(3) TEU that, in addition to the CFSP, the Union's other policies can include 'external aspects'. *It is therefore perfectly conceivable*, in principle, to have recourse, for the approval of an international agreement for the European Union, to competences in the area of freedom, security and justice or *to have a dual substantive legal basis* by exercising additional competences.[74]

It still remains clear that combinations may be difficult or impossible in practice due to diverging procedural requirements. In Case C-130/10, the European Parliament challenged the legality of a Council Regulation imposing certain specific restrictive measures directed against certain persons and entities associated with Usama bin Laden. The Court confirmed the following:

> 44. With regard to a measure that simultaneously pursues a number of objectives, or that has several components, which are inseparably linked without one's being incidental to the other, the Court has held that, where various provisions of the Treaty are therefore applicable, such a measure will have to be founded, exceptionally, on the various corresponding legal bases (see, in particular, Parliament v Council, paragraph 36 and case-law cited).
>
> 45. None the less, the Court has held also, in particular in paragraphs 17 to 21 of Case C-300/89 Commission v Council [1991] ECR I-2867 ('Titanium dioxide'), *that recourse to a dual legal basis is not possible where the procedures laid down for each legal basis are incompatible with each other* (see, in particular, Parliament v Council, paragraph 37 and case-law cited). (emphasis added)

[73] See already for instance Joined Cases C-164/97 and C-165/97, *Parliament v. Council* (EU:C:1999:99) para. 14, in which the Court confirmed that no combination of legal bases is possible 'where the procedures laid down for each legal basis are incompatible with each other'. Cf. Dashwood's 'Rule (iv)': 'However, no dual legal basis is possible where the procedures required by each legal basis are incompatible with each other.' Dashwood (n. 48) 218. Rule (iv) is formulated as an exception to Rule (iii) referred to earlier.

[74] Opinion of Advocate General Kokott delivered in Case-263/14, *European Parliament v. Council of the European Union* (EU:C:2015:729) paras 53 and 57 (emphasis added).

This is a clear example of a situation where different decision-making procedures and legal instruments render combinations of CFSP and other legal bases difficult.[75] With all this in mind, it is interesting to see that combinations do occur and have in the past been accepted by the Court in case of diverging procedures;[76] even when voting requirements were not compatible.[77]

These latter situations come close to a first example of a (necessary) combination of CFSP and other EU rules formed by the regulation of restrictive measures. In fact, legislative decisions taken by the Union in this area depend on a prior CFSP decision. Article 215(1) TFEU provides:

> Where a decision, adopted in accordance with Chapter 2 of Title V of the Treaty on European Union [the provisions on CFSP], provides for the interruption or reduction, in part or completely, of economic and financial relations with one or more third countries, the Council, acting by a qualified majority on a joint proposal from the High Representative of the Union for Foreign Affairs and Security Policy and the Commission, shall adopt the necessary measures. It shall inform the European Parliament thereof.

Paragraph 2 adds that this procedure is also to be followed whenever a CFSP decision provides for restrictive measures against natural or legal persons and groups or non-State entities. It is important to note, however, that, despite the 'twin' relationship between these decisions, they are adopted separately.[78]

In particular in relation to the conclusion of international agreements, it has not been unusual to use a dual legal basis. Even pre-Lisbon many examples of international agreements that were adopted both on the basis of what was then Article 24 TEU (CFSP) and Article 38 TEU (Police and Judicial Cooperation in Criminal Matters (PJCCM)) could be found. However, this 'cross-pillar mixity' was easier

[75] Previously also presented in Case C-155/07, *Parliament v. Council ('EIB Guarantees')* (EU:C:2008:605).

[76] Cf. Cases C-94/03, *Commission v. Council* (EU:C:2006:2) and C-178/03, *Commission v. European Parliament and Council* (EU:C:2006:4), in which the Court approved the combination of the CCP legal basis (then Art. 133 EC), which gave the European Parliament no formal role, with the legal basis for action on the environment (then Art. 175(1) EC), under which co-decision was the prescribed procedure. In these cases, however, QMV applied for both policy fields and the prerogatives of the European Parliament would not be encroached upon. Cf. also Dashwood (n. 48) 219.

[77] An example is given by Case C-166/07, *Parliament v. Council* (EU:C:2009:499) para. 69, where the Court saw no objection to complying with both the co-decision procedure and the requirement that the Council act by unanimity. But combinations of Art. 352 TFEU (previously Art. 308 EC), requiring unanimity, with provisions using the co-decision have occasionally also been acceptable. Cf. Joined Cases C-402/05 P and C-415/05P, *Yassin Abdullah Kadi and Al Barakaat International Foundation v. Council and Commission ('Kadi I')* (EU:C:2008:461) paras 235–236.

[78] The CFSP decision is based on Art. 29 TEU. See for instance Council Decision (CFSP) 2019/25 of 8 January 2019 amending and updating the list of persons, groups and entities subject to Arts 2, 3, and 4 of Common Position 2001/931/CFSP on the application of specific measures to combat terrorism, and repealing Decision (CFSP) 2018/1084, OJ 2019 L 6/6. See more generally on these issues, C. Eckes, *EU Counter-Terrorist Policies and Fundamental Rights—The Case of Individual Sanctions* (2009).

as the procedures as well as the effects were similar in both policy areas.[79] It could even be argued that those combinations were necessary as the procedure for both policy areas was laid down in Article 24 TEU and not in Article 38. CFSP and Community combinations were difficult, not only because of the diverging decision-making procedures, but also because of the unwillingness of Member States at that time to mix the Community method with the perceived 'intergovernmental' CFSP procedures. The solution was found in the conclusion of such agreements through the adoption by two distinct, although related, decisions: one 'on behalf of the European Union' (with a reference to the CFSP and/or PJCCM legal bases) and one 'on behalf of the European Community' (on the basis of EC legal bases).[80]

Post-Lisbon, a combination of TEU and TFEU legal bases has proven to be easier. In the *Mauritius* and *Tanzania* cases, the Council Decision challenged by the European Parliament was based on Articles 37 TEU (CFSP) and Article 218(5) and (6) TFEU.[81] It could be argued that this was an obvious combination as Article 218 TFEU also provides the procedure to conclude CFSP international agreements (and the combination is in fact used quite frequently: see Section 4.B). Hence, in this case the problem was not so much the incompatibility of procedures, but rather the main aim and content of the decision. As discussed previously, in those cases the Court decided in favour of 'CFSP-only' because of the foreign policy context, whereas in *Kazakhstan* adding a CFSP legal basis was not deemed necessary because of the 'incidental' nature of that policy in the agreement. Indeed, a proliferation of legal bases is not to be preferred. As the Court stated in *Philippines PCA*, only if 'several objectives which are inseparably linked without one being secondary and indirect in relation to the other, [then] the measure must be founded on the various corresponding legal bases'.[82] That said, it may be preferable from the point of view of the Union as a whole (as opposed to individual institutions) in

[79] Wessel, 'Cross-Pillar Mixity: Combining Competences in the Conclusion of EU International Agreements', in C. Hillion and P. Koutrakos (eds), *Mixed Agreements in EU Law Revisited* (2010) 30; as well as Wessel and Fernandez Arribas, 'EU Agreements with Third Countries: Constitutional Reservations by Member States', in S. Blockmans (ed.), *The European Union and International Crisis Management: Legal and Policy Aspects* (2008) 291.

[80] See the Agreement between the EU, the EC and Switzerland, OJ 2004 L 370/78 and the Agreement between the EU, the EC and Liechtenstein, Council Decisions 2008/262/EC, OJ 2008 L 83/5 and 2008/261/EC, OJ 2008 L 83/3.

[81] Council Decision 2011/640/CFSP of 12 July 2011 on the signing and conclusion of the Agreement between the European Union and the Republic of Mauritius on the conditions of transfer of suspected pirates and associated seized property from the European Union-led naval force to the Republic of Mauritius and on the conditions of suspected pirates after transfer, OJ 2011 L 254/1; Council Decision 2014/198/CFSP of 10 March 2014 on the signing and conclusion of the Agreement between the European Union and the United Republic of Tanzania on the conditions of transfer of suspected pirates and associated seized property from the European Union-led naval force to the United Republic of Tanzania, OJ 2014 L 108/1.

[82] Case C-377/12, *Commission v. Council* (EU:C:2014:1903) para. 34.

that having a multitude of legal bases may actually be beneficial to ensure 'full legal coverage', and therefore enhance the EU's external relations possibilities.

The reluctance to opt for a dual legal basis can mainly be found in the Council. As Naert discovered: 'at the stages of signature and conclusion, the Council has generally opted for not accepting that the CFSP competence should be exercised by the Union, leaving it to be exercised by the Member States as part of national competences in mixed agreements'.[83] This points to a preference for mixity rather than for a dual legal basis solution and is a somewhat peculiar reasoning. It could be argued that this is contrary both to the fact that CFSP is mentioned as a *Union* competence in the Treaties and that the same Union is to reach its external objectives in an integrated manner. By opting for mixity rather than for an EU-only agreement with a dual legal basis, the Council stands in the way of a further consolidation of the Union's external action and a possible violation of the loyalty principles (Articles 4(3) and 24(3) TEU) comes to mind.[84]

Similar confusion also arises in relation to some of the so-called 'horizontal' agreements. The CFSP parts of these agreements were (at least pre-Lisbon) often seen not as Union but as Member State competences, which would be covered by the mixed nature of the agreement. So-called horizontal agreements cover a wide range of issues; they may be 'deep and comprehensive' and usually take the shape of an Association Agreement or a Partnership and Cooperation Agreement. Although it is clear that these agreements do not 'exclusively or principally relate to CFSP' (Article 218(3) TFEU), the High Representative may in practice be appointed to negotiate CFSP matters.[85] Despite the CFSP being a *Union* competence, and Article 218 dealing with the conclusion of *all* international agreements,[86] it proves difficult in practice simply to take CFSP parts of agreements along during the negotiation, signing, and conclusion phase.

[83] Naert (n. 54) 412; as well as—for the contrary view—Passos, 'The External Powers of the European Parliament', in P. Eeckhout and M. López-Escudero (eds), *The European Union's External Action in Times of Crisis* (2016).

[84] Art. 24(3) TEU: 'The Member States shall support the Union's external and security policy actively and unreservedly in a spirit of loyalty and mutual solidarity and shall comply with the Union's action in this area. ... They shall refrain from any action which is contrary to the interests of the Union or likely to impair its effectiveness as a cohesive force in international relations.' See also on the choice for mixity, Chamon, 'Constitutional Limits to the Political Choice for Mixity', in E. Neframi and M. Gatti (eds), *Constitutional Issues of EU External Relations Law* (2018) 163; as well as M. Chamon and I. Govaere (eds), *EU External Relations Post-Lisbon: The Law and Practice of Facultative Mixity* (2020), and the contribution by Van Elsuwege in that volume (n. 54).

[85] See for instance Council Decision authorising the opening of negotiations with the Republic of Kazakhstan for an enhanced Partnership and Cooperation Agreements between the European Union and its Member States, of the one part, and the Republic of Kazakhstan, of the other part (Council doc. 8282/11 of 13 April 2011, Art. 2(2)).

[86] Cf. Dashwood (n. 48) 190: 'Article 218 TFEU contains the most complete procedural code governing the negotiation and conclusion of international agreements on behalf of the EU, as well as certain related matters, that have existed to date. ... As such, it tends to reinforce the view that the Treaty of Lisbon has created an integral Union structure ...'. This contribution also provides a good overview of the many aspects of the Art. 218 procedure.

B. The Practice of Combining Legal Bases for the Conclusion of International Agreements

In 2018, Alan Dashwood wrote:

> An important issue is whether the Court will prove willing to countenance the combination of legal bases for the exercise of EU competence in the field of the common foreign and security policy (CFSP) with legal bases figuring in the Treaty on the Functioning of the European Union (TFEU).[87]

In the context of the present contribution, the argument in favour of combinations would be that these would allow—if necessary—for a more comprehensive review of questions of legality, by plugging gaps that still exist in the system of legal review in the area of CFSP.

Since a combination of CFSP and other legal bases is not excluded in practice, the question is what obstacles hinder a further development of this notion, not only allowing the Court to exercise its 'full review', but also allowing for a more comprehensive assessment of legality questions. Examples from practice include the Agreement continuing the International Science and Technology Center and the Agreement establishing the EU-LAC International Foundation.[88] Other cases in point include the Partnership Agreement with New Zealand[89] and the accession of the EU to the Treaty of Amity and Cooperation in Southeast Asia.[90] In the latter case, the Decision's legal basis is defined as follows:

> Having regard to the Treaty on European Union, and in particular Article 37 in conjunction with Article 31(1) thereof,
>
> Having regard to the Treaty on the Functioning of the European Union, and in particular Articles 209 and 212 in conjunction with Article 218(6)(a) and Article 218(8), second subparagraph, thereof...[91]

[87] Ibid. 189–190.

[88] See Council Decision (EU) 2015/1989 of 26 October 2015 on the signing, on behalf of the European Union, of the Agreement continuing the International Science and Technology Centre, OJ 2015 L 290/7; Council Decision (EU) 2016/1873 of 10 October 2016 on the signing, on behalf of the European Union, of the Agreement establishing the EU-LAC International Foundation; OJ 2016 L 288/1.

[89] Council Decision (EU) 2016/2079 of 29 September 2016 on the signing, on behalf of the European Union and Provisional Application of the Partnership Agreement on Relations and Cooperation between the European Union and Its Member States, of the One Part and New Zealand, of the Other Part, OJ 2016 L 321/1.

[90] Many thanks to Dr Frederik Naert (Council Legal Service) for guiding me to these examples.

[91] Council Decision 2012/308/CFSP of 26 April 2012 on the accession of the European Union to the Treaty of Amity and Cooperation in Southeast Asia, OJ 2012 L 154/1.

The Decision thus combines Articles 37 TEU (CFSP), Article 31(1) TEU (laying down the voting requirements), and Articles 208 and 212 TFEU (development cooperation and economic, financial, and technical cooperation) and Article 218 TFEU (the procedure to conclude international agreements). The preamble explains this combination as follows (emphasis added):

> (2) The Treaty aims to promote peace, stability and cooperation in the region. To this end, it calls for the settlement of disputes by peaceful means, the preservation of peace, the prevention of conflicts and the strengthening of security in Southeast Asia. Hence, *the rules and principles set out in the Treaty correspond to the objectives of the Union's common foreign and security polity.*
>
> (3) Furthermore, the Treaty provides for enhancing cooperation in economic, trade, social, technical and scientific fields as well as for the acceleration of economic growth in the region by promoting a greater utilisation of the agriculture and industries of the nations in Southeast Asia, the expansion of their trade and the improvement of their economic infrastructure. Therefore, the Treaty promotes cooperation with the developing countries of that region as well as economic, financial and technical cooperation with countries other than developing countries.[92]

Naert pointed to the fact that in this case not only the Council, but also the Commission, the High Representative, and the European Parliament were of the opinion that dual legal bases were possible.[93] It could be argued that this should not come as a surprise. Article 218(3) TFEU mentions agreements that relate 'principally' (but not 'exclusively') to the CFSP and this may hint at the possibility of a dual legal basis.[94]

Because of their more 'comprehensive' scope, multiple legal bases are often used for the conclusion of 'horizontal' agreements, as the (mixed) Association Agreements with Ukraine, Georgia, and Moldova, or the Enhanced Partnership and Cooperation with Kazakhstan reveal. The respective Council Decisions[95] use Article 37 TEU as a substantive legal basis alongside legal bases in the TFEU.[96] Similarly, the negotiation, signing, as well as the conclusion of the (EU-only)

[92] A similar reason could already be found in the proposal that was jointly submitted by the High Representative and the Commission. Joint Proposal for a Council Decision on the accession of the European Union to the Treaty of Amity and Cooperation in Southeast Asia, Brussels, 16.2.2012. JOIN(2012) 1 final, available at https://eur-lex.europa.eu/legal-content/EN/TXT/PDF/?uri=CELEX:52012JC0001&rid=2 (accessed 11 November 2020).

[93] Naert (n. 54) 405.

[94] Wessel (n. 79).

[95] Council Decision 2014/295/EU of 17 March 2014; Council Decision 2014/494/EU of 16 June 2014; and Council Decision 2014/492/EU of 16 June 2014; Council Decision (EU) 2016/123 of 26 October 2015, OJ 2016 L 29/1.

[96] Naert found that in these cases the reason for the dual legal basis was to be found in the need for a swift provisional application which would include CFSP parts. Naert (n. 54) 412.

Stabilisation and Association Agreement with Kosovo was also done on the basis of Council Decisions using a CFSP legal basis.[97] The same goes for the Council Decision on the signing, provisional application, and/or conclusion of the agreements with Japan,[98] Armenia,[99] and Canada,[100] to mention some recent examples. While these decisions are not listed as 'CFSP Decisions' (using 'CFSP' in the numbering), but as 'EU' decisions, a dual legal basis may sometimes be found even in decisions that are categorized as a 'CFSP Decision'.[101] Whereas Article 37 TEU forms the key CFSP legal basis for CFSP agreements, the Ukraine, Kosovo, and Southeast Asia agreements are examples of the fact that occasional reference is also—or perhaps *even*—made to Article 31(1) TEU on the CFSP voting requirements (see on this also the *Kazakhstan* case in Section 3.B). This is interesting since here the incompatibility of different voting rules is even made explicit in the combination of legal bases used to adopt the decision. In that respect it is important to keep in mind that the TEU (Article 31(3)) foresees a 'passerelle clause' which allows changes in decision-making procedures without resort to treaty amendment. In the words of Butler, 'This passerelle clause provides elasticity away from unanimity, allowing for the adoption of certain CFSP Decisions by QMV in set areas as defined by the European Council'.[102] With the further consolidation of the various dimensions of the EU external action, there may come a moment when the

[97] Council Decision (EU) 2016/342 of 12 February 2016 on the conclusion, on behalf of the Union, of the Stabilisation and Association Agreement between the European Union and the European Atomic Energy Community, of the one part, and Kosovo, of the other part, OJ 2016 L 71/1 (referring to Art. 37 in conjunction with Art. 31(1) TEU, and Art. 217, in conjunction with Arts 218(7), 218(6)(a)(i), and the second subparagraph of Art. 218(8) TFEU). See on this agreement and the political reasons for the EU-only nature, Van Elsuwege, 'Legal Creativity in EU External Relations: The Stabilization and Association Agreement Between the EU and Kosovo', 22 *European Foreign Affairs Review* (2017) 393.

[98] Council Decision (EU) 2018/1197 of 26 June 2018 on the signing, on behalf of the European Union, and provisional application of the Strategic Partnership Agreement between the European Union and its Member States, of the one part, and Japan, of the other part, OJ 2018 L 216/1 (referring to Art. 37 TEU as well as Art. 212(1) TFEU, in conjunction with Art. 218(5) and the second subparagraph of Art. 218(8) thereof).

[99] Council Decision (EU) 2018/104 of 20 November 2017 on the signing, on behalf of the Union, and provisional application of the Comprehensive and Enhanced Partnership Agreement between the European Union and the European Atomic Energy Community and their Member States, of the one part, and the Republic of Armenia, of the other part, OJ 2018 L 23/1 (referring to Art. 37 TEU, and Arts 91, 100(2), 207, and 209, in conjunction with Art. 218(5) and (7) and the second paragraph of Art. 218(8) TFEU).

[100] Council Decision (CFSP) 2017/2322 of 29 May 2017 concerning the signing and conclusion of the Agreement between Canada and the European Union on security procedures for exchanging and protecting classified information, OJ 2017 L 333/1 (Art. 37 TEU, in conjunction with Art. 218(5) and the first subparagraph of Art. 218(6) TFEU).

[101] See for instance Council Decision (CFSP) 2017/718 of 27 March 2017 concerning the signing and conclusion of the Agreement between the European Union and the Republic of Moldova on security procedures for exchanging and protecting classified information, OJ 2017 L 106/1 (referring to Art. 37 TEU and Art. 218(6) TFEU); or Council Decision (CFSP) 2016/2360 of 28 November 2016 on the signing and conclusion of the Acquisition and Cross-Servicing Agreement between the European Union and the United States of America, OJ L 350/1 (Art. 37 TEU and Art. 218(5) and (6) TFEU). One may argue, however, that in these cases the reference to Art. 218 TFEU is merely of a procedural nature.

[102] Butler (n. 5) 265.

European Council allows QMV for certain CFSP acts, thus streamlining the different procedures.[103]

Association Agreements form a specific category. While some horizontal agreements are in need of various substantive legal bases as Article 218 TFEU merely provides the procedure, it could be argued that this is not the case for Association Agreements, for which Article 217 TFEU provides a full and complete legal basis.[104] In that respect, it is surprising (at least from a legal perspective) that in these cases a CFSP legal basis is added.[105] After all, by concluding an Association Agreement, the Union does not seem to be limited to certain policy areas and is in principle allowed also to use its CFSP competence.[106]

Apart from combined legal bases in decisions dealing with international agreements, practice also reveals the possibility of using both CFSP and other legal bases in other types of Council decisions. Thus, a combination can be found in decisions on the position of the Union in other international organizations or in the framework of a Cooperation Council based on an international agreement.[107]

[103] Proposals in this direction were also made by the Commission in *State of the Union 2018: Making the EU a stronger global actor*, 12 September 2018.

[104] Art. 217 TFEU: 'The Union may conclude with one or more third countries or international organisations agreements establishing an association involving reciprocal rights and obligations, common action and special procedure.' CFSP is not in any way excluded from this provision. At the same time, the Court has sometimes asked for an additional legal basis. See for instance Case C-81/13, *United Kingdom v. Council* (EU:C:2014:2449), where next to Art. 217 an additional legal basis had to be found in relation to the free movement of workers (Art. 48 TFEU). Cf. Smyth, 'Variable Geometry, Justice and Home Affairs and the Conduct of EU External Relations', in J. Czuczai and F. Naert (eds), *The EU as a Global Actor—Bridging Legal Theory and Practice: Liber Amicorum in honour of Ricardo Gosalbo Bono* (2017) 337.

[105] The EU-Kosovo agreement gives the following (unconvincing) reason: 'The Agreement provides for the establishment of an association between the Union and Kosovo involving reciprocal rights and obligations, common actions and special procedure. It also contains provisions falling within the scope of Chapter 2 of Title V of the [TEU] concerning the Common Foreign and Security Policy of the Union. The decision to sign the Agreement should therefore be based on the legal basis providing for the establishment of an association allowing the Union to enter into commitments *in all areas covered by the Treaties* and on the legal basis for agreements in areas covered by Chapter 2 Title V of the TEU.' (emphasis added)

[106] Art. 217 TFEU simply provides: 'The Union may conclude with one or more third countries or international organisations agreements establishing an association involving reciprocal rights and obligations, common action and special procedure.'

[107] Recent examples include: Council Decision (EU) 2018/1552 of 28 September 2018 on the position to be taken, on behalf of the European Union, within the Cooperation Council established by the Partnership and Cooperation Agreement between the European Communities and their Member States, of the one part, and the Republic of Azerbaijan, of the other part, with regard to the adoption of the EU-Azerbaijan Partnership Priorities, OJ 2018 L 260/20 (referring to Art. 37 TEU, and Arts 207, 209, 218(9) TFEU); Decision (EU) 2018/253 of 15 February 2018 on the position to be taken on behalf of the European Union within the Joint Committee established by the Partnership Agreement on Relations and Cooperation between the European Union and its Member States, of the one part, and New Zealand, of the other part, as regards the adoption of decisions on the rules of procedure of the Joint Committee and the adoption of the terms of reference of the subcommittees and working groups, OJ 2018 L 46/9 (Art. 37 TEU and Arts 207 and 212(1), in conjunction with Art. 218(9) TFEU); Council Decision (EU) 2017/2434 of 18 December 2017 on the position to be adopted on behalf of the European Union within the Joint Council established by the Political Dialogue and Cooperation Agreement between the European Union and its Member States, of the one part, and the Republic of Cuba, of the other part, as regards the adoption of a decision of the Joint Council on the rules of procedure of the

Combinations of CFSP and other legal bases are thus possible and applied in certain specific situations in relation to the conclusion of international agreements. It is interesting that different voting requirements do not seem to stand in the way of this combination; something that, as observed previously, was occasionally accepted by the Court in 'intra-TFEU' cases.[108] At the same time, it still seems to be impossible to combine the legislative procedure with CFSP decision-making, which explains why it is much harder for internal decisions to have a dual legal basis. In fact, EurLex currently lists 67 Council Decisions in which CFSP and TFEU legal bases are combined, and all of them relate to international agreements. The combination has often already started in the preparatory phase. Despite the rule in Article 218(3) TFEU that the initiative is *either* done by the Commission *or* by the High Representative, joint proposals occur.[109] Similar developments have been witnessed in relation to the composition and functioning of the 'negotiating team'. According to Article 218(3) TFEU, 'the Union negotiator or the head of the Union's negotiating team' are nominated with a view to the subject of the agreement envisaged.[110] In cases involving CFSP, the Council would usually nominate either the Commission representative or the High Representative as head of the negotiating team. In practice, when the Commission representative is nominated, the Commission representative may allow the EEAS representative to take the lead.[111] Naert has explained this by pointing to the fact that the establishment of

Joint Council and those of the Joint Committee, OJ 2017 L 344/26 (Art. 37 TEU and Arts 207 and 209 in conjunction with Art. 218(9) TFEU); Council Decision (EU) 2017/2431 of 11 December 2017 on the position to be taken, on behalf of the European Union, within the Joint Committee established by the Cooperation Agreement on Partnership and Development between the European Union and its Member States, of the one part, and the Islamic Republic of Afghanistan, of the other part, as regards the adoption of the Rules of Procedure of the Joint Committee and the setting-up of two special working groups, OJ 2017 L 344/11 (Art. 37 TEU and Arts 207 and 209 in conjunction with Art. 218(9) TFEU).

108 Dashwood (n. 48); and Naert (n. 54) 407; as well as Cremona, 'EU Treaty-Making after the Lisbon Treaty—A Test Case for Mutual Sincere Cooperation?', in J. Czuczai and F. Naert (eds), *The EU as a Global Actor—Bridging Legal Theory and Practice: Liber Amicorum in honour of Ricardo Gosalbo Bono* (2017) 424–439, at 431. These authors point to accepted combinations of QMV and unanimity in Case C-166/06, *Parliament v. Council ('International Fund for Ireland')* (EU:C:2009:499) paras 66–69 and in Joined Cases C-402/05 P and C-415/05 P, *Yassin Abdullah Kadi and Al Barakaat International Foundation v. Council and Commission ('Kadi I')* (EU:C:2008:461) paras 212 and 235–236.

109 Cf. Marquart, 'Still New Kids on the EU's Institutional Block? The High Representative and the European External Action Service Seven Years after the Entry into Force of the Treaty of Lisbon', in J. Czuczai and F. Naert (eds), *The EU as a Global Actor—Bridging Legal Theory and Practice: Liber Amicorum in honour of Ricardo Gosalbo Bono* (2017) 1. See for an example the Joint Recommendation for a Council Decision authorizing the opening of negotiations for a Framework Agreement between the European Union and Japan referred to earlier. In these cases, the Council Decision would state: 'Having regard to the joint proposal by the European Commission and the High Representative of the Union for Foreign Affairs and Security Policy'.

110 Cf. Marquart (n. 109); as well as Gatti and Manzini, 'External Representation of the European Union in the Conclusion of International Agreements', 49 *Common Market Law Review* (2012) 1703.

111 See for instance the Council Decision on the opening of negotiations of the Kazakhstan Agreement (Section 3.B). Cf. also Dashwood (n. 48) 202 in support of this development: 'There would clearly be a strong case for the High Representative to be formally associated with the Commission in negotiating such an agreement.'

the EEAS also implied the moving of geographical desks from the Commission to that Service.[112]

The conclusion is that combinations of legal bases only partly solve the problem of the restricted legality assessment in CFSP. While adding TFEU legal bases certainly allows for a more comprehensive approach in international agreements dealing with a variety of external relations themes, in many other instances all that is seen are references to the procedure to conclude the international agreements. In a more substantive sense, and leaving out the example of international agreements, combinations of CFSP and other EU policy areas remain difficult as the latter almost always involve decisions adopted on the basis of the legislative procedure. While challenges to CFSP legality thus remain, practice also shows that legality issues mainly concern institutional questions of competence. Where individual rights are at stake (such as in the case of restrictive measures, staff issues, procurement decisions, or access to documents), the Court interprets its competence to include a review of legality on the basis of Union-wide values and principles.

5. Conclusion: An Incomplete Review of Legality

Some 20 years ago, questions of legality would have raised eyebrows when brought up in a CFSP context. The aim of this chapter was to reveal that these days the principle of legality is to be applied across the board and is to guide all Union competences, including its competence 'to define and implement a common foreign and security policy, including the progressive framing of a common defence policy' (Article 2(4) TFEU). Review of legality by the Court is somewhat hampered by the restrictions on the Court's jurisdiction in relation to CFSP acts. At the same time, recent case-law has underlined the intention of the treaty drafters to see the limitations as exceptions to the more general idea that, in principle, all Union acts should be subject to a 'full review'.

The possibility for the Court to engage in this review largely depends on the choice of legal basis. This choice itself is now clearly subject to the rule in Article 40 TEU, and the claim has been made that the criteria on the basis of which the Institutions make a choice for the appropriate legal basis should be the same in TEU–TFEU situations as in TFEU–TFEU cases. At the same time, choosing a certain legal basis may affect the extent to which the legality of decisions can be assessed. This implies that key EU principles, including the principle of conferral, run the risk of becoming useless where there is a CFSP legal basis. This would run directly against the Court's view:

[112] Naert (n. 54) 419.

> the Union is founded on the principle of the rule of law and it respects fundamental rights as general principles ... It follows that the institutions are subject to review of the conformity of their acts with the treaties and the general principles of law, just like the Member States when they implement the law of the Union.[113]

This chapter thus pointed to a clear challenge: how to square some of the specific rules and procedures of CFSP with the fact that it is at the same time part and parcel of the Union's legal order. As the latter indicates the need not only to apply key EU principles to the CFSP area but also to allow for a review of these principles, this chapter investigated the possibility of combining legal bases for CFSP and other EU policies. Despite the abundant references to the principle of consistency in the Treaties, combining legal bases remains difficult. While practice has revealed a number of procedural combinations in relation to the conclusion of international agreements, extending any review of legality through adding a substantive TFEU legal basis typically runs up against either incompatible procedural requirements or the political wish of the Council to keep CFSP separate. The result is an incomplete system of legality review.

[113] Case C-355/04 P, *Segi and Others v. Council* (EU:C:2007:116) para. 51.

5

Accession to International Instruments as an EU Legality Constraint

Bruno De Witte

1. Introduction

This chapter deals with the extent to which international treaties concluded by the EU, or by all or some of its Member States, form an external constraint on the legality of EU action, and on action by its Member States within the scope of EU law. The term 'legality constraint' is interpreted as meaning that those international treaties serve to determine whether an act of EU law, or an act of national law determined by EU law, is legally valid or not. The chapter does not deal with the extent to which *customary* international law may also act as an EU legality constraint.[1]

International agreements are likely to act as an EU legality constraint, due to the principled openness of the EU legal order to international law. One of the opening provisions of the Treaty on European Union (TEU), namely Article 3(5), affirms that the Union shall contribute 'to the strict observance and the development of international law, including respect for the principles of the United Nations Charter'. The twin notions of observance and development are complementary. 'Development' refers to the way in which the Union helps to shape international law by means of unilateral action and the conclusion of treaties; 'observance' expresses the idea that the Union will respect its obligations under international law (especially those that it has freely accepted by means of treaties) and that it will also contribute to the observance of international law by its Member States. Thereby, the TEU expresses a strong commitment that the EU will abide by its international

[1] On customary law, the Court of Justice of the European Union (CJEU) held as follows, in Case C-366/10, *Air Transport Association of America and Others* (EU:C:2011:864) para. 101: 'Under Article 3(5) TEU, the EU is to contribute to the strict observance and the development of international law. Consequently, when it adopts an act, it is bound to observe international law in its entirety, including customary international law, which is binding upon the institutions of the EU.' However, because customary law 'does not have the same degree of precision as a provision of an international agreement', the CJEU's review is limited to whether there are manifest breaches (para. 110 of the same judgment). For recent doctrinal studies on that subject, see Konstadinides, 'Customary International Law as a Source of EU Law: A Two-Way Fertilisation Route?', 35 *Yearbook of European Law* (2016) 513; Delile, 'Les effets de la coutume internationale dans l'ordre juridique de l'Union européenne', 53 *Cahiers de droit européen* (2017) 159.

Bruno De Witte, *Accession to International Instruments as an EU Legality Constraint*. In: *Contemporary Challenges to EU Legality*. First edition. Edited by: Claire Kilpatrick and Joanne Scott, Oxford University Press (2021). © Bruno De Witte.
DOI: 10.1093/oso/9780192898050.003.0005

treaty obligations. The main way in which the EU can show its commitment is by correctly implementing treaty obligations through its internal legislation and, additionally, by participating in international monitoring and dispute settlement where they exist. Judicial enforcement of treaty obligations by its own 'domestic courts' is a third way for the EU to show strict observance of international obligations, and this is the way in which international treaties act most clearly as legality constraints.

2. International Agreements in the Hierarchy of Norms of EU Law

The commitment of Article 3(5) TEU is complemented by another norm of primary EU law, which was part of the original EEC Treaty and is now contained in Article 216(2) of the Treaty on the Functioning of the European Union (TFEU): 'Agreements concluded by the Union are binding upon the institutions of the Union and on its Member States.'

One could have understood this provision as simply meaning that the EU's external agreements are *binding under international law*, that is, as nothing more than a reaffirmation of the *pacta sunt servanda* rule. However, the European Court of Justice, in its seminal *Haegeman* judgment of 1974, adopted a more far-reaching interpretation. It stated that the Community's external agreements, from the time of their entry into force 'form an integral part of Community law'.[2] In a number of more recent rulings, the Court has confirmed that 'it is settled case-law of the Court that the provisions of an international agreement entered into by the European Union … form an integral part of the EU legal system as from the coming into force of that agreement'.[3] There is therefore no need for a dualist-type transformation of those agreements by either the Union or its Member States. International agreements are directly applicable within the EU legal order and a source of higher law within the hierarchy of norms of that legal order. They have primacy over EU secondary law, and acts of EU law are reviewable for compliance with international agreements. Shortly after *Haegeman*, the Court extended its 'automatic incorporation' doctrine to decisions adopted by international bodies operating under an EU agreement.[4]

[2] Case 181/73, *Haegeman v. Belgian State* (EU:C:1974:41) para. 5.
[3] Opinion 1/15, *EU-Canada PNR Agreement* (EU:C:2017:592) para. 67.
[4] Case C-30/88, *Greece v. Commission* (EU:C:1989:422) para. 13, where the Court, in relation to a decision of the EEC-Greece Association Council, stated: 'Since it is directly connected with the Association Agreement, Decision No 2/80 forms, from its entry into force, an integral part of the Community legal system.'

The consequences of the precedence of international agreements over secondary EU law are manifold. Before concluding an international agreement, the EU institutions (in particular, their legal services[5]) must check whether existing EU legislation might conflict with the agreement and, if so, must prepare for the amendment or repeal of the legislation before the entry into force of the agreement. Quite often, though, the Union will seek to 'upload' its internal norms to the international level and ensure that the agreement does not involve any need for legislative reform in the EU.[6] It may also happen that the European Commission negotiates agreements creating international obligations in order to 'pave the way' for the adoption of internal EU legislation which it favours. A further consequence of the precedence of international agreements is that incompatible EU legislation can, in principle, be reviewed and invalidated by the Court of Justice.

As stated by Article 216 TFEU, the EU's international agreements are binding both on the EU itself *and on its Member States*, irrespective of whether the latter are also contracting parties to the agreement (which then would be called, in EU parlance, a mixed agreement). By being integrated in the EU legal order, the external agreements benefit from the primacy of EU law over national law. The Member States must, *as a matter of EU law*, adapt their laws to comply with the Union's external agreements,[7] and national courts are called to disapply norms of national law that conflict with directly effective provisions of those external agreements. The agreements are thus a *multilevel legality constraint*, and the legality review is conducted by the Court of Justice of the European Union (CJEU) and by national courts, by means of direct actions and preliminary rulings on interpretation and validity.[8] The multilevel operation of these procedural mechanisms can be illustrated by considering three examples from the case-law.

(a) In the *FIAMM* case,[9] the CJEU had to decide whether the EU was liable for the damage caused to European companies by the EU's violation of World Trade

[5] The role played by the legal services of the EU institutions in monitoring the compatibility of EU legislation with existing or envisaged EU agreements is noted by Kuijper, 'An Introduction to Union External Action, Its Scope, Its Institutions and Its Instruments', in P. J. Kuijper *et al.* (eds), *The Law of the European Union* (5th ed., 2018) 1231, at 1258.

[6] Cremona, 'Extending the Reach of EU Law: The EU as an International Legal Actor', in M. Cremona and J. Scott (eds), *EU Law Beyond EU Borders* (2019) 64, at 107. See, as an illustration of this practice, the case study by de Burca, 'The European Union in the Negotiation of the UN Disability Convention', 35 *European Law Review* (2010) 174.

[7] For a judicial expression of this duty see Case C-12/86, *Demirel v. Stadt Schwabisch Gmund* (EU:C:1987:400) para. 11: 'in ensuring respect for commitments arising from an agreement concluded by the Community institutions the Member States fulfil, within the Community system, an obligation in relation to the Community, which has assumed responsibility for the due performance of the agreement'.

[8] In addition, the Commission can also bring infringement actions if it considers that a Member State has failed to comply with an EU external agreement; see e.g. Case C-293/03, *Commission v. France* (EU:C:2004:598).

[9] Case C-120/06 P, *FIAMM and Others v. Council and Commission* (EU:C:2008:476).

Organization (WTO) law, that violation having been ascertained by the WTO's dispute settlement body. The procedural mechanism used was a direct action for damages against the Council and the Commission. The action was brought by private firms before the (then) Court of First Instance and, on appeal, before the Court of Justice. The outcome was a rejection of the claim because of the lack of direct effect, within the EU legal order, of WTO dispute settlement decisions.

(b) In the *International Air Transport Association* case,[10] the legality question posed was whether the EU regulation for compensation of air passengers was compatible with the Montreal Convention for International Carriage by Air, a treaty ratified by the EU. The judicial mechanism used was a challenge before the UK's High Court of the British act implementing the EU regulation. That court sent a preliminary question to the Court of Justice about the validity of the EU regulation, but the CJEU found that there was no violation of the Montreal Convention.

(c) In the *Soysal and Savatli* case,[11] the legality question targeted national law rather than EU law. A German administrative court sent a preliminary reference asking whether a German law requiring entry visas from Turkish lorry drivers was in breach of the Additional Protocol to the EU-Turkey association agreement. The CJEU interpreted the Protocol as having direct effect in the EU legal order and as precluding the application of the German law; the visa requirement was held to be a new restriction of the provision of services which conflicted with the standstill obligation contained in the Protocol.

Whether the CJEU reviews the legality of EU secondary law or of national law, the assessment is made in three essential steps (which act as hurdles for the parties seeking the review). The Court examines: (1) whether the document invoked is an international treaty binding on the EU; (2) whether the relevant provision of that treaty has direct effect; and (3) whether there is, in substance, a conflict between the international and the EU/national law provision. The first question is usually not problematic,[12] and the third one has to be decided case by case. However, the second step has a structural nature, and the way in which the Court deals with it has important consequences for the degree to which international treaties act as legality constraints for the EU; this second step will be examined more closely in Section 3.

[10] Case C-344/04, *IATA and ELFAA* (EU:C:2006:10).

[11] Case C-228/06, *Soysal and Savatli* (EU:C:2009:101).

[12] Although this first condition is usually not problematic, there are cases where the existence of an EU agreement is doubtful. See the recent case of the EU-Turkey statement on refugees: it seemed, from a press release, that the statement was adopted by the European Council whereas the General Court found that in reality it had been concluded by the Member States acting collectively, so that it was not, in fact, an EU agreement. In addition, it was not clear whether the statement should be viewed as a binding treaty or as a non-binding gentlemen's agreement (however, the General Court did not reach that additional question). Case T-192/16, *N.F. v. European Council* (EU:T:2017:128).

3. The Court's Direct Effect Doctrine as a Filter for Legality Review

The notion of direct effect has no univocal meaning in international law. In its narrowest meaning, direct effect means that a treaty provision creates rights for individuals that they can enforce before domestic courts. A somewhat broader meaning includes treaty provisions, which, although they do not confer rights on individuals, are precise enough to be enforceable by domestic courts. A third, even broader, meaning includes treaty provisions that are not judicially enforceable per se, but which are used by domestic courts as a benchmark for the consistent interpretation of national law.[13]

The starting point in EU law is the following formula, which the Court of Justice first coined in the *Kupferberg* judgment in the early 1980s, and has regularly repeated and confirmed since then:

> In conformity with the principles of public international law, Community institutions which have power to negotiate and conclude an agreement with a non-member country are free to agree with that country what effect the provisions of the agreement are to have in the internal legal order of the contracting parties. Only if that question has not been settled by the agreement does it fall for decision by the courts having jurisdiction in the matter, and in particular by the Court of Justice ... in the same manner as any question of interpretation relating to the application of the agreement in the Community.[14]

In reality, international treaties seldom prescribe the mode of their domestic effect (not even the TEU and TFEU do so!). This is left to the domestic law and practice of the parties to the treaty. In deciding such matters, national courts look at the formulation of the treaty norms but also at broader implications of international reciprocity and domestic separation of powers.[15] A rare example of a treaty requiring direct effect is the Agreement between the EU, its Member States, and some Balkan states on the establishment of a Common European Aviation Area, whose Article 15(1) states: 'each contracting party shall ensure that the rights which devolve from this agreement may be invoked before national courts'.[16]

[13] See Nollkaemper, 'The Duality of Direct Effect of International Law', 25 *European Journal of International Law* (2014) 105, at 110.

[14] Case 104/81, *Hauptzollamt Mainz v. Kupferberg & Cie* (EU:C:1982:362) para. 17.

[15] Forteau, 'The Role of the International Rules of Interpretation for the Determination of the Direct Effect of International Agreements', in H. P. Aust and G. Nolte (eds), *The Interpretation of International Law by Domestic Courts* (2016) 96.

[16] OJ 2006 L 285/3. Another, recent, example is the Withdrawal Agreement between the EU and the UK which contains provisions requiring direct effect of its provisions in the domestic order of the UK (OJ 2020 L 29/7, Arts 4(1) and 127(3)).

Therefore, in the absence of guidance in the text of the agreement, the question of direct effect falls to be decided by the CJEU. The general formula used by the Court is the following:

> a provision in an agreement concluded by the European Union with a non-member country must be regarded as directly applicable when, regard being had to its wording and to the purpose and nature of the agreement, the provision contains a clear and precise obligation which is not subject, in its implementation or effects, to the adoption of any subsequent measure.[17]

Two elements of this formula are noteworthy, as they subject the direct effect of international agreements to a stricter standard than in the case of 'internal' EU law (regulations or directives): there is a condition attached to the 'purpose and nature' of the agreement as a whole (irrespective of the wording of its single provisions) and, in relation to the single provisions, the Court attaches great importance to whether they require the adoption of implementing ('subsequent') measures. This general formula covers a judicial practice which varies widely, depending on the type of external agreement, ranging from the generous recognition of the direct effect of (mostly) bilateral association agreements, to the rejection of the direct effect of some important multilateral treaties such as the WTO agreements.[18] This bifurcation in the Court's case-law will be illustrated later by a brief discussion of some characteristic examples.[19]

As a preliminary point, it should be noted that the Court's determination of whether EU agreements have direct effect in the EU legal order is also binding for the national courts when they are being asked to apply an EU agreement (in particular, when they are being asked to examine the compatibility of a Member State act with the agreement). Paradoxically, the recognition of the direct effect of an EU agreement, by encouraging national courts to enforce it, may also

[17] Case C-240/09, *Lesoochranarske zoskupenie* (EU:C:2011:125) para. 44; Case C-464/14, *SECIL* (EU:C:2016:896) para. 96.

[18] M. Mendez, *The Legal Effects of EU Agreements: Maximalist Treaty Enforcement and Judicial Avoidance Techniques* (2013).

[19] For fuller discussion of the Court's case-law on the effect of international treaties, see Mendez (n. 18) and, for a more recent update, Mendez, 'The Application of International Law by the Court of Justice of the European Union', in C. A. Bradley (ed.), *The Oxford Handbook of Comparative Foreign Relations Law* (2019) 601; see also Kuijper, '"It Shall Contribute to ... the Strict Observance and Development of International Law ..." The Role of the Court of Justice', in A. Rosas, E. Levits, and Y. Bot (eds), *The Court of Justice and the Construction of Europe: Analyses and Perspectives on Sixty Years of Case-Law* (2013) 589; Klabbers, 'The Reception of International Law in the EU Legal Order', in R. Schutze and T. Tridimas (eds), *Oxford Principles of European Union Law* (2018) 1208; P. Koutrakos, *EU International Relations Law* (2nd ed., 2015) chs 6 and 8; Martines, 'Direct Effect of International Agreements of the European Union', 25 *European Journal of International Law* (2014) 129; Ghazaryan, 'Who Are the "Gatekeepers"? In Continuation of the Debate on the Direct Applicability and the Direct Effect of EU International Agreements', 37 *Yearbook of European Law* (2018) 27.

increase the risk of its inconsistent application by the courts in various Member States.[20]

A. Maximal Direct Effect: The Bilateral Trade and Association Agreements

The CJEU recognized the direct effect of the key provisions of a large number of *bilateral* trade and association agreements concluded by the EU in the course of the past decades. These include: the association agreements with ACP (African, Caribbean and Pacific) countries; the free trade agreements with (former) EFTA (European Free Trade Association) states; cooperation agreements with Russia and other successor states of the Soviet Union; and association agreements with Mediterranean countries such as Morocco, Tunisia, and Lebanon.[21] In interpreting those treaties, the Court recognized the direct effect of provisions granting individual rights to trade, requiring equal treatment of persons, and prohibiting restrictions on the free movement of capital. It extended direct effect to decisions adopted by the joint bodies created under those bilateral agreements, such as the EU-Turkey Association Council.[22] More rarely, the Court has also granted direct effect to *multilateral* conventions, such as the Montreal Convention.[23]

The most conspicuous example of this 'generous' approach is the large body of CJEU case-law that affirms the direct effect of rights granted to Turkish citizens under the Ankara Agreement (1963), its Additional Protocol, and the implementing Decisions of the Association Council.[24] The Court thus 'created' (to the initial surprise of the Member States) an enforceable right to equal treatment for Turkish citizens in employment and social security, and it also precluded a host of national measures that contravened the standstill provisions of those documents. For example, in the *Soysal and Savatli* case,[25] the Court, by recognizing the direct effect of an old standstill provision contained in a protocol to the association

[20] This point is made by Rosas, 'International Responsibility of the EU and the European Court of Justice', in M. Evans and P. Koutrakos (eds), *The International Responsibility of the European Union—European and International Perspectives* (2013) 139, at 147.

[21] For a list of judgments in which the Court of Justice recognized the direct effect of individual rights contained in agreements of this type, see Casolari, 'The Acknowledgment of the Direct Effect of EU International Agreements: Does Legal Equality Still Matter?', in L. S. Rossi and F. Casolari (eds), *The Principle of Equality in EU Law* (2017) 83, at 89–91 (fns 21–34). In addition, see Case C-464/14, *SECIL* (EU:C:2016:896) (association agreements with Tunisia and Lebanon).

[22] Case C-192/89, *Sevince v. Staatssecretaris van Justitie* (EU:C:1990:322) paras 14–26.

[23] Montreal Convention for the Unification of Certain Rules for International Carriage by Air, OJ 2001 L 194/38. The direct effect of some of its provisions was expressly recognized in Case C-344/04, *IATA and ELFAA* (EU:C:2006:10) para. 39, and implicitly accepted in Case C-258/16, *Finnair* (EU:C:2018:252).

[24] For an overview of those rights, see K. Eisele, *The External Dimension of the EU's Migration Policy: Different Legal Positions of Third-Country Nationals in the EU: A Comparative Perspective* (2014).

[25] Case C-228/06, *Soysal and Savatli* (EU:C:2009:101).

agreement with Turkey, precluded the application of the 'Schengen' visa requirement to Turkish service providers entering Germany, thereby disrupting a major piece of the Union's harmonized immigration control regime. Similarly, the Court found that a new German scheme imposing integration requirements as a condition for family reunification could not be applied to Turkish citizens because of the direct effect of the same standstill provision.[26] Again, this affected a central piece of national immigration law that could have seemed unconnected with the economic cooperation content of the Ankara Agreement and its ancillary instruments. In these and other cases,[27] the legality constraint imposed by an international obligation of the EU had important effects on the conduct of Germany's immigration policy.

B. Judicial Exclusion of Direct Effect

In many other cases, the CJEU adopted a much more restrictive attitude, either by taking a stricter view of when a provision is 'precise and unconditional', or by excluding the direct effect of international agreements because of the general 'nature and purpose' of those agreements, even when the wording of the individual provision at stake could seem sufficiently precise.

1. WTO Law

The WTO Agreements, like most international treaties, do not contain rules on their domestic effect. All major trading partners of the EU deny the direct effect of WTO law, as does the CJEU, ever since *Portugal v. Council* (1999),[28] except when WTO norms have been 'incorporated' into EU law through express reference in a piece of EU legislation. The Court has consistently reaffirmed this position *despite* the fact that many of the WTO rules seem rather precise and *because* of the alleged need to preserve the room for manoeuvre of the EU's political institutions in WTO dispute settlement.[29] As a result of this attitude, the WTO Agreements do not operate as a *judicial* constraint on EU action, although these Agreements remain binding, which means that the EU institutions should strive to comply with them even in the absence of a judicial sanction in case of non-compliance. Also, it is not entirely clear whether this judicial 'hands-off' attitude equally applies to the Member States. In a recent, still pending, case before the CJEU, the question arose

[26] Case C-138/13, *Dogan* (EU:C:2014:2066).

[27] For another recent judgment impacting on Germany's immigration policy, see Case C-652/15, *Tekdemir* (EU:C:2017:239).

[28] Case C-149/96, *Portugal v. Council* (EU:C:1999:574).

[29] Bronckers, 'From "Direct Effect" to "Muted Dialogue": Recent Developments in the European Courts' Case Law on the WTO and Beyond', 11 *Journal of International Economic Law* (2008) 885; Ruiz Fabri, 'Is There a Case—Legally and Politically—for Direct Effect of WTO Obligations?', 25 *European Journal of International Law* (2014) 151.

whether a Member State can be held to have infringed EU law by acting in breach of the EU's (and Member State's) commitments under the General Agreement on Trade in Services (GATS).[30]

2. The Aarhus Convention

The EU and its Member States are parties to this treaty, which aims to strengthen the procedural side of environmental protection by providing a right to information, a right to participation, and a right to administrative and judicial review of environmental measures.[31] In partial implementation of the Aarhus Convention, the EU adopted Regulation 1367/2006 allowing non-governmental organizations (NGOs) to request internal review of *individual* environmental measures of the EU, although Article 9(3) of the Aarhus Convention does not make a distinction between individual and general measures.[32] The compatibility of the Regulation with the Aarhus Convention was tested in the *Vereniging Milieudefensie* case. The EU Commission had authorized the Netherlands to postpone the introduction of certain EU clean air requirements. Dutch NGOs requested an internal review of this Commission decision, but the Commission refused to undertake the review because this was a general measure and only *individual* measures were, in its opinion, subject to the internal review mechanism. The NGOs challenged the refusal, invoking a breach by the EU of Article 9(3) of the Aarhus Convention. The CJEU rejected the claim for lack of direct effect: although Article 9(3) is binding on the EU, it is not sufficiently precise and unconditional to be judicially enforceable.[33] The same is true for the EU Member States: they are bound by the Aarhus Convention as a matter of EU law but Article 9(3) does not have direct effect in the national legal orders, even though the CJEU insisted that national courts should interpret their national law, if at all possible, in conformity with Article 9(3).[34] As a result, the EU was found by the Aarhus Convention's Compliance Committee to have failed to comply with Article 9 of the Convention 'with regard to access to justice by members of the public because neither the Aarhus Regulation, nor the

[30] Case C-66/18, *Commission v. Hungary*, Opinion of Advocate General Kokott (EU:C:2020:172) paras 39–68.

[31] Convention on Access to Information, Public Participation in Decision-making and Access to Justice in Environmental Matters, done at Aarhus, Denmark, 25 July 1998, [1999] UNTS 447.

[32] Art. 9(3) requires 'access to administrative or judicial procedures to challenge acts and omissions by private persons and public authorities which contravene provisions of . . . national law relating to the environment'.

[33] Joined Cases C-401/12 P and C-403/12 P, *Council and Others v. Vereniging Milieudefensie and Stichting Stop Luchtverontreiniging Utrecht* (EU:C:2015:4).

[34] Case C-240/09, *Lesoochranarske zoskupenie* (EU:C:2011:125) paras 45, 50, and 51. See also the more recent Case C-664/15, *Protect Natur-, Arten- und Landschaftschutz Umweltorganisation* (EU:C:2017:987), in which the CJEU held that Art. 9(3) of the Aarhus Convention, whilst not having direct effect 'as such', helps to define the material scope of the (directly effective) obligation under Art. 47 of the EU Charter of Fundamental Rights to offer effective judicial protection for EU-based rights.

jurisprudence of the CJEU implements or complies with the obligations arising under [Article 9]'.[35]

3. The UN Disability Convention

The CJEU's reluctance to recognize the direct effect of multilateral agreements has also affected the one human rights treaty concluded by the EU, namely the UN Convention on the Rights of Persons with Disabilities (CRPD). This Convention was ratified by the EU, and has therefore become part of the EU legal order. Since the entry into force of the CRPD, a number of cases required the Court of Justice to reflect on its significance for the EU's regime of fundamental rights protection. Briefly stated, whereas the CJEU accepted that EU legislation (and national legislation implementing EU law) could, and should, be interpreted in conformity with the provisions of the CRPD,[36] it has refused to use the CRPD as a standard for reviewing the validity of EU law. This was decided by a Grand Chamber judgment of March 2014, upon a reference by the Irish Equality Tribunal.[37] The applicant in the main dispute, Ms Z, had been refused maternity or adoptive leave by her employer when she became a mother through surrogacy. As the reason for her recourse to surrogacy was her inability to support a pregnancy, she claimed that the refusal of leave constituted discrimination on (among others) grounds of disability in the sense of EU Directive 2000/78 on equal treatment in employment.[38] The Irish court added a specific question as to whether the CRPD was 'capable of being relied on for the purposes of interpreting, and/or challenging the validity, of Directive 2000/78'. The CJEU answered yes to the first prong of that question, adding that EU secondary legislation, such as Directive 2000/78, must be interpreted in a manner that is consistent with the Convention. As to the second prong of the question, the Court emphatically insisted that the validity of Directive 2000/78 could not be assessed in the light of the CRPD because that Convention's provisions were not unconditional and sufficiently precise and therefore did not have direct effect in EU law.[39] The main reason for this restrictive view was that the CRPD requires its States Parties to take implementing measures to achieve the objectives of the Convention. As EU Directive 2000/78 could be considered an implementing measure of the CRPD, the

[35] Communication ACCC/C/2008/32. See Ankersmit, 'An Incoherent Approach Towards Aarhus and CETA: The Commission and External Oversight Mechanisms', in I. Govaere and S. Garben (eds), *The Interface between EU and International Law—Contemporary Reflections* (2019) 321, at 327–329. The complete file of this Aarhus compliance case can be accessed at http://www.unece.org/env/pp/compliance/compliancecommittee/32TableEC.html (accessed 11 November 2020).

[36] Indeed, the interpretative impact of the CRPD on EU non-discrimination law has been quite substantial; see Waddington, 'The Influence of the UN Convention on the Rights of Persons with Disabilities on EU Non-Discrimination Law', in U. Belavusau and K. Henrard (eds), *EU Anti-Discrimination Law Beyond Gender* (2018) 339.

[37] Case C-363/12, *Z.* (EU:C:2014:159).

[38] OJ 2000 L 303/16.

[39] Case C-363/12, *Z.* (EU:C:2014:159) para. 90. Confirmed, shortly afterwards, in Case C-356/12, *Glatzel* (EU:C:2014:350) para. 69.

Court might have examined whether it constituted an *adequate* implementation of the EU's international obligations and, if not, the Court could have declared the Directive to be (partially) invalid; but the Court did not take that course. The least one can say is that it did not make a great effort to ensure the effective enforcement of the sole human rights treaty concluded by the EU. It decided to shield EU law from the disruption that would be caused by the enforcement of an international human rights instrument.

The Court's attitude to WTO law, the Aarhus Convention, and the CRPD raises the question whether it applies double standards—taking a stricter view of the direct effect of an external agreement compared to the direct effect of an internal EU norm. Indeed, when it deals with internal EU norms, contained in a directive or regulation, the Court recognizes the direct effect of provisions that give clear rights to individuals but also of other kinds of provisions that can serve as a standard for reviewing national implementing measures. Whereas originally direct effect was often defined, not least by the Court of Justice itself, as the creation of *rights* for individuals which the national courts must protect, that expression was gradually superseded by what the French call *invocabilité*, namely the capacity of the norm to be invoked by individuals in national courts which are bound to apply them. Norms contained in directives might not have as their object the attribution of a benefit to individuals, but may nevertheless serve as a standard for reviewing the legality of Member State action when individuals can show a sufficient interest in the outcome of such a review. Thus, the Court of Justice has repeatedly accepted that individuals could invoke provisions of a directive that merely set out procedural obligations for the Member States, in order to oppose measures adopted in breach of those obligations. This happened, for instance, with the obligation to make an environmental impact assessment under Directive 85/337.[40] A standard formula used by the Court in such cases is that:

> where the Community authorities have … imposed on Member States an obligation to pursue a particular course of conduct, the effectiveness of such an act would be diminished if individuals were prevented from relying on it in legal proceedings and if national courts were prevented from taking it into consideration … in determining whether the national legislature … had kept within the limits of its discretion.[41]

EU law norms can therefore be used by parties in a national court case both as a sword (i.e. as a source of new rights) and as a shield (i.e. as a protection against

[40] Case C-72/95, *Kraaijeveld and Others* (EU:C:1996:404), and Case C-287/98, *Linster* (EU:C:2000:468).

[41] For example, in Case C-287/98, *Linster* (EU:C:2000:468) para. 32, and Case C-664/15, *Protect Natur-, Arten- und Landschaftschutz Umweltorganisation* (EU:C:2017:987) para. 34.

conflicting national norms). The terms most frequently used by the Court are the 'capacity to invoke' or 'to rely on' a provision of EU law, and the Court has occasionally specified that this is, indeed, what 'direct effect' nowadays means.[42] Contrasting with this line of case-law, the direct effect of external agreements is subject to a different and more restrictive standard.[43] Here, direct effect seems limited to provisions that formulate precise rights for individuals and 'review of legality' is excluded when provisions need implementation—even when, in fact, they have been implemented.

The Court's policy on direct effect[44] is an important complement to the 'simple' rule of Article 216 TFEU and its interpretation in *Haegeman*. The monist perspective of the relation between international treaties and the 'domestic' legal order of the EU, expressed in *Haegeman*, must be qualified by the direct effect requirement which makes it maybe more plausible to call the EU legal order a 'neo-monist' (in the sense of: 'not-so-monist') one.[45]

4. Political Exclusion of Direct Effect: The New Trend

According to the *Kupferberg* formula cited earlier, when the effect of an agreement in the internal legal orders is not settled by the text of the agreement itself, the Court of Justice can step in to decide the question of direct effect by way of interpretation. However, most free trade agreements concluded by the EU nowadays (since 2008) *do* settle the question as they contain clauses excluding direct effect, and thereby exclude that these agreements may serve as an effective legality constraint in the EU legal order. This is the case in the Free Trade Agreement with Korea, the Economic Partnership Agreement with the CARIFORUM States, the Trade Agreement with Colombia and Peru, and those concluded with Ukraine and with Singapore.[46] Another recent example is Article 30.6 of the trade agreement with Canada (CETA), stating that 'nothing in this Agreement shall be construed as

[42] See e.g. Case C-226/07, *Flughafen Köln/Bonn* (EU:C:2008:429) para. 39: '... Article 14 (1)(a) of Directive 2003/96 ... *has direct effect in the sense that it may be relied upon by an individual before national courts* ... in a dispute, such as that in the main proceedings, between that individual and the customs authorities of that State, for the purpose of having national legislation which is incompatible with that provision disapplied ...' (emphasis added).

[43] In a recent Chamber judgment, the Court claims unconvincingly that it 'does not assess the direct applicability of the provisions of an agreement signed by the European Union according to criteria other than those it uses in order to determine whether the provisions of a directive are directly applicable' (Case C-167/17, *Klohn* (EU:C:2018:833) para. 33).

[44] For an early description of the Court's case-law as a 'policy' of direct effect, see Klabbers, 'International Law as Community Law: The Law and Policy of Direct Effect', 21 *Yearbook of European Law* (2001) 263.

[45] See Cannizzaro, 'The Neo-Monism of the European Legal Order', in E. Cannizzaro, P. Palchetti, and R. Wessel (eds), *International Law as Law of the European Union* (2012) 35.

[46] Semertzi, 'The Preclusion of Direct Effect in the Recently Concluded EU Free Trade Agreements', 51 *Common Market Law Review* (2014) 1125; Casolari (n. 21).

conferring rights or imposing obligations on persons other than those created between the Parties under public international law, nor as permitting this Agreement to be directly invoked in the domestic legal systems of the Parties'.[47] Similarly, Article 23.5 of the EU-Japan Economic Partnership Agreement, states: 'Nothing in this Agreement shall be construed as conferring rights or imposing obligations on persons'.[48]

There has been no official explanation of why the EU (together with its co-contracting parties) has taken this course of excluding the direct effect of recent trade agreements. Semertzi suggests that the reason could be that those agreements incorporate WTO norms, so that allowing for direct effect of the agreements would undermine the EU's room for manoeuvre under WTO law (which has no direct effect).[49] This practice may also denote, more generally, a growing scepticism about the legitimacy of international law-making. However, the exclusion of direct effect is accompanied, in all these agreements, by the creation of various mechanisms for international dispute settlement, including investment arbitration for the benefit of private firms. This raises the question whether investment-state dispute settlement is normatively preferable to allowing 'domestic' courts to enforce the agreements.[50]

The negative political approach towards direct effect has even been extended to the EU's neighbourhood relations, albeit in a different form. The EU's association agreements with Ukraine do not contain a no-direct-effect clause, but the EU Council, when signing them, stated that 'the Agreement shall not be construed as conferring rights or imposing obligations which can be directly invoked before Union or Member State courts or tribunals'.[51] The Council thus seeks to pre-empt the Court of Justice from applying its usual favourable approach to the direct effect of bilateral association agreements. As this is a unilateral statement by one of the parties to the Agreements, it is not entirely sure whether the Court of Justice will follow the Council's lead on this question, but it is too early to tell.[52]

The recent practice of the Union may seem problematic in the light of the EU's constitutional commitment to the rule of law. According to the CJEU, the EU legal order is based on the rule of law, meaning that all EU legal acts are subject to judicial review of their compatibility with higher law.[53] How to explain and justify, then,

[47] Comprehensive Economic and Trade Agreement between Canada, of the one part, and the European Union and its Member States, of the other part, OJ 2017 L 11/23.

[48] Agreement between the European Union and Japan for an Economic Partnership, OJ 2018 L 330/3.

[49] Semertzi (n. 46).

[50] See discussion of this question by Bronckers, 'Is Investor-State Dispute Settlement (ISDS) Superior to Litigation Before Domestic Courts? An EU View on Bilateral Trade Agreements', 18 *Journal of International Economic Law* (2015) 655.

[51] Council Decision 2014/295, OJ 2014 L 161/1, Art. 5, and Council Decision 2014/669, OJ 2014 L 278/6, Art. 3.

[52] See discussion of this point by G. Van der Loo, *The EU-Ukraine Association Agreement and Deep and Comprehensive Free Trade Area* (2016) 195–197.

[53] Case 294/83, *Les Verts v. Parliament* (EU:C:1986:166) para. 23.

the situation whereby precise provisions of an international agreement (which is 'higher law' in the EU legal order) cannot serve for reviewing internal EU (or Member State) acts? Also, this approach ignores the EU's own historical experience, where the direct effect of EU treaty norms allowed them to have a concrete impact on the daily lives of European citizens.

5. Limits to the Primacy of International Treaties in the EU Legal Order

Whereas the priority of international treaties over secondary EU law is recognized by Article 216(2) TFEU, those treaties do not prevail over norms of primary EU law, that is, the norms contained in the founding Treaties and the human rights that are part of the general principles of Union law and now of the EU Charter of Rights. In order to avoid conflicts with primary law, external agreements can be scrutinized by the Court of Justice before their entry into force, by means of a request for an Opinion. Thus, in Opinion 1/15, the CJEU held that the EU could not conclude the agreement that it had negotiated with Canada on the exchange of passenger name records, because that agreement contained a number of provisions conflicting with the right to respect for private life.[54] In Opinion 1/17, the Court subjected the CETA agreement with Canada to review against a number of rights and principles of EU primary law (namely, the autonomy of the EU legal order, the principle of equal treatment, the effectiveness of EU competition law, and the right of access to an independent tribunal) before concluding on its compatibility with EU law.[55]

However, even if a treaty, or a decision of an international organ, has already entered into force and the EU is bound by it under international law, the Court can still be asked to intervene, and can still decide that it breaches fundamental rights and should therefore not be a source of legality in the EU legal order. A typical but rather low-key application of this conflict rule occurred in the case *Germany v. Council* of 1998. The Court of Justice held there that the Framework Agreement on Bananas, which the European Community had validly concluded with four Latin American countries, could not receive application within the EC legal order because it breached the general principle of non-discrimination by harming the interests of particular categories of banana importers in a disproportionate way.[56] In coming to that conclusion, the Court assumed, without much explanation, that the Member States of the EU had established a specialized legal order in which certain values and rights were entrenched, so that the Court of Justice could

[54] Opinion 1/15, *EU-Canada PNR Agreement* (EU:C:2017:592).
[55] Opinion 1/17, *EU-Canada CET Agreement* (EU:C:2019:341) paras 106 ff.
[56] Case C-122/95, *Germany v. Council* (EU:C:1998:94) paras 54–73.

legitimately decide that international obligations conflicting with those rights and values must be set aside. By enforcing the EU's constitutional norms against conflicting international norms, the Court was acting in a similar way to most national constitutional courts which, increasingly, tend to accept the primacy of international treaty norms over domestic legislation, but not over domestic constitutional law.

Ten years later, in the *Kadi* judgment, the CJEU adopted the same solution as in *Germany v. Council*. Once again, it decided to refuse the application of a norm originating in international law in order to preserve some fundamental norms of the internal legal order of the Community, namely the rights of defence and the right to property. Yet, this time, and unlike in *Germany v. Council*, its detailed discussion of the relevant fundamental rights was preceded by a more general argument that highlighted the autonomy of the Community legal order. The Council Regulation that was challenged in *Kadi* aimed to implement a UN Security Council Resolution, but this feature could not exempt the Regulation from judicial review. According to the CJEU, 'the review by the Court of the validity of any Community measure in the light of fundamental rights must be considered to be the expression, in a community based on the rule of law, of a constitutional guarantee stemming from the EC Treaty as an autonomous legal system which is not to be prejudiced by an international agreement'.[57] The reason for the greater solemnity of the *Kadi* judgment is rather obvious. Unlike in the *Germany v. Council* case, this time the Court's judgment had important repercussions in international law, in that it indirectly challenged the authority of the Security Council's anti-terrorism policy, even though it is doubtful whether the *Kadi* judgment actually caused the EU to breach international law.[58]

The *Kadi* judgment did not call into question the CJEU's traditional view that international agreements of the EU form part of the EU legal order upon their ratification and entry into force. The Court affirmed, however, that these agreements cannot be a source of 'external' legality when they themselves come into conflict with the EU's 'internal' legality (in this case, the fundamental rights protected by the EU legal order). In defending that view, the CJEU considered it useful to highlight the autonomy of the special legal order that the EU Member States have brought into being. This highlighting also seems quite appropriate because, in doing so, the CJEU did not seek to distance itself from international human rights law. Indeed, the part of the *Kadi* judgment in which the Court outlines the content of the rights of defence and the right to property as general principles of EU law relies on the

[57] Joined Cases C-402/05P and C-415/05P, *Kadi and Al Barakaat International Foundation v. Council and Commission* (EU:C:2008:461) para. 316.

[58] For the argument that the judgment was compatible with international law, see Scheinin, 'Is the ECJ Ruling in *Kadi* Incompatible with International Law?', 28 *Yearbook of European Law* (2009) 637.

corresponding provisions of the European Convention on Human Rights (ECHR) and on the case-law of the European Court of Human Rights (ECtHR).[59]

6. International Treaty Obligations of the Member States as EU Legality Constraints

Whereas most of this chapter is concerned with the extent to which treaties concluded by the EU can act as EU legality constraints, this section, and the following one, examine the related question whether international treaties concluded by the EU's *Member States* (rather than by the EU itself) may also act as EU legality constraints. In this section, the treaties which EU Member States conclude with third countries will be discussed, and in Section 7, the particular case of treaties concluded exclusively among EU Member States, without the participation of third countries, will be examined more closely.

The starting point of the analysis, and the default rule, is that international obligations of the Member States, even if accepted by all of them, are *not* a source of EU legality. The Court of Justice stated this clearly, in the *Intertanko* judgment, in relation to the Marpol Convention, which is an international treaty concluded by all the EU Member States but not by the EU itself. Such treaties can be taken into account by national courts when *interpreting* EU law, but cannot be relied on to *set aside* EU law that is in conflict with these treaties.[60] Similarly, the Member States cannot rely on their international obligations towards third countries in order to limit the application of EU law on their territory, as the CJEU held in relation to a bilateral extradition treaty between Latvia and Russia in the *Petruhhin* judgment.[61] This case-law, which seeks to protect the privileged place of EU law in the domestic legal orders of the Member States, grates on the Union's commitment, laid down in Article 3(5) TEU, to contribute to the strict observance of international law.

The exception to the general rule is when Member State agreements are integrated into primary EU law by reference. This is the case, above all, with the ECHR, a treaty to which all the EU Member States are parties, but the EU itself is not. Article 6 TEU declares the ECHR rights to be general principles of Union law, and

[59] *Kadi* judgment (n. 57): ECtHR case-law is cited in paras 344, 360, 363, and 368.

[60] Case C-308/06, *Intertanko* (EU:C:2008:312). See, in the same sense, the earlier judgment in Case C-379/92, *Peralta* (EU:C:1994:296) para. 16.

[61] Case C-182/15, *Petruhhin* (EU:C:2016:630). In this connection, Art. 351 TFEU makes an exception for international agreements concluded earlier than the time of the Member State's accession to the EU. Such treaties can be invoked as an excuse for not applying EU law, but they do not become a source of EU legality. The Court of Justice has sought to limit the scope of this exception clause; see the discussion by J. Klabbers, *Treaty Conflict and the European Union* (2008) ch. 6, and by Rosas, 'The Status in EU Law of International Agreements Concluded by EU Member States', 34 *Fordham International Law Journal* (2011) 1304, at 1321–1324.

Article 52(3) EU Charter requires the interpretation of Charter rights to follow the corresponding rights of the ECHR.

The Convention's role in shaping the EU's own regime of fundamental rights protection was rather different in the periods before and after the entry into force of the Lisbon Treaty, which gave the full force of primary EU law to the EU's Charter of Rights. Before Lisbon, the CJEU had to rely on external sources to give substance to the protection of human rights in the EU legal order; international human rights treaties, and especially the ECHR, served as sources of inspiration. The Court of Justice presented this rather complex legal situation in the following way:

> it should be recalled that, according to settled case-law, fundamental rights form an integral part of the general principles of law the observance of which the Court ensures, and that, for that purpose, the Court draws inspiration from the constitutional traditions common to the Member States and from the guidelines supplied by international treaties for the protection of human rights on which the Member States have collaborated or to which they are signatories. The ECHR has special significance in that respect.[62]

According to this formula, the ECHR had 'special significance', but its formal status seemed to be the same as that of other international instruments, namely that of offering 'guidelines' from which the Court 'draws inspiration' in fine-tuning its own general principles of EU law. The ECHR was thus an *indirect* legality constraint for the EU.

Since the EU's own Charter of Fundamental Rights (CFR) became fully part of primary EU law, in 2009, this state of dependence on external sources of human rights protection has seemingly ended. Since the CFR contains a long list of rights, there is no longer any need to 'borrow' rights elsewhere, and the EU legal order could be seen as self-sufficient in this respect. However, the Charter text itself prevents this self-sufficiency from happening. Its Article 52(3) states: '[I]n so far as this Charter contains rights which correspond to rights guaranteed by the Convention for the Protection of Human Rights and Fundamental Freedoms, the meaning and scope of those rights shall be the same as those laid down by the said Convention.' This remarkable clause seems to imply that not only the Convention itself, but also the jurisprudence of the ECtHR, are incorporated into EU law and act as a legality constraint in the same way as the EU's Charter itself.

In fact, however, the CJEU does not systematically use the case-law of the ECtHR in its interpretation and application of the EU Charter of Rights.[63] The failure to

[62] Case C-479/04, *Laserdisken* (EU:C:2006:549) para. 61; identical or almost identical paragraphs appeared in most Court judgments dealing with fundamental rights in the pre-Lisbon period, including also in the *Kadi* judgment (n. 57) para. 283.

[63] See De Witte, 'The European Union in the International System of Human Rights Protection: Solo Singer or Voice in the Choir?', in E. Bribosia and I. Rorive (eds), *Human Rights Tectonics—Global*

systematically *refer* to the case-law of the ECtHR is not problematic from the point of view of Convention law, as the ECtHR has never made it a duty for national courts to expressly refer to its own case-law when adjudicating cases involving rights protected under the Convention. The only relevant requirement, laid down in Article 13 ECHR, is, rather, that the national legal systems should offer remedies for the alleged violation of Convention rights, whether on the basis of national constitutional rights corresponding to those of the ECHR, or on the basis of the directly effective provisions of the ECHR itself. Yet, things might look different from the point of view of EU law, because of Article 52(3) CFR. Based on the text of that provision, it could be argued that the CJEU should proceed to a double check whenever a right contained in the Convention is at stake. It should assess the EU or national measures in light of the CFR first, and then move on to check whether that interpretation of the CFR also corresponds to the views adopted by the ECtHR regarding the corresponding Convention right. However, the CJEU does not do so systematically, or at least, it does not always provide evidence in its judgments that it took account of the case-law of its counterpart in Strasbourg.

The Convention relating to the Status of Refugees[64] (the Geneva Convention) also has a particular legal status within the EU legal order. Indeed, Article 78(1) TFEU specifies that the EU's common policy on asylum 'must be in accordance with the Geneva Convention of 28 July 1951 and the Protocol of 31 January 1967 relating to the status of refugees, and other relevant treaties'. In addition, Article 18 of the EU Charter protects the right of asylum 'with due respect for the rules of the Geneva Convention'. Although the EU (unlike its Member States) is not a party to the Geneva Convention, that treaty is binding on the EU institutions by means of those references in Article 78(1) TFEU and Article 18 CFR.[65] The preambles to the various pieces of EU legislation in the field of asylum refer, indeed, to the Geneva Convention. By now, though, the complex asylum regime enacted by the EU is generally more detailed and protective than the Geneva Convention and it is hard to see how, in practice, the Geneva Convention could act as a standard for *reviewing* the legality of EU asylum law. However, the Geneva Convention plays a role as a standard for the *interpretation* of various EU asylum instruments. The Court of Justice affirmed this, as a matter of principle, in the *Abdulla* case,[66] and actually adopted such Geneva-conforming interpretation in some later cases.[67]

Dynamics of Integration and Fragmentation (2018) 225, and Krommendijk, 'Opinion 2/13 as a Game Changer in the Dialogue between the European Courts?', in *idem*, 243.

64 Convention relating to the Status of Refugees, Geneva, 28 July 1951, in force 22 April 1954, 189 UNTS 150.

65 This was expressly confirmed by the CJEU: Joined Cases C-391/16, C-77/17, and C-78/17, *M (Révocation du statut de réfugié)* (EU:C:2019:403) para. 74.

66 Joined Cases C-175/08, C-176/08, C-178/08, and C-179/08, *Salahaddin Abdulla and Others* (EU:C:2010:105) para. 53.

67 See Bay Larsen, 'Quelques remarques sur les relations entre le droit international et le régime d'asile européen commun', in *Liber Amicorum Vasilios Skouris* (2015) 73, at 75–77.

However, the Court made it clear in the *Qurbani* judgment that it will not interpret the Geneva Convention itself.[68] A German court had, by means of a preliminary reference, asked some questions about the interpretation of Article 31 of the Geneva Convention, but the Court of Justice declined jurisdiction. It stated that its power 'to provide interpretations by way of preliminary rulings extends only to rules which are part of EU law'[69] and therefore does not include the Geneva Convention. This is only otherwise where a provision of EU legislation specifically refers to the Geneva Convention, in which case the interpretation of that EU law provision may imply the need also to interpret the Geneva Convention. In the case at hand, the German court had exclusively referenced the Geneva Convention without pointing out any corresponding provision on EU asylum law, and therefore the request for a preliminary ruling was refused. Whereas there is some logic to the Court's restrictive view, there was also a missed opportunity for the Court to become a leading authority in the interpretation of the Geneva Convention which, as is well known, does not possess a judicial or quasi-judicial monitoring system and therefore relies heavily on the interpretative efforts of the domestic courts of its contracting parties.[70]

7. International Agreements Concluded Exclusively among EU Member States

In the original text of the EEC Treaty, treaties concluded by the Member States jointly were expressly included among the available legal instruments. Such treaties can be called *complementary* or *parallel agreements*, since they were to be adopted in connection with the founding Treaties by the very same contracting parties, namely all EEC Member States together, without the participation of any third countries. The reference to this instrument was not unusual at the time, since other international organizations, such as the International Labour Organization (ILO) and the Council of Europe, used 'conventions' as their principal law-making instrument (as they still do today). Article 293 EC Treaty used to provide for complementary agreements between the Member States in a number of areas but only three agreements came into being on this basis: the Convention of 27 February 1968 on the Mutual Recognition of Companies and Firms,[71] the Convention of 27 September 1968 on Jurisdiction and the Enforcement of Judgments in Civil

[68] Case C-481/13, *Qurbani* (EU:C:2014:2101) paras 17–29.
[69] Ibid. para. 21.
[70] On the potential role of the Court of Justice in this regard, see Bank, 'The Potential and Limitations of the Court of Justice in Shaping International Refugee Law', 27 *International Journal of Refugee Law* (2015) 213.
[71] Bull EC Suppl. 2/1969. This treaty has never entered into force.

and Commercial Matters (usually called the Brussels Convention),[72] and the Convention of 23 July 1990 on the Elimination of Double Taxation in connection with the adjustment of profits of associated enterprises.[73] Later, the Treaty of Maastricht provided for the possibility for conventions to be concluded between the EU Member States in the new policy area of the 'third pillar' (Justice and Home Affairs). At that stage of the European integration process, the choice for inter-state conventions (rather than the more incisive legal instruments of Community law) was inspired by the wish to preserve control by the Member States of the adoption and application of these instruments. In the years following the entry into force of the Treaty of Maastricht, a large number of such conventions were concluded, but only one of these actually entered into force during the following years, namely the Europol Convention.[74] From the perspective of this chapter, the Court of Justice tended to treat these intra-EU agreements as sources of *secondary* law that were binding on the Member States, but which did not prevail (unlike agreements with third states) over other instruments of secondary EU law, and thus could not act as 'legality constraints'.

On the whole, parallel agreements proved to be a disappointment for their authors, mainly because of the fact that, by requiring ratification by the national parliaments, their entry into force and subsequent amendment became a very cumbersome operation. Because of this disillusionment with the convention instrument, the Lisbon Treaty entirely scrapped complementary conventions from the range of EU legal instruments. Existing intergovernmental agreements were transformed into EU legislative acts (whilst keeping the memory of their international law origin in their commonly used denomination, as with the 'Brussels Regulation' and the 'Dublin Regulation').

As a counterpoint to this decline of the *parallel* agreements, there has been a recent revival of *partial* agreements between limited groups of EU Member States on subjects closely connected to the operation of the Union. The international treaty instrument is here used as one of the instruments allowing for differentiated integration by enabling a group of EU states to conclude agreements outside the institutional and decision-making strictures of the EU legal order. The conclusion of the 'Fiscal Compact' between 25 of the then 27 Member States, and of the Treaty establishing the European Stability Mechanism between the then 17 euro area states, are recent examples of this use of international law as a mechanism of differentiated integration.[75] They were followed more recently (in May 2014) by

[72] OJ 1972 L 299/32. It was later replaced by EC Regulation 44/2001. The currently applicable version is EU Regulation 1215/2012 on jurisdiction and the recognition and enforcement of judgments in civil and commercial matters, OJ 2012 L 351/1.

[73] OJ 1990 L 225/10.

[74] Convention on the establishment of a European Police Office, OJ 1995 C 316/1 (entered into force 1 October 1998). It has since been replaced by an EU Regulation (Regulation 2016/794, OJ 2016 L 135/53).

[75] On the political and legal circumstances explaining, and justifying, this recourse to *inter se* international agreements in the context of the euro crisis, see De Witte, 'Using International Law in the

the signature of yet another international agreement in the sphere of Economic and Monetary Union (EMU) law, namely the Agreement on the Single Resolution Fund, which is the intergovernmental part of the banking union package.[76] A further international agreement closely connected with the functioning of the EU was signed on 19 February 2013 between 25 Member States (all except Croatia, Poland, and Spain), namely the Agreement on a Unified Patent Court.[77]

Although recourse to international side agreements was a novelty in the EMU context, it is a traditional instrument in the toolbox of European integration, which has mainly been used to give legal form to differentiated integration projects, the most prominent examples being the Schengen Agreement of 1985 and Schengen Convention of 1990. The legal possibility for EU states to conclude such *inter se* agreements is based on the fact that in areas in which the EU has (only) shared competence, and as long as the EU has not exercised that competence, the Member States preserve the power to adopt their own rules either individually or together with a group of like-minded EU states (or, indeed, together with third states). In doing so, they are, however, constrained by the requirement, affirmed repeatedly by the Court of Justice[78] and seemingly accepted by all EU states, that such cooperation 'on the side' must not contain any rules that conflict with existing EU law obligations. In that sense, partial agreements clearly do *not* constitute a legality constraint for the EU. Any provision of those agreements can at any time be overruled by EU legislation and, if that happens, national courts must set aside the provision of the agreement, and the states concerned must terminate the agreement.[79]

Euro Crisis—Causes and Consequences', ARENA Working Paper No. 4 (2013). See also the explanations offered by a member of the Council legal service: de Gregorio Merino, 'Legal Developments in the Economic and Monetary Union During the Debt Crisis: The Mechanisms of Financial Assistance', 49 *Common Market Law Review* (2012) 1613, esp. at 1635–1640. Among the more critical assessments of this development, highlighting the threat to the EU's institutional integrity, see Dimopoulos, 'The Use of International Law as a Tool for Enhancing Governance in the Eurozone and its Impact on EU Institutional Integrity', in M. Adams, F. Fabbrini, and P. Larouche (eds), *The Constitutionalization of European Budgetary Constraints* (2014) 41.

[76] Agreement on the Transfer and Mutualisation of Contributions to the Single Resolution Fund, [2014] Council doc. 8457/14.

[77] Agreement on a Unified Patent Court, OJ 2013 C 175/1.

[78] Case C-370/12, *Pringle* (EU:C:2012:756).

[79] See Case C-284/16, *Achmea* (EU:C:2018:158), where the CJEU held that a bilateral investment agreement between Slovakia and the Netherlands was incompatible with primary EU law. The Member States collectively drew the consequence from that judgment that intra-EU bilateral investment agreements should be terminated: *Declaration of the representatives of the governments of the Member States of 15 January 2019 on the legal consequences of the judgment of the Court of Justice in Achmea and on investment protection in the European Union*, available at https://ec.europa.eu/info/sites/info/files/business_economy_euro/banking_and_finance/documents/190117-bilateral-investment-treaties_en.pdf (accessed 11 November 2020).

8. Conclusion

When the EU decides to become a party to an international legal instrument, whether bilateral or multilateral, the effect of this is not limited to creating obligations for the EU under public international law. The international agreement is also incorporated automatically in the EU legal order and becomes a legality constraint within that legal order, due to the recognition, by EU law itself, of the precedence of those international commitments over secondary EU law. In the multilevel European legal space, agreements concluded by the EU also become a legality constraint for the Member States of the EU, even if they are not parties to the international instrument themselves.

This legality constraint is primarily reflected in the rule-making activity of the EU's political institutions. Ensuring compliance with the EU's international obligations will set in motion the adoption of internal legislation to implement those international obligations or to repeal existing EU law measures that are inconsistent with them. This activity of the EU's institutions operates, in principle, under the control of the CJEU, which can review the compliance of EU secondary law (and Member State law) with the EU's international agreements. However, the Court has self-limited this review power through the development of a doctrine on the direct effect of international agreements. The result of this doctrine is that some agreements effectively act as legality constraints on the EU and its Member States, whereas others (mostly multilateral ones) do not, because of their lack of direct effect. This court-led mitigation of the primacy of international treaties has been supplemented, in the past 10 years, by a treaty practice through which the Union excludes the direct effect of its substantively most ambitious trade agreements. The Court of Justice also clearly affirms the precedence of the EU's *primary law* (the Treaties and the Charter of Rights) over the EU's international obligations. This attitude is similar to that displayed by national constitutional courts which tend to affirm the primacy of the national constitution over international treaties, but it nevertheless shows how the CJEU:

> is struggling with the task of shaping a distinctive relationship between the European legal order and the international legal order which is neither one of simple hierarchy and obedience nor one which prioritizes political sovereignty and independence, but one which acknowledges the important place of international law within EU law and of the EU within the international legal order.[80]

The last part of the chapter completed this picture by examining the extent to which agreements concluded by the EU's Member States (as opposed to the Union

[80] De Burca, 'Internalization of International Law by the CJEU and the US Supreme Court', 13 *International Journal of Constitutional Law* (2015) 987, at 1006–1007.

itself) could also act as legality constraints in the EU legal order. The default answer to that question is negative—the Union is not bound by the commitments undertaken by other international actors, even if they happen to be its Member States—but there are some exceptions where EU primary law itself makes international instruments concluded by the Member States into indirect legality constraints for the EU, namely, the European Convention on Human Rights and the Geneva Convention on Refugees.

6
Disintegration through Law
Brexit, Article 50, and the Court

*Kieran Bradley**

1. Brexit: Look on my Works, ye Mighty . . .

The withdrawal of the United Kingdom from the European Union, universally dubbed 'Brexit', dominated the British political landscape from the conclusion of the legally problematic, but ultimately irrelevant, 'New Settlement for the United Kingdom within the European Union' adopted by the European Council on 19 February 2016,[1] until the global coronavirus pandemic put it into perspective. It also dominated Union affairs from the date of the fateful consultative referendum, 23 June 2016, albeit that the withdrawal process was not initiated for another nine months; even where Brexit was not an item on the meeting agenda, it was the elephant in every room.

Brexit has challenged the legal and political foundations of the Union in unprecedented ways, and to an unprecedented extent. It may continue to do so for some years to come, though the nature and scope of any continued disruption depends in large measure on how the 2020 Withdrawal Agreement and the EU-UK Trade and Cooperation Agreement are applied, and how the Union and the United Kingdom regulate their future relations.[2] From the institutional and legal perspective, the withdrawal process hinges on Article 50 of the Treaty on European Union (TEU), a provision introduced into Union law at the time of the Lisbon Treaty reforms. While a fringe group of Brexiteers might have preferred a sudden, chaotic, and presumably illegal withdrawal of the United Kingdom from the Union,[3] successive British governments have preferred to comply with the relevant Treaty

* Former judge of the EU Civil Service Tribunal, former Special Adviser to the CJEU. The views expressed are exclusively personal to the author, and may not be attributed to any institution, or any member or official of any institution, with which he is or has been associated. Best thanks are due to Michael Dougan for his enlightening comments on an earlier version of the text; he bears no responsibility for any errors.

[1] European Council Conclusions, EUCO 1/16, Brussels, 19 February 2016.

[2] Respectively OJ 2020 L 29/7 and OJ 2020 L 444/14; on the challenges facing the Union and its legal order more generally, see Dawson, 'Coping with Exit, Evasion, and Subversion in EU Law', 21 *German Law Journal* (2020) 51.

[3] See Bradley, 'On the Cusp: Brexit and Public International Law', in I. Govaere and S. Garben, *The Interface between EU and International Law* (2019) 203, at 203–204.

Kieran Bradley, *Disintegration through Law: Brexit, Article 50, and the Court*. In: *Contemporary Challenges to EU Legality*. First edition. Edited by: Claire Kilpatrick and Joanne Scott, Oxford University Press (2021). © Kieran Bradley.
DOI: 10.1093/oso/9780192898050.003.0006

procedure. Overnight, Article 50 TEU became the single most famous provision in the entire EU statute book. At the same time, its incoherent design and laconic drafting have exacerbated the inherent complexity and uncertainty generated by the decision of a Member State to withdraw from an international organization of the scope and ambition of the European Union. A surprising number of individuals associated with the European Convention of 2002–2003 have claimed paternity of this provision; the most vociferous claimants disagree as to whether it was inserted with the United Kingdom in mind.[4] Whether or not this was the case, the assertion that Article 50 was never intended to be used[5] hardly explains, still less excuses, its omissions and deficiencies.

The possibility that Article 50 could be invoked again or amended in the future, possibly even the near future, should not be discounted. It may therefore be appropriate to attempt to draw some lessons from the Brexit exercise, with a view to avoiding, or at least mitigating, the disruptive effects of the withdrawal process on the Union's legal order. Moreover, the withdrawal procedure laid down in Article 50 TEU—as it played out in practice and has been interpreted by the Court—together with the 2020 Withdrawal Agreement, pose a number of challenges to Union and international legality. This chapter will examine in order: how Article 50 TEU transgresses the scheme of the Treaties and of accepted norms of international law; whether and how the United Kingdom's hostility to the Court of Justice[6] was justified in the withdrawal context; how the legal uncertainty of the Brexit process impacted the Court's rulings on Brexit-related questions submitted to it in the interim period between notification and withdrawal; and the role of the Court under the Withdrawal Agreement.

2. Article 50 TEU and the Scheme of the Union Treaties

In the classical case-law of the Court of Justice, 'it is necessary to consider the spirit, the general scheme and the wording' of provisions of Union law.[7] Given the far-reaching effects of its operation, it would be useful to assess how Article 50 TEU fits into the general scheme of the Union Treaties considered in their historical context.

The trajectory of European integration was set by the authors of the 1951 Treaty of Paris establishing the European Coal and Steel Community (ECSC). In order

[4] Cf. Amato, 'Brexit: Article 50 was Never Actually Meant to be Used, Says Its Author', *The Independent*, 26 July 2016 (*yes*) and Lord Kerr of Kinlochard, 'Article 50 Author Lord Kerr: I Didn't Have UK In Mind', *Politico*, 29 March 2017 (*no*).

[5] Amato (see n. 4).

[6] Properly speaking, now the 'Court of Justice of the European Union', hereinafter 'the CJEU', or 'the Court' for convenience.

[7] Case 26/62, *Van Gend en Loos* (EU:C:1963:1) 12, 1st para.

to safeguard world peace, they sought by 'establishing an economic community, [to create] the basis for a broader and deeper community among peoples long divided by bloody conflicts[,] and to lay the foundations for institutions which will give direction to a destiny henceforth shared'.[8] While the 1951 Treaty has lapsed, the thinking that underpinned the establishment of the now defunct coal and steel community, as reflected in its admirably succinct preamble, is still largely relevant, even if the threat of war between States of the Union has, hopefully, disappeared. The 'deepening' of the 'community among peoples' was launched by the adoption of the 1957 Treaties of Rome, establishing the European Economic and Atomic Energy Communities.[9] The momentum thereby created has been sustained by successive Treaty revision exercises, starting with some, mostly minor, institutional reforms in the 1960s and 1970s, and continuing with the major substantive expansions of the Community's (now Union's[10]) competences, and the loosening of the grip of Member State governments on the policy-making process, since the mid-1980s. In parallel, the Union has been 'broadened' by the accession of 22 Member States to join the original six. This reflects the Union's vocation to expand, in line with the call issued by the first Member States to 'the other peoples of Europe who share their ideal to join their efforts'.[11]

None of the founding Treaties provided for an exit clause.[12] The 50 years' duration of the ECSC Treaty[13] could even be seen as a 'no exit' clause for that half-century, and reflects the innovative, and daring, character of the first Community Treaty. No doubt it was intended on expiry either to extend the Treaty, abolish the time limitation, or replace it with something more progressive if this were available, as indeed transpired in 2002. The Treaties of Rome were more self-confidently 'concluded for an unlimited period'.[14] Failing proof to the contrary, it is suggested that the absence of an exit clause in these instruments was not the result of an oversight. Had they wished to allow for this possibility, the Treaty authors had the example of the International Labour Organization, another multilateral organization whose constitution provides both for further implementing instruments, and for the possibility of unilateral withdrawal, subject to the compliance of the withdrawing state with certain obligations.[15]

By far the more plausible explanation is that, to borrow from the Schuman Declaration's projection regarding the possibility of future hostilities between

[8] Preamble to the Treaty establishing the European Coal and Steel Community, 5th para.

[9] For convenience, references will be restricted henceforth to the European (Economic) Community (E(E)C) Treaty.

[10] For convenience, and at the risk of anachronism, reference will be made to the 'Union', except where it is necessary to refer to one or other of the 'Communities'.

[11] Preamble to the Treaty establishing the European Economic Community, 8th para.

[12] On exit clauses generally, see Helfer, 'Exiting Treaties', 91 *Virginia Law Review* (2005) 1579.

[13] Art. 97 ECSC.

[14] Arts 240 EEC and 208 Euratom; see now Art. 356 TFEU.

[15] Art. 1(5) ILO Constitution 1919.

France and Germany, withdrawal from the Community Treaties was considered 'not merely unthinkable, but materially impossible'.[16] This would certainly be consistent with the indications in the preambles to the Community Treaties quoted above. In the same line of reasoning, the Court of Justice proclaimed in 1964 that 'the transfer by the States ... of the rights and obligations arising under the Treaty carries with it a permanent limitation of their sovereign rights'.[17] In so far as it is relevant,[18] Article 56 of the 1969 Vienna Convention on the law of Treaties (VCLT) only permits unilateral withdrawal from a treaty which does not have an exit clause in two circumstances: if 'it is established that the parties intended to admit the possibility of denunciation or withdrawal', or if 'a right of denunciation or withdrawal may be implied by the nature of the treaty'. It is difficult to see how either of these could have been demonstrated in respect of the Community Treaties; indeed, the predominant, though not unanimous,[19] academic opinion prior to the Treaty of Lisbon was that there was no such legal possibility, notwithstanding the fact that two governments had threatened unilaterally to withdraw in the 1970s and 1980s.[20] If the Community served to safeguard world peace, then withdrawal could even have been seen politically as a hostile act.

The inclusion in the TEU of an exit clause clearly goes against the grain of the underlying assumptions on which the Union is based, and has been operating under for the last 60 plus years. While the addition of Article 50 TEU was a considered political choice, both the existence of Article 50 and its operation in the case of the United Kingdom have perturbed the Union's political and legal order, which is founded on the idea that once a Member State, always a Member State. It exacerbates the tension between the Union's aspiration to be something more than a classical international organization, to which the Member States have transferred a part of their sovereign rights, and the hard fact that the Union has no control over certain existential aspects of its existence and functioning. Union legality was also predicated on the understanding that rights granted under the Union legal order will be respected and protected within that legal order; Article 50 TEU challenges Union legality by failing to provide any protection, even on a transitional basis, for legal situations which were created in good faith in accordance with the Union legal order.

16 Schuman Declaration, 9 May 1950, English translation offered by the European Union, available at https://europa.eu/european-union/about-eu/symbols/europe-day/schuman-declaration_en (accessed 11 November 2020).

17 Case 6/64, *Costa v. ENEL* (EU:C:1964:66) 594, 5th para.

18 See later, in Section 3.

19 According to M. Dougan, a right of unilateral withdrawal 'was widely assumed to exist well before and regardless of the Lisbon Treaty Reforms': Dougan, 'So Long, Farewell, Auf Wiedersehen, Goodbye: The UK's Withdrawal Package', 57 *Common Market Law Review* (2020) 631, at 632.

20 See e.g. Hill, 'The European Economic Community: The Right of Member State Withdrawal', 12 *Georgia Journal of International and Comparative Law* (1982) 335; Weiler, 'Alternatives to Withdrawal from an International Organisation: The Case of the European Economic Community', 20 *Israeli Law Review* (1985) 282.

3. Article 50 TEU and the Development of International Law

Amongst the most fundamental objectives of the European Union is to 'contribute to . . . the strict observance and development of international law'.[21] One might be entitled to expect that the constituent power of the Union, which in this case was the Member States that adopted the Treaty of Lisbon (albeit relying largely on the work of the 2002–2003 European Convention), would also take some account of international legality, even if Member States are entitled to ignore such provisions of international law as do not formally apply. While Article 50 TEU has been said to have been inspired by the relevant provisions of the VCLT,[22] the Union's withdrawal provisions fly in the face of the scheme of the VCLT and the underlying concern of the international community for ensuring the stability of treaty relations. Whether or not all of the provisions of the VCLT reflect customary international law and hence bind the Union, it would be difficult to argue against the proposition that the stability of treaty relations is an underlying concern of international law, as appears from the judgment of the International Court of Justice in *Gabčíkovo-Nagymaros Project (Hungary v. Slovakia)*, cited approvingly by the Court of Justice in *Racke*.[23]

The rule of the VCLT which would be pertinent in the present context is set out in Article 42(2), which provides that withdrawal from a treaty 'may take place only as a result of the application of the provisions of the treaty or of the present Convention'. Article 42(1) VCLT provides that '[t]he validity of a treaty or of the consent of a State to be bound by a treaty may be impeached only through the application of the present Convention'. In its commentary on the draft articles, the International Law Commission 'considered it desirable, as a safeguard for the stability of treaties, to underline in a general provision in the beginning of this part that the validity and continuance in force of a treaty is the normal state of things which may be set aside only on the grounds and under the conditions provided for in the present articles'.[24] *Prima facie*, these are mutually exclusive alternatives. Where the treaty in question contains an exit clause, in accordance with *pacta sunt servanda*, the withdrawal provisions of the VCLT do not apply;[25] indeed, any other interpretation could give rise to legal and procedural chaos, as states to the same multilateral treaty could choose whether to apply, fully or in part, or to reject the

[21] Art. 3(5) TEU.

[22] Case C-621/18, *Wightman*, Opinion (EU:C:2018:978) paras 76 and 108 respectively; see further later, in Section 5.B.2.

[23] Case C-162/96, *Racke v. Hauptzollamt Mainz* (EU:C:1998:293) para. 50.

[24] Commentary on Article 39 in ILC, 'Draft Articles on the Law of Treaties', *Reports of the* [International Law] *Commission to the General Assembly*, at its eighteenth session in 1966 (2005) 236, available at https://legal.un.org/ilc/texts/instruments/english/commentaries/1_1_1966.pdf (accessed 11 November 2020).

[25] Eden, *The Revocability of Instruments of Withdrawal from Multilateral Treaties with Particular Emphasis on the United Kingdom's Article 50 TEU Notification*, 22, available on ssrn.com, updated to '05/10/2018', that is, either 10 May or 5 October 2018.

application of the provisions of, the exit clause of that treaty. It has not been suggested, for example, that any provision of the VCLT procedure other than Article 68 should apply to withdrawal under Article 50 TEU.[26]

Article 42(2) VCLT is complemented by Article 54 VCLT. This provides that:

> the withdrawal of a party [from a treaty] may take place:
>
> (a) in conformity with the provisions of the treaty, or
> (b) at any time by consent of all the parties after consultation with the other contracting parties.

The International Law Commission took the view that 'whatever may be the provisions of a treaty regarding its own termination, it is always possible for all the parties to agree together to put an end to the treaty', under whatever form of agreement they should choose.[27]

Articles 65 to 68 VCLT lay down, inter alia, the procedure which applies for withdrawal from a treaty 'under the provisions of the present Convention'. In rejecting an absolute rule which would require the consent of the other parties to the treaty to the withdrawal, the International Law Commission noted that 'in the case of treaties . . . there is the special consideration that the parties . . . have brought themselves into a relationship in which there are particular obligations of good faith'.[28] It also noted the consensus of the governments that 'the general object of this article [is] the surrounding of the various grounds of . . . termination [of a treaty] . . . with procedural safeguards against their arbitrary application for the purpose of getting rid of inconvenient treaty obligations'.[29]

The procedure laid down by Articles 65 to 68 VCLT, for withdrawal from treaties which do not have an exit clause, differs very significantly from that laid down by Article 50 TEU:

- a withdrawing party must invoke a 'ground for . . . withdrawing from [the treaty]';
- it must notify the other parties to the treaty of its 'claim' to withdraw and refrain from withdrawing during the notification period;
- it must provide reasons for this claim;
- other parties may raise objections to this claim;
- in case of objections, the parties must engage in a dispute settlement procedure under Article 33 of the UN Charter before withdrawal can take effect;

26 See later, in Section 5.B.
27 ILC (n. 24), 'Draft Articles on the Law of Treaties', Commentary on Article 51, 249.
28 Ibid. Commentary on Article 62, 262.
29 Ibid. Commentary on Article 62, 262.

- withdrawal is subsequently effected by means of an 'instrument communicated to the other parties' signed by the competent authority;
- the right unilaterally to revoke a notification of intention to withdraw is not assumed on the basis of the right of unilateral withdrawal, but is explicitly provided for in a separate provision of the VCLT.

It appears to follow from the text of these provisions that the right of withdrawal from a treaty under the VCLT is in no way unconditional; it may only be invoked in good faith, in accordance with Article 26 VCLT, and it is subject to important procedural conditions. In particular, there must be a 'ground' which is sufficiently plausible that it can be notified to the other parties, and can then be relied upon as a basis for objection by the other parties.

By providing a withdrawal procedure which can be invoked without safeguards of any kind, other than the possibly redundant proviso that the Member State's decision be taken in accordance 'with its own constitutional requirements', the Union's constituent authority has prima facie failed to contribute to the development of international law, and challenged head-on the objective of the stability of treaties.

4. The European Court of Justice in the Brexit Debate: Red Line or Red Herring?

A. The Proper Role of the Court

The establishment of a system of third-party dispute resolution was something of an afterthought in the Schuman Declaration, which refers simply to a 'means of appeal against the decisions of the [High] Authority', and the jurisdiction of the ECSC Court of Justice was correspondingly limited.[30] The political order imagined by the founding fathers of the later European Communities, on the other hand, encapsulated in their 'determination to lay the foundations of an ever closer union among the peoples of Europe',[31] was wildly more ambitious, albeit adopting an incremental, 'Vorsprung durch Technik', approach. This was built on legal structures, shored up by a well-functioning judicial system. Thus, though the substantive law of the ECSC was largely set out in the Treaty of Paris, this was true only to a limited extent of the EEC Treaty. This later treaty provided the institutional procedures and substantive outlines of that Community's policies, but left it to the autonomous institutions to 'give direction to a destiny henceforth shared' by adopting common policies and the measures necessary to make the common market a reality.

[30] Schuman Declaration (n. 16).
[31] Ibid. 1st para.

At a time when international tribunals were still a comparative rarity, including where international trade relations were concerned,[32] the Treaty authors did not hesitate to create a fully independent Court of Justice, with a comprehensive gamut of jurisdictional powers, and whose bounden duty was to ensure that 'the law', and not merely the Treaty, 'is observed'.[33] The Court was thus explicitly empowered to censure Member States for their failure to comply with Union law at the suit of a wholly autonomous institution in infringement proceedings, and to interpret Union law as it should apply in disputes between individuals before the national courts. If it would be too easy in retrospect to say that the Court's pivotal role in European integration was structurally inevitable, certainly the Treaty authors contemplated such a possibility with equanimity, and did nothing to prevent the Court playing such a role,[34] notwithstanding relatively recent transatlantic experience which might have given them pause.[35]

Whether or not the role played by the Court has been exaggerated,[36] it is undeniable that since the 1985 Single European Act, the Member State governments have reassumed their primary responsibility for the process of the constitutional reform of the Union, through successive amendments of the Treaties which have limited in practice the incentive, if not the opportunity, for the Court to determine the shape of the Union constitution. The point remains nonetheless that it has always fallen to the Court—and in principle it will always do so as long as the Union system remains—to take decisions which on occasion have a very direct impact on the interests of the Member States and Union citizens.

B. 'Does Magna Carta Mean Nothing to You? Did She Die in Vain?'[37]

The traditional British attachment to the rule of law, including 'the freedom of the individual against the arbitrary authority of the despot',[38] needs no illustration. It is therefore somewhat surprising that the UK government sought, largely *ex post*

[32] Neither GATT 1947 nor EFTA 1960 had a third-party dispute settlement mechanism when they were adopted; while endowed with dispute settlement procedures, neither has a court even today.

[33] Art. 31 ECSC and Art. 164 EEC; see now Art. 19(1) TEU.

[34] As detailed in the magnificent multi-volume study *Integration Through Law* (M. Cappelletti, M. Seccombe, and J. Weiler (eds), *Integration Through Law* (1986)); see also Weiler, 'The Transformation of Europe', 100 *Yale Law Review* (1991) 2403.

[35] As educated citizens and politicians, they would presumably have been well aware of the struggle between the US Supreme Court and the elected branches of government just 20 years before; see e.g. J. Shesol, *Supreme Power* (2010).

[36] J. Baquero Cruz, *What's Left of the Law of Integration* (2018) 18.

[37] Tony Hancock, 'Twelve Angry Men', Hancock's Half Hour (1959); this is a skit on the 1957 Sidney Lumet film of the same name.

[38] Lord Denning's assessment of the Magna Carta, in Lee, 'Lord Denning, Magna Carta and Magnanimity', 27 *Denning Law Journal* (2017) 268.

facto, to pin a sizeable portion of the blame for its decision to withdraw from the Union onto the Court, and then to prevent the Court's being given the necessary jurisdiction to help clear up the legal mess that decision has caused.

In the first place, in his letter to Donald Tusk of 10 November 2015, Prime Minister David Cameron did not raise the jurisdiction of the Court of Justice as one of the 'concerns of the British people over [their] membership of the European Union'.[39] If, as was subsequently claimed, the Court's role was a factor which justified withdrawal from the Union, then at the very least the Prime Minister would have been obliged to raise it, in accordance with the duty of sincere cooperation under Article 4(3) TEU. But that is not all; having failed to raise any such concern in Brussels, in a speech for home consumption delivered the same day, Cameron vowed to examine how the United Kingdom could exercise its 'right to review legal acts by European institutions and courts to check that they remain within the scope of the EU's powers, or whether they have overstepped the mark'.[40] If the UK government considered that the role of the Court was a sufficient reason for leaving the Union, which no reform could address, then the 'New Settlement' exercise begins to look like a somewhat hollow fiasco.

There is, however, little or no evidence that the impact in the United Kingdom of the Court's case-law, or the role of the Court in general, played any significant part in the decision of the British people to withdraw from the European Union. The Court barely rated a mention in most analyses of the run-up to the referendum vote.[41] For one commentator, indeed, 'the absence of serious public engagement with the great issues that were bandied about, such as … the European Court of Justice' was '[o]ne of the shocking aspects of the referendum'.[42]

It is true, of course, that a previous Conservative government had complained very publicly about the Court some 20 years before. In a submission to the intergovernmental conference preparing the Treaty of Amsterdam, tellingly entitled *A Partnership of Nations*, the Court was accused of 'impos[ing] disproportionate costs on Governments or businesses, even where they have made every effort to meet their EC obligations'; proposals to clip the Court's wings were revived following the Conservatives' surprise outright general election victory in 2015.[43] That said, the mild implicit rebuke Cameron delivered in Chatham House was hardly a rallying cry for leaving the Union; it is, however, in tune with remarks by certain members of the UK Supreme Court, who were then waging a 'campaign of low-key

[39] Available at https://assets.publishing.service.gov.uk/government/uploads/system/uploads/attachment_data/file/475679/Donald_Tusk_letter.pdf (accessed 11 November 2020).

[40] Chatham House speech, 10 November 2015, available at https://www.gov.uk/government/speeches/prime-ministers-speech-on-europe (accessed 11 November 2020).

[41] See e.g. A. Glencross, *Why the UK Voted for Brexit* (2016); C. Oliver, *Unleashing Demons* (2016); G. Gibbon, *Breaking Point* (2017).

[42] A. Barnett, *The Lure of Greatness* (2017) 146.

[43] Cm 3181, London, HMSO, March 1996, para. 37; D. Gowland, *Britain and the European Union* (2017) 105–106.

civil disobedience' as regards the Court of Justice, though without resorting to open hostility.[44] The Chatham House announcement was apparently designed to convince Boris Johnson (at that time an influential backbench MP and Mayor of London) to back the Remain campaign.[45] The Prime Minister continued to woo Johnson for his support by proposing various forms of 'sovereignty lock' which would be introduced into British law if the United Kingdom were to vote to stay in the European Union. In time, however, Johnson himself came to the conclusion that the proposed sovereignty Act was untenable;[46] the proposal was subsequently described in the *Financial Times* as 'a ludicrous legislative device that meant that an act of parliament would declare, by means of circular logic, acts of parliament were sovereign'.[47] This 'ludicrous legislative device' has now become law.[48]

Ten days before the 'New Settlement' for the United Kingdom was adopted by the European Council, Marina Wheeler QC, who was at the time married to Boris Johnson, published a scathing attack on the case-law of the Court of Justice interpreting Protocol No. 30 to the Union Treaties on the application of the EU Charter on Fundamental Rights to Poland and to the United Kingdom. In her view, the reforms to persuade the United Kingdom to remain in the Union 'need[ed] to address the EU legal order, in particular the jurisdiction muscle-flexing of the Court in Luxembourg'.[49] While cogently argued in a manner that might appeal to some lawyers, it does not appear to have stoked a public debate on the question amongst the electorate. In her major contribution on the referendum debate, Home Secretary Theresa May advocated the United Kingdom's withdrawal from the European Convention on Human Rights (ECHR), judging the European Court of Human Rights in Strasbourg unfavourably when compared to its counterpart in Luxembourg.[50] The only negative note she struck was a vague call to 'work to limit the role of the Court of Justice'. The 'Vote Leave' campaign published an initiative proposing rapidly to end the Court's jurisdiction in the United Kingdom in respect of asylum policy and national security matters;[51] this dates from mid-June 2016, just before the referendum was held, and is unlikely to have had a major impact on the outcome.

Armstrong presents a somewhat more nuanced view on the possible relevance of case-law from Luxembourg, suggesting that '[t]he role of the Court of Justice as

44 Bradley, 'International and Other Apex Courts: Dublin viewed from Luxembourg', 1 *Irish Supreme Court Review* (2019) 31, 37.

45 T. Shipman, *All Out War* (revised and updated, 2017) 162.

46 Shipman (n. 45) 165.

47 Green, 'Brexit: why did the ECJ become a UK "Red Line"?', *Financial Times*, 12 April 2017.

48 European Union (Withdrawal Agreement) Act 2020, s. 38.

49 'Cavalier with our Constitution: a Charter too far', *UK Human Rights Blog*, 9 February 2016; a shorter version of the piece was published in *The Spectator* on 13 February 2016 as 'The Crucial Missing Part of Cameron's EU Deal'.

50 Speech of 25 April 2016, available at https://www.gov.uk/government/speeches/home-secretarys-speech-on-the-uk-eu-and-our-place-in-the-world (accessed 11 November 2020).

51 H. Clarke *et al.*, *Why Britain* [sic] *voted to leave the European Union* (2017) 55.

the authoritative interpreter of EU law was at the fore of criticisms about a loss of control over law'.[52] By way of illustration, he cites the Court's 'extension of gender equality protection in respect of pay to include occupational pensions schemes' in the 1990 *Barber* judgment, as well as the case-law on the Working Time and Posted Workers directives. That said, the temporal effects of the *Barber* ruling were limited by the Member States in a subsequent protocol to the Treaties; the adoption of this protocol was a striking, if untypical, illustration of the limits of the power of the Court, and the ultimate predominance of the Member State governments, which is exactly the sort of initiative which should have appealed to, and appeased, the UK government. It would also be surprising if a majority of the UK electorate voted to leave the European Union on the grounds that certain judgments of the Court of Justice gave a priority to workers' rights over other, economic, interests. In any case, Armstrong goes on to admit that 'it is difficult to pinpoint clear examples of judgments of the Court of Justice which generated the sort of level of political or social controversy that might lead voters to consider that the UK should leave the EU'.[53] The same cannot be said of judgments of the European Court of Human Rights, such as those concerning voting rights for prisoners, which famously caused the Prime Minister of the day, David Cameron, to suffer an upset stomach.[54]

Whatever the dark mutterings in Conservative central office over the years, the general view is that the United Kingdom's outright hostility to the Court only became government policy on the occasion of the speech of newly appointed Prime Minister Theresa May at the Conservative Party conference in October 2016, four months after the referendum had been held. According to one press report, '[w]e do not (yet) know how or why the prime minister decided to include this definite objective [of ending the jurisdiction in the United Kingdom of the CJEU] in her conference speech ... there was little sign that this was to be a government "red line" before the conference'.[55]

This sequence of events is reflected in the careful, if slightly demagogic, drafting of the relevant Brexit objective outlined in the government's White Paper on *The United Kingdom's exit from and new partnership with the European Union*.[56] There the government commits to taking 'control of our own affairs as those who voted in their millions to leave the EU demanded we must, and bring an end to the jurisdiction of the ... CJEU', but stopping short of claiming that millions consciously voted against CJEU jurisdiction. The government's assessment of the Court in this White Paper is at times oddly ambivalent. On the one hand, it acknowledges that the Court 'aims to provide both consistent interpretation and enforcement of EU

[52] K. Armstrong, *Brexit Time* (2017) 118.

[53] Ibid. 121.

[54] 'Cameron Sickened by Prisoner Vote', *The Times*, 3 November 2010, reporting on Prime Minister's Questions that day.

[55] Green (n. 47).

[56] Cm 9147, HM Government, London, 2 February 2017.

law across all 28 Member States and a clear process for dispute resolution when disagreements arise'; on the other hand, in the same paragraph, the government pledges to 'end the jurisdiction of the CJEU in the UK'.[57] It later contrasts the dispute settlement mechanism of the World Trade Organization (WTO) Agreements with that of the European Union. In the former, 'the outcome was prescribed, but not the means', whereas in the Union system, 'there is a right to an effective remedy from a judicial body', as if this were something to be avoided at all costs.[58]

The UK government thereby sought to make the Court a scapegoat, at least in part, for its discontent with the Union. It has been suggested that 'escaping from the jurisdiction of the Court … [was] one of the very few objectives for Brexit which Mrs May [identified] which can ONLY be achieved by the United Kingdom's actually leaving the European Union', given that all the other objectives, excepting the restoration of control of immigration from the Union, could 'arguably be best achieved by the United Kingdom's remaining in the European Union'.[59] In reality, the government's gripe appears to have been less with particular rulings of the Court that adversely affected the perceived interests of the United Kingdom, than with the very effectiveness of the Union's legal order, which the Court undeniably helped fashion. The principal attributes of this legal order—notably the primacy of Union law, the direct effect of certain Treaty provisions, and the irreversibility in principle of the transfer of Member State powers to the Union—had been established well before the United Kingdom acceded to the Union.[60] Indeed, the possibility that the UK courts would become 'subordinate in some respects to the European Court of Justice' had percipiently been brought to the government's attention in November 1960, even before the first application for accession to the European Communities had been lodged.[61]

If the UK government's real complaint was with the range and intensity of the Union's policies and activities, it should instead have pointed the finger at the Union's political process, and in particular the long series of Treaty reforms which were undertaken by the Member States, from the Single Act (1986) to the Treaty of Lisbon (2009).[62] The United Kingdom was able to play a full part in the successive extensions of the Union's powers, and, in that context, was very successful in

[57] Ibid. 13, para. 2.3.

[58] Ibid. Annex A, para. A.20.

[59] K. Bradley, presentation at the Panel Discussion on Brexit at the Closing Session of the XXVIII Congress, Estoril, 26 May 2018, 140, 141, available at https://drive.google.com/file/d/1dpwkGmZhM6dckFk2NrelY7-9VAzNukul/view (accessed 11 November 2020) (emphasis in original).

[60] Apart from Case 26/62, *Van Gend en Loos* (EU:C:1963:1) and Case 6/64, *Costa v. ENEL* (EU:C:1964:66), see also Case 7/71, *Commission v. France* (EU:C:1971:121), esp. 19 and 20.

[61] The Lord Chancellor, Lord Kilmuir, to Ted Heath, Minister for European Affairs, cited in Gowland (n. 43) 67.

[62] There is much truth in the suggestion that in fact the 'transfer of huge areas of competences … actually came to a halt with the Maastricht Treaty in 1992': Mayer, 'The EU in 2030: An Anticipated Look Back at the 2020s', 21 *German Law Journal* (2020) 63, at 64.

carving out for itself large exemptions from some of the Union's flagship political initiatives; future historians may wonder just why the other Member States tolerated the United Kingdom behaving like an outlier for so long.

For all its grandstanding, however, the United Kingdom accepted the principle, albeit grudgingly and subject to some exceptions, that for the purposes of the application of the bulk of the provisions of the Withdrawal Agreement the Court of Justice is best placed to rule on Union law matters, even where the facts arise in the UK territory, and where relations between it and the Union are governed by provisions of Union law.[63]

Whatever the mitherings of the British government before and after the referendum debate, and during the negotiations on the Withdrawal Agreement, its hostility to the Court is a rejection of the principle and the practice of Union legality, at the same time as it recognizes *sua sponte* that the Court is providing an effective judicial remedy. Having contributed largely to the origin and development of the rule of law, starting with the Magna Carta,[64] the United Kingdom appears to be cooling in its support for this fundamental value, at least in this transnational context.

5. Uncertainty and the Law: Pre-Brexit Rulings of the Court of Justice

A. 'No Deal Brexit': *Le Vide Juridique*

While providing explicitly for the possibility of a Member State's withdrawing from the Union, the Treaties fail entirely to make any provision governing the consequences of such withdrawal, in effect leaving the entire gamut of legal questions to be decided in an uncertain agreement of unknown content. Union law does not provide for the maintenance of individual rights or legal situations where a Member State withdraws from the Union, though it has been argued that shared obligations under the European Convention on Human Rights may require the maintenance of certain fundamental rights.[65] It equally fails to condition withdrawal to the payment of the debts which the Union has incurred on the basis of the financial backing of all the Member States, including that which decides to withdraw. This glaring omission led the House of Lords Select Committee on the European Union to conclude conveniently, though not wholly convincingly,

[63] Revised Political Declaration of 17 October 2019 setting out the Framework for the Future Relationship between the European Union and the United Kingdom (OJ 2020 C 34/1); it is unclear to what extent the UK government will be willing to follow up on this commitment in any future relations agreement.

[64] See e.g. Fernandez-Villaverde, 'Magna Carta, the Rule of Law, and the Limits of Government', 47 *International Review of Law and Economics* (2016) 22.

[65] Vidmar, 'Brexit, Democracy, and Human Rights: The Law between Secession and Treaty Withdrawal', 35 *Wisconsin Journal of International Law* (2018) 425.

that the United Kingdom could, if it chose to, walk away from the Union without paying a cent.[66]

It is difficult to conceive that the Treaty authors, even those responsible for Article 50 TEU, intended to countenance such potential for legal chaos. Prior to accession, there are in principle no individual rights or situations in the acceding state governed by Union law which need to be taken into account or preserved; more precisely, any such rights or situations as exist will have been created and governed by a specific legal regime, such as an association agreement or a trade and economic development agreement, which is EU law as such for the Union and the then existing Member States, but not in the acceding state. On withdrawal from the Union, on the other hand, there are literally millions of situations for which the governing legal framework disappears at the stroke of midnight, like Cinderella's horse-drawn carriage, though the situations themselves do not disappear. Thus it can be assumed that most of the three and a half million remaining in the Union ('EU27') citizens who reside in the United Kingdom and the one plus million UK citizens who live in the territory of the EU27[67] will probably wish to stay where they are, or at least not be forced to leave against their will. Similarly, companies from EU27 with ongoing contracts or other ongoing commercial relations in the United Kingdom, and UK companies with dealings with the EU27, presumably want to be able to complete their transactions, sort out VAT and import/export formalities, and so on.

These are matters which are dealt with in the Withdrawal Agreement.[68] However, until the solid victory of the Johnson government in the elections of 12 December 2019, it was far from certain that any agreement would be concluded, while some even harboured hopes going into the elections that Brexit itself could be reversed—a possibility the Court had sanctioned a year before. At different junctures in the long saga, a no-deal Brexit seemed the most likely outcome.

B. 'Decisions and Revisions that a Minute Will Reverse': *Wightman* and the Right of Revocation

1. The Strange Disappearance of Article 50(3) TEU: What Was the Question Again?

As is well known, in *Wightman*, the Court was asked whether a withdrawing state had a right unilaterally to revoke its notification of intention to withdraw from the

[66] *Brexit and the EU Budget*, 15th Report of Session 2016–2017, HL Paper 125, London, 2017; their lordships were on more solid legal ground in concluding that the enforcement of any financial obligations in a no deal Brexit scenario was highly problematic.

[67] These figures are at best rather approximate.

[68] See n. 2; see also Dougan (n. 19), and Bradley, 'Agreeing to Disagree: The European Union and the United Kingdom after Brexit', 16 *European Constitutional Law Review* (2020)379.

Union and, if so, under what conditions.[69] In a nutshell, the Court held, relying primarily on a reading of the Treaties as a whole, that because the United Kingdom has an unconditional right to withdraw from the Union, it also has an unconditional right to reverse that decision. The Court's reasoning has largely, but not universally,[70] been approved by the commentariat. One quite comprehensive analysis of the judgment concluded that, although the judgment raised a number of legal and political questions beyond the immediate Brexit context, '[n]ormatively . . . the principled position of the ECJ is . . . convincing', while a would-be critic gave it as his view that 'there is much to commend in the ruling and . . . the judgment is deeply satisfying in terms of the cogency of its legal reasoning'.[71]

It would nonetheless be a mistake to think, as has been suggested, that '[t]he 'principal argument against unilateral revocation relies on a parallel between revocation and extension', or to prevent the unanimity requirement for extension being circumvented.[72] Under an alternative narrative which was not considered explicitly by the Court, the principal argument against unilateral revocation is that Article 50 TEU does not permit revocation at all. One of the peculiarities of the proceedings in *Wightman* is that none of the parties challenged the existence of a right to revoke,[73] but divided instead on the conditions for the exercise of such right. The applicants and interveners in the main proceedings favoured a unilateral right, while the Council and the Commission argued for European Council supervision, with the UK government resolutely refusing to take a position other than on the admissibility of the request for a preliminary ruling.[74] As a result, while the Court goes to some lengths to demonstrate the existence of a right of revocation, it does so without examining the principal arguments against this position.[75]

The 'no-revocation' thesis is founded primarily on the wording of Article 50 TEU. Article 50(1) TEU does not provide that a Member State may withdraw from

[69] Case C-621/18, *Wightman and Others v. Secretary of State for Exiting the European Union* (EU:C:2018:999). The term 'revocation' is used, to avoid talking about the 'withdrawal of the notification of withdrawal'; it is also the term used in Art. 68 VCLT.

[70] Tierney, 'Professor Stephen Tierney: Article 50 Decision Calls into Question Political Neutrality of the CJEU', *Scottish Legal News*, 10 December 2018, available at https://www.scottishlegal.com/article/professor-stephen-tierney-article-50-decision-calls-into-question-political-neutrality-of-the-cjeu (accessed 11 November 2020); Weiler (writing before the judgment), 'A Second Brexit Referendum—What Makes You Think They Will Have You Back?', *EJIL: Talk!*, 26 November 2018, available at https://www.ejiltalk.org/a-second-brexit-referendum-what-makes-you-think-they-will-have-you-back/ (accessed 11 November 2020).

[71] Cuyvers, '*Wightman*, Brexit and the Sovereign Right to Remain', 56 *Common Market Law Review* (2019) 1303, at 1331; Cotter, 'Ten Months Later: A Retrospective of *Wightman*', *DCU Brexit Institute News*, 21 October 2019.

[72] Cuyvers (n. 71) 1314 and 1323 respectively.

[73] This is the converse of the situation in *Miller I*, where the parties agreed that revocation was legally impossible, and the courts proceeded on this basis: *Miller et al. v. Secretary of State for Exiting the European Union* [2017] UKSC 5.

[74] The agent for the UK was invited at the hearing to take a position on the revocability issue, but declined.

[75] Advocate General Campos Sánchez-Bordona noted the existence of this thesis, with references to the legal literature, but did not examine it in any detail either: Opinion (n. 22) para. 59, fn. 32.

the Union, merely that it may 'decide' to do so. Under this thesis, the unilateral (national) decision to withdraw from the Union is not legally effective without the second (Union) phase of the process, that is, Article 50(3) TEU, which provides that '[t]he Treaties shall cease to apply to the State' that has notified its intention to withdraw, from a given date (two years after notification or the date determined by a withdrawal agreement). By this token, the initial decision has no effect in Union law; notification is required to initiate the withdrawal procedure. Thus, while the *date* of the withdrawal is uncertain (though the fixing of the date is subject to strict procedural parameters), the *fact* of withdrawal is not. It would follow that the injunction in Article 50(3) TEU that the 'Treaties shall cease to apply' to the withdrawing state is substantive; it is an essential, operative, part of the mechanism for withdrawal, and takes the place of the 'instrument' of withdrawal provided for under Article 67(2) VCLT.[76] The decision to withdraw does not require the consent of the Union, but its effectiveness is subject to the application of Article 50 TEU. Article 50(1) TEU establishes the unilateral 'sovereign' right of a Member State to initiate the withdrawal procedure; however, that procedure could not work without Article 50(3) which, under this thesis, both allows and requires withdrawal.

While it is true, as the Court noted, that 'the wording of Article 50 TEU ... does not explicitly address the subject of revocation ... [and] neither expressly prohibits nor expressly authorises revocation',[77] Article 50 TEU is arguably not silent as regards the legal effects of notification. Under the 'no revocation' thesis, once the Member State in question has notified its intention to withdraw, the procedure is out of its hands, and its role is limited to deciding whether to accept or reject a proposed withdrawal agreement, and, as need be, agreeing or refusing an extension of the deadline for the withdrawal to take effect (Articles 50(3) and (4) TEU respectively). By that token, the Member State has an unconditional right to initiate the procedure, but having done so, withdrawal follows ineluctably in accordance with Article 50(3) TEU.

Instead, the Court treats Article 50(3) TEU as being limited to determining 'when the withdrawal ... will take effect'.[78] In this, it appears to be following the analysis of the Advocate General who had opined that 'the obligation to notify ... and the two-year period to negotiate the agreement ... are only formal elements and do not limit the unilateral nature of the initial decision to withdraw'.[79] The question in *Wightman*, however, was not whether Article 50(2) and (3) TEU constrain the right to decide to withdraw, but whether they provide for a right to revoke a notification to do so. If these so-called 'formal elements' do not in any way constrain the right of withdrawal, then it follows that the withdrawing Member State would

[76] See previously, in Section 3.
[77] Case C-621/18, *Wightman* (n. 69) para. 48.
[78] Ibid. para. 54.
[79] Opinion (n. 22) para. 92.

not even be obliged to notify its intention to withdraw, and could simply exit the Union without more—a sovereigntist thesis so extreme that not even the mainstream Brexit community espoused it at the time.[80] If the obligation to notify under Article 50(2) TEU is a substantive requirement, then so should be the obligation to withdraw at the end of the period set in accordance with Article 50(3).

Moreover, interpreting Article 50(2) and (3) TEU as 'formal elements' which do not condition the right of withdrawal could be said to overturn the balance of power within the negotiation context intended by the Treaty. If notification is irrevocable, it is the Union which has the whip hand, and can present the withdrawing state with a take-it-or-leave it option on the text of such an agreement.[81] This is not as surprising or unjust as it might first appear; given the structure of Article 50 TEU, and its failure to mitigate, or even regulate, any of the practical or legal consequences of withdrawal, it is clear that the Union will probably have a stronger interest in ensuring an orderly withdrawal by concluding an agreement than the withdrawing state, for financial if for no other reasons. Furthermore, as withdrawal without a deal is a scenario which is expressly provided for, at the end of the day one of the parties will have a stronger hand in putting pressure on the other to accept a deal. It is the withdrawing state, not the Union, which initiated the withdrawal exercise, and it is the Union's primordial duty to protect its citizens, its businesses, its (remaining) Member States, and the Union itself, in a situation not of its own making.[82] Being essentially dictated by the necessity to reconcile these interests as best it can, the Union's substantive negotiating position is unlikely to vary greatly according to whether or not notification is revocable, and, indeed, the vast majority of the provisions of the 2020 Withdrawal Agreement were negotiated before the *Wightman* proceedings had been resolved.

According the Union, the upper hand in negotiations on any withdrawal agreement might be considered the price the withdrawing state must pay for its untrammelled right to decide to withdraw and force a disorderly withdrawal if it so chooses. Nor would it offend in any way the spirit of the VCLT procedure, in so far as it is relevant, which prima facie allows remaining states to object to and delay withdrawal, and influence the conditions of any such withdrawal. Overturning this balance, by allowing the withdrawing state simply to walk away from any draft agreement it does not care for, would mean that that state could ... eat its cake and have it too.[83]

[80] See Bradley (n. 3).
[81] See e.g. H.-B. Shäfer and A. Radwan, 'Brexit Poker—Who Has a Better Hand in the Withdrawal Negotiations?', Allerhand Working Paper 17/2016.
[82] European Council guidelines for Brexit negotiations, 29 April 2017.
[83] This was implicitly acknowledged in the 'Three Knights opinion': Edward *et al.*, 'In the matter of Article 50 of the Treaty on European Union', 10 February 2017, para. 48.

2. The VCLT as a 'Considerable Source of Inspiration'

The shadow of Article 68 VCLT fell long on the revocation debate both before and during the *Wightman* proceedings. It stipulates that '[a] notification or instrument provided for in Article 65 or 67 may be revoked at any time before it takes effect'; as the Court noted, it applies in principle even in circumstances where the treaty has an exit clause.[84] Never mind that the Union has its own legal order whose 'autonomy ... with respect to ... international law is justified by the essential characteristics of the European Union and its law', as the Court reminded the reader in *Wightman*.[85] Never mind that neither the Union nor all its Member States are party to the VCLT, or that Article 68 VCLT does not reflect a rule of customary international law, as Advocate General Campos Sánchez-Bordona very correctly noted before launching into his analysis of the revocation issue. For revocationists, the 'with one bound, our hero was free' appeal of Article 68 VCLT proved irresistible. Wherever revocation was being promoted, there Article 68 VCLT was to be found, albeit hedged about with the necessary reservations and qualifications—the usual quiddets and quillits of legal discourse. Thus, for example, in their carefully crafted opinion, the Three Knights noted that the VCLT provides 'some support' for the revocationist thesis, and 'may be taken into account in interpreting Article 50'.[86]

The Court and the Advocate General in *Wightman* were in agreement that the VCLT was relevant, though the Court was more prudent as regards the intensity of that relevance.[87] Early in his analysis, the Advocate General suggested that 'Article 68 of the VCLT ... may be a considerable source of inspiration as regards [the] interpretation' of Article 50 TEU. Warming to the theme, he later took the more affirmative line that 'what is true is that Article 50 TEU is based on the VCLT', and that there was therefore 'no reason not to apply, by analogy, the same rule in the framework of the procedure for withdrawing from the European Union'.[88]

The VCLT procedure for withdrawal from a treaty which has no exit clause has already been examined (see Section 3); of all the features of that procedure, Article 50 TEU has retained only one, the two-stage procedure of notification, including a waiting period before withdrawal. Article 50 TEU may thus be said to have been 'inspired' by the VCLT in the same way as a child's go-cart was inspired by a Formula One sports car: each has four wheels and assists the occupant in forward motion, though this particular go-cart has neither steering wheel nor brake.

At the same time as it recognizes a right of unilateral withdrawal, the VCLT imposes certain procedural restrictions on the exercise of this right, in the interests of the other parties to the treaty. As the state in question would already have identified sufficient grounds for withdrawal to defend its decision in front of the other states

[84] Case C-621/18, *Wightman* (n. 69) para. 71.
[85] Ibid. para. 45.
[86] Three Knights opinion (n. 83) 20 and 21, para. 54.
[87] Case C-621/18, *Wightman* (n. 69) para. 70.
[88] Case C-621/18, *Wightman*, Opinion (n. 22) paras 76 and 108 respectively.

party, revocation would be based on a recognition that those grounds are not, or are no longer, valid; there would therefore be no reason to limit, still less prohibit, the right of revocation. It is thus in respect of a very different right of withdrawal that the International Law Commission took the view that the right of revocation was 'implicit in the fact' that the coming into effect of withdrawal was delayed in time.[89]

Though it only relied marginally on the VCLT, preferring instead to base its reasoning on Article 50 TEU, the Court did note that its conclusion was 'corroborated by the provisions' of the VCLT.[90] The right of withdrawal under the VCLT is not unconstrained *à la Wightman*, but if the VCLT provisions had indeed been 'taken into account' in the drafting of what subsequently became Article 50 TEU, then it is surely more likely than not that the Treaty authors would have provided rules and a procedure governing revocation, if this possibility were to be allowed. It is not clear that the VCLT provides any justification for the interpretation into the Treaties of a revocation clause which simply is not there.

3. Sovereign Thinking and the Rule of Law

The Court was at pains to emphasize the 'sovereign' character of the Member State's decision under Article 50(1) TEU. In the present case, this arises from the fact that the decision to withdraw is taken unilaterally, that is, 'not ... in concert with the other Member States or with the EU institutions'; it is 'for that Member State alone to take, in accordance with its constitutional requirements, and therefore depends solely on its sovereign choice'. This 'sovereign nature' was in turn relied upon to 'support[ ] the conclusion that the Member State has a right to revoke the notification', which if exercised would 'reflect[ ] a sovereign decision by that State to retain its status as a Member State'.[91]

Generally speaking, '[t]he term sovereignty is invested with heavy meaning in much of the writing on constitutionalism, political theory and international relations, as well as in political debate'.[92] It may be used with different meanings: 'the supreme authority in the internal order of a state', the 'characteristics of a state' for the purposes of international law, or 'the extent to which a state has power of effective or unfettered action'.[93] In particular, the divide between those who view sovereignty as indivisible, and those who consider indivisible sovereignty as an anachronistic folly, reflects the tension between conceptions of the Union mentioned previously.

[89] ILC (n. 24), 'Draft Articles on the Law of Treaties', Commentary on Article 64, 264.

[90] What should the Court have done if those provisions had *not* corroborated its interpretation: change its interpretation or ignore those provisions?

[91] Case C-621/18, *Wightman* (n. 69) paras 50, 57, and 59.

[92] R. Hardin, *Liberalism, Constitutionalism, and Democracy* (1999) 153. The quotation continues: '[t]he heavy meaning is typically incoherent and the term is therefore often misleading'.

[93] House of Lords Select Committee on the European Communities, *Economic and Monetary Union and Political Union*, 27th Report Session 1989–1990, paras 11–13.

Given that the remaining strands to the Court's reasoning depend on a semantic argument which did not wholly convince the Advocate General who suggested it, an appeal to general values of vast and uncertain scope, and the somewhat ambiguous legislative history of Article 50 TEU, much rides on the Court's reliance on the 'sovereign character' of the initial decision of the United Kingdom to withdraw. The Court was obviously aware that the sovereignty flag had been regularly brandished in the Brexit debate in the United Kingdom, and of the wry comment in the government's White Paper under the rubric 'Taking control of our laws', that '[w]hilst Parliament has remained sovereign throughout our membership of the EU, it has not always felt like that'.[94] In any case, the Court's choice of this term conveyed the unmistakable message that the exercise of the right of revocation would be no less an expression of the sovereignty of the United Kingdom than the exercise of the right to withdraw from the Union.

It appears from the Advocate General's Opinion, to which the Court refers in this regard, that 'sovereign' here is essentially a synonym for 'unilateral'; '[i]f a State's decision to conclude a treaty is unilateral, so is its decision to withdraw from it'.[95] That may be so of the initial decision to withdraw, but the unilateral character of that decision does not mean that the right necessarily contains within it a right to revoke its decision; only the first stage of the withdrawal process (Article 50(1) TEU) is unilateral, the second stage requires the participation of both the Union and the withdrawing state (Article 50(2) TEU). Where the second stage fails to produce an agreement, under the 'no revocation' thesis the third stage—automatic withdrawal (Article 50(3) TEU)—is out of the hands of either party.

Under the VCLT scheme, where the treaty in question contains an exit clause, the right to withdraw, and any possible right to revoke a notification of intention to withdraw, are both subject to whatever substantive and procedural conditions may be derived from that treaty, in accordance with the principle *pacta sunt servanda*. In any case, it was the Court itself which had noted a few paragraphs previously that the Treaties had created 'a new legal order ... for the benefit of which the Member States ... have limited their sovereign rights'.[96] Arguably, the 'sovereign' character of a right does not in and of itself mean that its exercise is free from all constraint under Union law, for example the operation of Article 50(3) TEU, if this is applicable. To use the terminology of the House of Lords Select Committee cited earlier (see text accompanying footnote 93), the fact that withdrawal from the Union represents an affirmation of the United Kingdom's status as a sovereign state does not mean that it enjoys unfettered discretion over all aspects of the withdrawal procedure.

[94] White Paper, *The United Kingdom's exit from and new partnership with the European Union*, Cm 9147, HM Government, London, 2 February 2017.

[95] *Wightman* Opinion (n. 22) para. 93.

[96] Case C-621/18, *Wightman* (n. 69) para. 44.

The 'sovereign' character of the right of a Member State to decide to withdraw appears to be based on Article 50(1) TEU, which only requires compliance with its own constitutional requirements. This is a distinctly anomalous proviso, which on its face makes compliance with national law a rule of Union law, though the German *BundesVerfassungsgericht* would not agree.[97] In any case, it is not in any way comparable to the equivalent requirement under Article 48(4), 2nd, TEU and Article 49, 2nd, TEU, as in each case the resulting act would comprise primary law, whose validity falls outside the Court's jurisdiction.[98] It has been suggested by one of the putative authors of Article 50 TEU that this provision was intended to ensure that the decision would not have to comply with any pesky EU rules.[99] If that were indeed true, it would be difficult to reconcile with the Union's values as set out in Article 2 TEU, which include 'respect . . . for the rule of law'.

Be that as it may, while the matter did not arise in *Wightman*, it could be argued that the decision to withdraw is not in principle exempt from all forms of judicial review at the Union level. In *Shindler*, the General Court held that the Member State's decision to withdraw under Article 50(1) TEU does not 'give[ ] rise to a decision of acceptance from the EU institutions, by which they confirm that the State in question has respected' its own constitutional requirements, on the grounds that '[s]uch a decision of acceptance ... by any ... EU institution is not needed and is not provided for by Article 50 TEU'.[100] It is obviously true that no such decision is explicitly provided for in Article 50; however, this does not answer the applicants' argument that Article 50 TEU requires an *implicit* acceptance, which is a different matter.

The Union phase of the withdrawal procedure may only be initiated if the European Council receives a notification of intention to withdraw from '[a] Member State which decides to withdraw'. In deciding to initiate the procedure, the European Council is not merely a letter box, but it must itself take a decision on whether or not it has received a valid notification. In so doing, the European Council is required to comply with the values of the Union, including, for example, the Charter of Fundamental Rights. If the European Council considers that the notification is null and void, either because the Member State has not respected its own constitutional requirements, or for some other reason, is it really expected to ignore such invalidity? Should it remain indifferent, for example, if the decision underlying the notification had been taken on the basis of a referendum vote where suffrage was only granted to white, male, card-bearing members of the political party which won the largest number of seats in the European Parliament elections of 2019? Any refusal of the European Council to operate the withdrawal procedure

97 Lisbon Treaty judgment, 2 BvE 2/08, 30 June 2009, para. 330.

98 Case C-370/12, *Pringle* (EU:C:2012:756) para. 33.

99 Lord Kerr, cited in 'Article 50 annotated—with comments from its author', *Politico*, 28 March 2017.

100 Case T-458/17, *Shindler v. Council* (EU:T:2018:838) para. 58; appeal rejected, Case C-755/18 P, *Shindler v. Council* (EU:C:2019:221).

would in principle leave it open to judicial review in either annulment proceedings or proceedings for illegal failure to act.

For the European Council to ignore the presumptively illegal character of a national decision to withdraw would ignore the express terms of Article 50(1) TEU, if non-respect of constitutional requirements is at issue, or the rule of law, if the alleged breach concerns a provision of Union law. Union legality demands that 'neither [the] Member States [of the Union] nor its institutions can avoid a review of the question whether the measures adopted by them are in conformity with the basic constitutional charter, the Treaty',[101] including the protection of fundamental rights as stipulated by Article 6(1) TEU. Moreover, the Court itself hinted that the sovereign character of a revocation decision did not absolve it from all possibility of review, in holding that revocation must be 'expressed through its democratic process in accordance with constitutional requirements', and 'be submitted in writing to the European Council and ... unequivocal and unconditional'.[102] The European Council would therefore be entitled—indeed obliged—to reject a revocation notification which did not comply with these requirements, and its rejection would be open to annulment proceedings. If a revocation decision is subject to the rule of law, then it would be anomalous if the even more far-reaching decision to withdraw were not.

The Court has referred to the notion of the 'sovereignty' of the Member States in other contexts of Union law. The 'specialty rule' in the Framework Decision on the European Arrest Warrant is said to be 'linked to the sovereignty of the executing Member State'.[103] The same is true of the discretionary option under Article 17 of the Dublin III Regulation on international protection (the so-called 'sovereignty clause'). In each case, the matter at issue is one upon which the Member State may decide 'in its absolute discretion', in the sense that it is not obliged under Union law to opt for one outcome over another.[104] The sovereign character of such a decision does not, however, entail that the Member State remain master of all the legal consequences of its decision once this has been taken. Thus, for example, where a Member State does decide to assume the function of 'Member State responsible' for examining an application for international protection under the discretionary clause, or waive the application of the specialty rule, it would then be required to comply with the relevant provisions of the Dublin III Regulation or the Framework Decision respectively. By that token, the sovereign character of a withdrawing state's decision under Article 50(1) TEU would not absolve it from compliance with the requirements of Article 50(3) TEU, if this latter precluded unilateral revocation.

[101] Case 294/83, *Les Verts v. Parliament* (EU:C:1986:166) para. 23.
[102] Case C-621/18, *Wightman* (n. 69) paras 66 and 74.
[103] Case C-388/08, *Leymann and Pustovarov* (EU:C:2008:669) para. 44.
[104] See the *M. A.* case: Case C-661/17, *M. A. et al. v. International Protection Appeals Tribunal* (EU:C:2019:53).

The presentation of the Court's reasoning is also curious. After paraphrasing the provisions of Article 50(1) to (3) TEU governing the right of withdrawal, the Court refers to a 'conclusion' on the right of revocation, without any of the intermediate argumentation that one might have expected. The only previous mention of the right of revocation in the Court's reasoning is the finding that an 'intention' is not irrevocable.[105] Moreover, the sovereign nature of the right of withdrawal merely 'supports' such a conclusion, which otherwise appears to be free-standing.[106]

4. 'Intentions' and Consequences

Unlike its Advocate General, the Court did not rely on the VCLT to any significant extent. The Court based its analysis primarily on the classical canons of interpretation of EU law: the wording, the objectives, and the context of Article 50 TEU, as well as a nod in the direction of its legislative history. It kicked off by referring to the undoubted fact that the withdrawing Member State notifies its 'intention', rather than its 'decision', to the European Council: '[a]n intention is, by its nature, neither definitive nor irrevocable'. As a semantic argument considered in isolation, this might seem quite convincing, though, as the Advocate General pointed out, 'it is not as compelling as it at first sight appears, since Article 50(2) TEU also uses the term *decision* (the "Member State which *decides* to withdraw shall notify . . .")'.[107]

In the first place, an intention which is formulated but not communicated (an intention *simpliciter*) is not the same as one which is communicated to a third party (an expressed intention), and on the basis of which the third party then takes an agreed course of action. The former 'by its nature' may indeed be 'neither definitive nor irrevocable'; the latter, on the other hand, may have consequences from which the party who expressed the intention may be unable to escape with impunity. Whereas in common parlance an expression of intention may normally be retracted without further consequences, that is not necessarily the case in the legal context. It has been argued that 'in international treaties, just as in contract law, *intention* means the determination of a party to perform a certain act with legal consequences'.[108]

In this regard, the VCLT may be, for once, of some assistance in explaining the wording of Article 50(2) TEU.[109] As already noted, withdrawal from a treaty in accordance with the VCLT procedure, that is, where the treaty does not provide an exit clause, may only be effected in two stages. The first requirement is the

[105] See Section 5.B.4.

[106] This does not appear to be an infelicity of translation; the French version of this phrase, 'milite en faveur de l'existence d'un droit . . . de révoquer la notification' does not display any greater degree of conviction than the English.

[107] *Wightman* Opinion (n. 22) para. 101.

[108] Vidmar, 'Unilateral Revocability in *Wightman*: Fixing Article 50 with Constitutional Tools', 15 *European Constitutional Law Review* (2019) 359, 368 (emphasis in the original).

[109] The Court noted that the VCLT 'was taken into account in the preparatory work' for what became Art. 50 TEU; Case C-621/18, *Wightman* (n. 69) para. 70.

notification of a 'claim' to withdraw (Article 65(1) VCLT), followed by a cooling-off period of at least three months (Article 65(2) VCLT). Withdrawal itself may only be effected at the end of this procedure by the lodging of a written 'instrument' of withdrawal (Article 67(2) VCLT). While the Treaty authors jettisoned most of the useful features of the VCLT procedure,[110] they appear nonetheless to have been influenced by its general scheme. The notification of the 'intention' to withdraw is the equivalent of a VCLT 'claim', rather than the final instrument of withdrawal. If this were the case, it would follow that a Member State withdrawing from the Union could not in any case notify a 'decision' giving effect to its withdrawal, as it is obliged either to wait out the two-year cooling-off period or conclude an agreement. By this token, the use of the term 'intention' does not in fact speak to the issue of revocability at all.

5. Withdrawal, Accession, and Expulsion

With something of a flourish, in the middle of its reasoning the Court held that 'given that a State cannot be forced to accede to the European Union against its will, neither can it be forced to withdraw from the European Union against its will'.[111] There is a pleasing air of simple and inexorable logic about this finding—a look of unarguability. That said, the right of withdrawal is not obviously the 'counterpart' of the possibility of accession, and requiring a Member State to withdraw, after a putative change of mind, is not in fact tantamount to an expulsion.

It is true, of course, that a request to accede to the Union, like the initial decision by a Member State to withdraw, is inherently unilateral; the Union is not involved in the decision to request accession, and is in principle entirely indifferent as to what and how the state decides, or indeed whether the state in question subsequently revokes its request. Article 49 TEU does not create any right, unconditional or otherwise, for the state to accede to, or otherwise change its legal status vis-à-vis, the Union; the Union institutions and Member States are under no obligation to accept its request, which may easily fall by the wayside. At this stage, the candidate has only some rather general obligations under the Treaty as a third state, that of showing it respects the Union's values and a commitment to promoting them. It is only when, and if, the Member States agree on the terms of accession, and the accession agreement comes into force, that the new state acquires any rights and obligations as a Member State.

The situation of a withdrawing Member State is entirely different. During the multilateral process of negotiating an agreement, it enjoys all its rights under Union law, except the right to participate in decisions the Union takes regarding the organization of the negotiations and the extension of the deadline, where it participates in its own right in any case.[112] The withdrawing Member State is

[110] See Section 3.
[111] Case C-621/18, *Wightman* (n. 69) paras. 65–67.
[112] Article 50(4) TEU.

also subject to all its obligations under Union law, including those to notify the European Council of its intention to withdraw, and to wait out the two-year period from notification before doing so. The positions of a state requesting to accede and one deciding to withdraw are not comparable, and the fact that a state cannot be forced to accede to the Union is *prima facie* not germane to the issue of whether a Member State may be required to withdraw on foot of its having notified an intention to do so.

The Court also hints, when considering the legislative history of what became Article 50 TEU, at the argument mooted in various quarters that forcing a Member State out of the Union on foot of a withdrawal notice, where it no longer wishes to leave, would be the equivalent of expelling that state against its will. Though considered at the time, amendments to allow expulsion had been rejected by the European Convention.[113] There is, however, the world of difference between forcing a state which has at no time notified its intention to withdraw from the Union to do so, and giving effect to such a notification in respect of a state which had previously decided to do so 'in accordance with its own constitutional requirements', even if the government now wishes to stop the process. If such a withdrawal is dictated by the rules of the game, then it is not strictly speaking an 'expulsion'.

It has also been suggested that 'where a decision to do something is unilateral there is a certain inherent logic to the claim that a later decision not to do it should be unilateral as well'.[114] If, as proposed earlier, in Section 5.B.1, the 'something' is the right to decide to withdraw, and therefore to initiate but not fully to control the withdrawal process, then the absence of a right of revocation does not contradict this 'inherent logic'. By this token, the Member State in question may change its mind, but only before notification. The matter may be illustrated by a comparison with the Commission's right to withdraw a legislative proposal established in the *Macro-financial assistance* case.[115] The Commission is entitled not merely to '*decide* to submit' a proposal, but also to submit such a proposal. While exercised unilaterally, this right is far from unconditional; in particular, the Commission must seek to 'promote the general interest of the European Union' and must comply with the substantive conditions and limits on Union competence which derive from the chosen legal basis. Although it follows the progress of the legislative procedure, and may amend its proposal at any time before Parliament's first reading, the Commission's consent is not required for the adoption of the act, in the way the withdrawing Member State must agree to any withdrawal agreement for this to be concluded. The possibility of withdrawing the Commission proposal is justified as a means of protecting its right of initiative, from which it is 'inseparable'; the

113 Case C-621/18, *Wightman* (n. 69) para. 68.
114 Cuyvers (n. 71) 1315.
115 Cuyvers (n. 71); Case C-409/13, *Council v. Commission* (EU:C:2015:217).

Commission's decision to withdraw its proposal must be reasoned and is amenable to judicial review.[116]

The right to decide to withdraw from the Union under Article 50 TEU is, by contrast, entirely unilateral, depends on the sole interest of the state concerned (which is not required to provide reasons), and does not obviously require any form of legal protection. Moreover, the submission of a proposal by the Commission is not attended by legal consequences in the way that a withdrawal notification is; there is no Treaty provision stipulating, for example, that 'failing its adoption by the legislature, the act proposed by the Commission shall be deemed adopted and enter into force two years after the submission of the proposal'.

6. Democracy, Liberty, and Citizens' Rights

Under the general rubric of the context of Article 50 TEU, the Court referred to a number of Treaty objectives—an ever closer union amongst the peoples of Europe and the elimination of the barriers which divide Europe—and values, notably liberty and democracy, which 'form part of the very foundations of the European legal order'. It also noted that 'any withdrawal of a Member State from the European Union is liable to have a considerable impact on the rights of all Union citizens'.[117]

Fundamental as these values are, liberty and democracy are very slippery concepts in the interpretation of provisions the Court has deemed essentially procedural.[118] It has been remarked that in both ancient and modern times 'democracy is very much about changing one's mind'.[119] This may very well be true where it is only the members of the particular demos who are directly affected by the change of mind; it is quite other in the context of relations between sovereign states. Which demos is to be considered: that of the withdrawing State alone, or those of the Union and its Member States (with or without the withdrawing state) as a whole? It is not that the 'no revocation' thesis would preclude a state changing its mind; it is based instead on the idea that this facility may legitimately be closed off after a certain point in time, or a particular stage of a decision-making procedure, in pursuit of other fundamental values, such as the rule of law or the principle of legal certainty. This is generally the case in the Union, where the Member States are required to comply with Union rules even if, as may happen on occasion, the majority of their particular demos would not agree. Under this reasoning, before notifying an intention to withdraw, a Member State would be required to ensure the necessary degree of political support over a sufficient period of time for such a course of action. Just as a state may not rely on domestic constitutional difficulties

[116] Case C-409/13, *Council v. European Commission* (n. 115) paras 74, 76, 77, and 94.

[117] Case C-621/18, *Wightman* (n. 69) paras 61 and 62.

[118] Though possibly no more so than the 'national identities' of the Member States, which the Court is called upon to preserve by virtue of Art. 4(2) TEU.

[119] Howse, 'The Road to Reversing Brexit: Local and Transnational Constitutional Principles', 39 *Cardozo Law Review* (2018) 1041, 1043.

to escape its obligations under an international agreement, between deciding and notifying a withdrawing state must guarantee that its withdrawal decision is also constitutionally irreproachable.[120] In these circumstances, the fact of revocation's becoming legally impossible does not offend the principle of democracy.[121]

The notion of liberty is even more difficult to pin down. Whose liberty, and what exactly does 'liberty' entail in concrete terms in this context? Would the interpretation of Article 50 TEU be different if the Member State in question aspired to being an 'illiberal democracy'?[122]

The Court also underlined the importance of Union citizenship, as 'the fundamental status of nationals of the Member States' on which 'withdrawal is liable to have a considerable impact'.[123] This much is unarguable, but citizenship rights are only one category of Union rights which would suffer a loss of protection as a result of withdrawal: social rights, economic rights, the integrity of the environment, and so forth. As Advocate General Szpunar remarked crisply in his opinion in *RO*, 'arguably the whole point for a Member State leaving an organisation such as the EU [is to] no longer be[ ] bound by obligations. The other side of the coin is . . . that rights are lost'.[124]

In the same context, it has been argued that 'considering the obligation to protect rights individuals derive from their EU citizenship, it is difficult to see how the EU or its Member States could deny a request from millions of EU citizens to remain in the EU'.[125] This is, however, precisely the situation which obtains in the Brexit context, where the wishes of the 16 million plus British electors who voted against withdrawal from the Union in a 'consultative' referendum are to be ignored, a situation which is *prima facie* perfectly compatible with Article 50 TEU.[126] Moreover, Article 50 TEU does not take any account of the possible wishes of the demoi of the remainder of the European Union.

In underlining the Union's objective of upholding 'an ever closer union', the Court can hardly have been unaware that the UK government had explicitly rejected any such aspiration as a condition of staying in the Union in the pre-referendum pact of 19 February 2016.[127] According to the Preamble to the Treaty

[120] This latter would also make sense of the somewhat obscure injunction in Art. 50(1) TEU that, as a matter of Union law, a Member State is to act 'in accordance with its own constitutional requirements'.

[121] For the sake of completeness, an appeal to the principle of democracy cut no ice in the *Macro-financial assistance* case (n. 115) para. 96.

[122] As Weiler has forcefully pointed out, this is 'ontologically an impossibility, an oxymoron': Weiler, 'The European Circumstance and the Politics of Meaning: Not on Bread Alone Doth Man Liveth (Deut. 8.3; Mat 4.4)', 21 *German Law Journal* (2020) 96.

[123] Case C-621/18, *Wightman* (n. 69) para. 64.

[124] Case C-327/18 PPU, *Minister for Justice and Equality v. RO*, Opinion (EU:C:2018:644) para. 60; see later, in Section 5.C.

[125] Cuyvers (n. 71) 1317.

[126] That said, the desire of the relevant majority of UK voters to exit the European Union has also, in effect, been affirmed in three general elections: in 2015 (when Cameron promised an 'in-out referendum' never dreaming he would be held to his promise), 2017, and 2019.

[127] European Council conclusions, EUCO 1/16, Brussels, 19 February 2016.

of Rome, the 'ever closer union' was intended to be open only to states which share the ideals of the founder members of the then European Economic Community. Arguably, this underlying objective is part of what distinguishes the Union from other international organizations,[128] and its outright rejection by a Member State is neither banal nor trivial. As the pro-Remain Cameron government claimed an opt-out from this objective in November 2015, it could hardly be maintained that the United Kingdom shared this particular Union ideal.

Under the 'no revocation' view, a Member State that wishes to terminate the withdrawal process after notification would still be required to withdraw, and then apply for re-accession under Article 49 TEU. Given that on withdrawal the state is in perfect regulatory alignment with the Union, the sooner it makes such an application, the better for all concerned. In so doing, it would have to demonstrate under the 1993 Copenhagen criteria that it once again embraces the objective of an ever closer union, as well as that of economic and monetary union. In addition, this would provide the remaining Member States with the opportunity of deciding whether or not they wish to readmit the state into the fold, and under what conditions. This is not demonstrably unfair in the circumstances; why should a single Member State be entitled to hold the entire European Union to ransom by threatening withdrawal and then reneging on its decision at will?

While this solution might be considered inconvenient in practical terms, it would not necessarily be more inconvenient than the years of uncertainty as to whether withdrawal would in fact go ahead, the possible conditions under which this would occur, and the Union's long-term relations with the withdrawing state. Knowing that, like winter, Brexit was coming might have facilitated the achievement of a withdrawal agreement rather more speedily,[129] and provided much-needed time for the preparation of the obviously more important agreement, or other arrangements, for the future relations between the Union and the United Kingdom. Brexit has proven to be a weapon of mass disruption;[130] automaticity of withdrawal would avoid the risks of notification based on less than solid political support, precisely because 'democracy is very much about changing one's mind'.[131]

[128] See earlier, in Section 2.

[129] While it may be a coincidence, it is also a fact that on the day when the Court handed down the *Wightman* judgment, the May government decided to pull the planned vote on the draft withdrawal agreement.

[130] It has been suggested that having been through the exercise once, the Union would be well prepared to cope with a withdrawal request from another Member State and the disruption would be less. This may or may not be the case; it should be recalled, however, that the UK was in many areas—such as the euro and the area of freedom, justice, and security—at best semi-detached from the Union, and that, in any case, most possible exiting Member States have common borders with not one but several remaining Member States.

[131] Howse (n. 119) 1043.

7. The Sounds of Silence

The perils of interpreting the sounds of silence in legal texts are notorious and manifold.[132] In *Wightman*, the Court relied, albeit as a very subsidiary argument, on the fact that on the occasion of the adoption of the text which inspired Article 50 TEU—that is, Article 46 of the first draft of the Treaty establishing a Constitution for Europe—the members of the Convention had rejected different amendments to that provision. These amendments were intended to allow for the expulsion of a Member State from the Union, 'to avoid the risk of abuse during the withdrawal procedure or to make the withdrawal decision more difficult', but were 'all rejected on the ground . . . that the voluntary and unilateral nature of the withdrawal decision should be ensured'.[133] However, in *Wightman* it was not the character of the withdrawal decision which was at issue, but the existence of a right of revocation (considered a quite separate matter by the VCLT) and the conditions for its eventual operation. It appears that another amendment tabled to the same Article 46 of the draft Convention, which was not brought to the attention of the Court, would have expressly allowed a state unilaterally to revoke its withdrawal notification by means of a simple declaration to the President of the European Council.[134] If the absence from Article 50 TEU of any prohibition on revocation can be considered to favour a right of unilateral revocation, then the absence of any provision allowing, and regulating, any such right may be considered a strong counterargument.

8. Should *Wightman* Have Been Decided Differently?

While the reasoning of the judgment in *Wightman* may leave something to be desired, it could be argued that the Court nonetheless reached a correct result, notwithstanding the poor design and drafting of the Treaty provision at stake, and the limited scope of the arguments put to it in the framework of the proceedings. Had it dealt with the matter, the Court might have found an explanation as to why the Article 50(3) TEU 'guillotine' could have spared a contrite United Kingdom which wished to remain in the fold; it would not have been the first time it rejected a literal interpretation of a provision of Union law.[135]

There is clearly merit in the view that 'it [was] one of those cases where the law would allow [more than one] interpretation',[136] and the Court would have been criticized whichever one it adopted. Had it decided that revocation was impossible, in a situation where the United Kingdom wished to change course, the Court would probably have been accused of forcing the unprecedented

[132] For a thoughtful consideration of the matter, see L. Tribe, *Constitutional Choices* (1985) ch. 4.
[133] Case C-621/18, *Wightman* (n. 69) para. 68.
[134] Eden (n. 25) 29.
[135] See e.g. Case C-540/13, *Parliament v. Council* (EU:C:2015:224) para. 37.
[136] Weiler, 'Brexit—Apportioning the Blame', *EJIL:Talk!*, 17 April 2020.

withdrawal of a Member State in the absence of an explicit Treaty rule to this effect. It is also difficult to see how the conditional right of revocation proposed by the Council and the Commission could have worked in practice; is it conceivable that a single Member State should have the power to determine whether a repentant Member State must nonetheless leave the Union?[137] At the hearing the agents of the Council and the Commission were asked why the Union supervision of the exercise of the right of revocation should require the positive vote of the 27 Member States in the European Council rather than, say, automaticity of revocation unless the 27 Member States all objected. That they had no convincing answer merely illustrates, however, that revocation is quite a different decision from withdrawal.

The practical inconveniences which follow from the judgment arise essentially because of the unconditional character of the right of withdrawal, rather than the existence of a right of revocation per se. In these circumstances, it could reasonably be argued that if the Treaty authors had intended the right of withdrawal to include an unconditional right of revocation, it was singularly remiss of them not to so provide explicitly.[138] Instead, the absence of an explicit rule on revocation left the Court to rummage in the attic of legal jumble for items from which to construct a plausible answer to a singularly difficult question. In the result, the Court was faithful to what it considered Article 50 TEU should have provided, within the general framework of European integration and the shared values of the Member States, in preference to a more literal interpretation of the relevant provisions.

The Court has not chosen the easiest path for itself. Having held the right of revocation was 'sovereign', the Court nonetheless assumed jurisdiction to rule on whether a purported revocation was 'unequivocal and unconditional'; thus, if the Court were to rule close to the withdrawal deadline that the notification of revocation lodged by a Member State was not intended 'to confirm the EU membership of the Member State concerned', the state could find itself excluded from the Union without any possibility of an agreement by operation of Article 50(3) TEU, unless of course the deadline were extended in time to facilitate the conclusion of an agreement. The political consequences of such a ruling would make those of the judgment of the United States Supreme Court in *Bush v. Gore* seem trivial by comparison.[139]

[137] While a single Member State may impede the accession of a candidate state, it is argued earlier that withdrawal is in no way the 'counterpart' of accession.

[138] Along with, inter alia, rules safeguarding acquired residence and social security rights, and subjecting withdrawal to the settlement of the withdrawing state's financial obligations.

[139] *Bush v. Gore* 531 U.S. 98 (2000).

C. The European Arrest Warrant and Mutual Trust in a Third Country

1. The *RO* Case: The Facts and the Judgment

RO was the subject of two European Arrest Warrants issued by the UK authorities in respect of a rape allegedly committed in 2003, and murder and arson allegedly committed in 2015. At the time of the proceedings before the Court of Justice, RO had been remanded in custody in Dublin. It was not disputed that if he were to be found guilty on these charges, he would be in prison in the United Kingdom after 29 March 2019, that is, the then expected date of the United Kingdom's withdrawal from the Union. He challenged his surrender to the United Kingdom essentially on the ground that his rights under EU law would no longer be guaranteed after Brexit, and that in any case, even if he could enforce equivalent rights before the national courts, these courts would be unable to make a reference to the Court of Justice. In May 2018, the High Court in Dublin asked the Court of Justice whether, given the uncertainty of the law, it should refuse surrender, or postpone its decision 'to await greater clarity about the relevant legal regime which is to be put in place' after Brexit.[140]

RO complained in particular that he would lose four categories of rights:

- The right to the deduction from his UK jail sentence of any period already spent in custody in Ireland (the 'offset rule').
- The right not to be tried in the United Kingdom for any crimes other than those for which he was surrendered (the so-called 'speciality rule').
- The right not to be surrendered or extradited to a state other than the United Kingdom (the 'onward surrender rule').
- More generally, his fundamental rights as guaranteed by Union law, and in particular the Union Charter of Fundamental Rights.

The Court started by recalling its standard case-law that EU law is based on the idea that the Member States share a set of common values, and that, on the basis of this mutual trust, every Member State must assume that every other Member State respects Union law, including the protection of fundamental rights. A Member State must therefore surrender any suspect it is holding under a European Arrest Warrant, except 'in exceptional circumstances' where the executing judicial authority takes the view that 'that surrender may result in the requested person being subject to inhuman or degrading treatment'.[141] The referring court had already

[140] Case C-327/18 PPU, *Minister for Justice and Equality v. RO* (EU:C:2018:733).

[141] Ibid. para. 40, citing Joined cases C-404/15 and C-650/15 PPU, *Aranyosi and Căldăraru* (EU:C:2016:198), and Case C-216/18 PPU, *Minister for Justice and Equality (Deficiencies in the System of Justice)* (EU:C:2018:586).

established that no such exceptional circumstances obtained in fact in the present case. The Court concluded that the 'mere notification by a Member State of its intention to withdraw from the Union ... cannot be regarded, as such, as constituting an exceptional circumstance' within the meaning of the case-law 'capable of justifying a refusal to execute a European Arrest Warrant'.[142]

RO argued, however, that with the notification of the United Kingdom's intention to withdraw 'the principle of mutual trust . . . has been irreparably eroded' and that for this reason his surrender should not go ahead. To answer this, the Court examined each of the four rights which RO had argued could be undermined:

- Regarding the deduction of time already served in the Irish jails, the Court accepted the assurance of the United Kingdom that it had incorporated the offset rule into domestic legislation, and that it applied the rule to any person extradited to the United Kingdom.
- RO had provided no evidence of existing or prospective legal proceedings which would contravene the rules of specialty and onward surrender.
- In any case, the United Kingdom had ratified the 1957 European Convention on Extradition and its legislation transposing the Convention into national law also incorporated the three rules at issue.
- The United Kingdom is party to the ECHR, of which it has incorporated Article 3 (prohibition on inhuman and degrading treatment) into its law; 'its continuing participation in that convention is in no way linked to its being a member of the European Union, [its] decision . . . to withdraw from the Union has no effect on its obligation to have due regard to Article 3' ECHR. Notification of withdrawal from the Union did not therefore justify refusing surrender for a risk of such treatment.[143]

As to RO's access to judicial review at the level of the European Union by means of a preliminary ruling request, the Court acknowledged that, in the absence of a withdrawal agreement, disputes on the existence or extent of his rights could not be referred to the Court of Justice. However, he 'should be able to rely on all those rights before a [UK] court or tribunal'. In any case, the Court itself had only become fully vested with jurisdiction as regards the European Arrest Warrant from 1 December 2014, five years after the Treaty of Lisbon entered into force.

In summary, the Court held that it is essential that in deciding on surrender, the Irish court be 'able to presume that . . . the issuing Member State [the United Kingdom] will apply the substantive content of the rights derived from' EU law 'in the period subsequent to the surrender, after withdrawal from the European Union'.[144]

[142] Ibid. paras 45–48.
[143] Ibid. paras 52–59.
[144] Ibid. para. 61.

2. Pyongyang Here We Come!

The reasoning of the Court in *RO* is disquieting in a number of respects.

The Court appears at times to treat the United Kingdom post-Brexit as a potentially wayward Member State, rather than a third state to which Union law, by virtue of Article 50(3) TEU, would simply not apply during almost the entire period of RO's eventual incarceration.[145] However, upon withdrawal, the United Kingdom ceases to be 'the issuing Member State', but becomes an 'issuing third state', which will have no more obligation to respect the Framework Decision and RO's rights under Union law than would the Democratic People's Republic of Korea. This contravenes the underlying premiss of the Framework Decision, according to the preamble to which '[t]he mechanism of the European arrest warrant is based on a high level of confidence *between Member States*' (emphasis added), and not between an executing Member State and a third state. The reason such a 'high level of confidence is required' is that the executing Member State is responsible for ensuring that the accused's fundamental rights and rights as a criminal defendant are respected for the future, not just at the time of the surrender, in the territory of the issuing Member State. The continuity of protection of the accused's rights is inherent in the very nature of the rights on which RO relied, which only kick in after surrender and are to be respected throughout the duration of the surrendered person's (possible) incarceration; the withdrawal of the United Kingdom cannot but undermine the value of the surrendering Member State's guarantee.

In this regard, it is no answer to say that neither the Irish High Court nor RO provided 'concrete evidence' of ongoing or possible future legal proceedings which could lead to his rights under the rules of specialty or onward surrender being disregarded. It may be that at the time of the national proceedings, and those before the Court, such proceedings were not yet in contemplation; even if they had been, neither the High Court in Dublin nor the accused would necessarily have been informed of their existence. Given the likely length of RO's incarceration if found guilty, there would be ample time for proceedings to be initiated at some future, post-Brexit date.

3. Protection of a Surrendered Person's Rights under UK Law

The Court placed great reliance on the fact that the rights RO relied on are guaranteed under UK law. No doubt some or all of these rights were also guaranteed under the law of some or all of the Member States before the adoption of the Framework Decision, particularly given the widespread, though not uniform, adherence of the Member States to the different European and international conventions in this field. That would not in itself suffice to justify an obligation to surrender under the Framework Decision. The system of the European Arrest Warrant is anchored

[145] For the purposes of argument, it was assumed that the UK would leave without an agreement, what Advocate General Szpunar called the 'default position', ibid. para. 46.

to the protection of the accused's rights *in the Union legal order*, with all that that entails, notably the supervision of the Commission and ultimately the Court of Justice, and the possibility for the individual to recover damages for the improper application of, or failure to apply, Union law, under the conditions defined in the Court's case-law, which reflects the autonomy of the Union's legal order.[146]

In particular, under Article 1(3) of the Framework Decision, surrender does not absolve the executing Member State of its duty to ensure the fundamental rights of the accused person 'as enshrined in Article 6' TEU are not undermined as a result of the surrender. That simply cannot be the case where the issuing state (the United Kingdom) will not be bound by Article 6 TEU right up to the end of the incarceration of the person surrendered. There is, moreover, no guarantee that the accused person's fundamental rights, including those protected under the EU Charter, will continue to be guaranteed under UK law after withdrawal. While withdrawal from the Union does not in any way entail withdrawal from the ECHR or the relevant conventions on extradition and related matters, having got rid of its Charter obligations by means of Brexit, nothing would stand in the way of the United Kingdom's also withdrawing from other international obligations guaranteeing fundamental rights and rights for accused persons. Such a course of conduct would be consistent with the government's stated objective of 'taking back control' of the law applicable in the territory of the United Kingdom, and 'repatriating' the vindication of individual rights, as has been advocated by successive UK prime ministers.

4. Access to Judicial Review at the CJEU

Even where the domestic courts are willing and able[147] to ensure compliance with the rights guaranteed under UK law, the interpretation they adopt may not comply with the specificities of Union law which an executing Member State must respect.[148] It is cold comfort for RO, who was at the time, as the referring court took pains to recall, 'presumed to be innocent', to be told that after surrender to the United Kingdom he 'should be able to rely on all th[e] rights [at issue] before a court or tribunal of that Member State'.[149] This sanguine assessment would carry some weight if the United Kingdom were indeed still a 'Member State' at the time, or at least treated as one for the purposes of Union law.[150] Otherwise, it might prove to be little more than a pious wish, particularly given the hostility of the United

[146] Opinion 1/09, *European Patent Jurisdiction* (EU:C:2011:123) and Opinion 2/13, *EU Accession to the ECHR II* (EU:C:2014:2454).

[147] Following stinging government defeats in the Supreme Court in two Brexit-related cases, the Conservative party has promised to examine the scope of judicial review, presumably not with the intention of widening or facilitating it: Bradley, '"Oh, to be in England now that Brexit's there"; some personal literary reflections', *EULawLive*, 26 February 2020.

[148] See *mutatis mutandis* the strictures of the Court in Opinion 2/13, *EU Accession to the ECHR II* (EU:C:2014:2454), to the effect that EU fundamental rights may only properly be guaranteed by Member State courts and the CJEU (paras 170 and 171).

[149] Case C-327/18 PPU, *Minister for Justice and Equality v. RO* (EU:C:2018:733) paras 28 and 60.

[150] As is the case during the transition period: see later, in Section 4.B.

Kingdom to the Charter—which includes a highly developed right to effective judicial protection—in all its manifestations. Indeed, out of all the enactments of Union law in existence, the Westminster parliament singled out the Charter as being excluded from the notion of 'retained EU law', as well as explicitly ruling out the possibility of obtaining *Francovich* damages, after exit day.[151]

It is also difficult to reconcile the Court's reasoning on this point with its statement in *Kadi*, holding that a particular legal basis, *in casu* Article 307 EC, 'may in no circumstances permit any challenge to the principles that form part of the very foundations of the Community legal order, one of which is the protection of fundamental rights, including the review by the Community judicature of the lawfulness of Community measures as regards their consistency with those fundamental rights'.[152] *RO*, however, imposes an obligation to surrender a Union citizen in circumstances where neither his rights under Union law, nor the possibility of judicial review at the Union level of the respect of those rights, is guaranteed during the entirety of his (possible) incarceration.[153]

It was widely reported that in early 2019 the Portuguese Supreme Court took account of the imminence of Brexit as a relevant consideration for refusing the surrender of an accused person to the United Kingdom under a European Arrest Warrant. It rejected this ground, though refusing the surrender on other grounds.[154]

Article 185 of the 2020 Withdrawal Agreement allows Member States to refuse to surrender their nationals to the United Kingdom with effect from 1 February 2020; three Member States, though not including Ireland, took up this option.[155]

5. The *RO* Proceedings: Overview

The prospect of RO's not being brought to justice was certainly an uncomfortable one; yet treating the United Kingdom as if it were a Member State for the purposes of the application of the Framework Decision during RO's incarceration was also problematic. The European Arrest Warrant scheme has the particularity of requiring one Member State to stand guarantor for the future rights in another

[151] European Union (Withdrawal) Act 2018, s. 5(4) and Sch. 1, clause 4, as originally adopted on 26 June 2018; the Act was referred to twice by Advocate General Szpunar in his Opinion in Case C-327/18 PPU, *Minister for Justice and Equality v. RO* (EU:C:2018:733) fns 49 and 56.

[152] Joined Cases C-402/05 P and C-415/05 P, *Kadi v. Council and Commission* (EU:C:2008:461) para. 304, cited in the *Wightman* judgment (n. 69) para. 62.

[153] It has been suggested that Ireland could have requested 'diplomatic assurances' as to RO's proper treatment during the entire period of incarceration: Sáenz Pérez, '*Minister of Justice v RO*: Brexit Means Nothing Has Changed . . . Yet', 44 *European Law Review* (2019) 548, 555.

[154] Case 120/17.2YREVR.S1, *AA*, judgment of 14 February 2019, available at http://www.dgsi.pt/jstj.nsf/954f0ce6ad9dd8b980256b5f003fa814/4126043be3210900802583a1004f6d19?OpenDocument (accessed 11 November 2020). My best thanks to Ricardo Passos, Michael Dougan, Alberto Saavedra, and most especially Margarida Martins, for their help with this judgment.

[155] OJ 2020 L 29/7 and 188 respectively; on the German constitutional ban on surrendering its nationals to a non-Member State, see *Financial Times*, 17 February 2019.

jurisdiction of the person it is surrendering. It can do so under this scheme safe in the knowledge that, whatever happens, the other jurisdiction is a Member State and subject to the full battery of mechanisms to ensure it complies with Union law. That is obviously not the case for a third state, and indeed Article 28(4) of the Framework Decision requires specific consent from the authorities of the executing Member State for each individual onward surrender to a third state, which is not required for onward surrender to a Member State.

In rejecting RO's arguments, the Court relied on the state of UK law as it stood at the time of the proceedings. The absence of 'concrete evidence' of any threat to RO's rights reflected the fact that the United Kingdom was still a Member State at the time, complying with its Union law obligations. This is, however, no real guide as to what its behaviour will be during the whole period when the surrender decision affects that person's rights, on which the Court can only speculate. To hold that it is not possible to say how a future ex-Member State would act once it has thrown off the shackles of Union membership is not to suggest that it will turn into the Wild West overnight; however, as has been remarked more than once, the whole point of Brexit is for the United Kingdom to escape from Union obligations.[156] The British government subsequently indicated that it had no intention of continuing with the European Arrest Warrant scheme after the end of the transition period.

D. Other Brexit-related Proceedings before the CJEU

The issues raised by the applicants in the annulment proceedings in *Shindler et al. v. Council*[157] were rather more far-reaching than those the General Court could usefully deal with in its judgment. In particular, the applicants sought to rely on the rule in Article 50(1) TEU that, as a matter of Union law, the decision of a Member State to withdraw from the Union be taken in accordance with that Member State's own constitutional requirements. However, the act being challenged—the Council decision authorizing the Commission to open negotiations with the United Kingdom—manifestly did not directly affect the applicants' legal situation, and the action was ruled inadmissible. Moreover, the General Court was clearly correct in holding that the Council was not vested, either expressly or implicitly, with a power to decide that the United Kingdom had complied with its own constitutional requirements.[158]

[156] Advocate General Szpunar, Case C-327/18 PPU, *Minister for Justice and Equality v. RO* (EU:C:2018:733), Opinion; David Frost, United Kingdom Brexit negotiator, speech at the ULB, Brussels, 17 February 2020.

[157] Case T-458/17, *Shindler v. Council* (EU:T:2018:838); appeal rejected, Case C-755/18 P, *Shindler v. Council* (EU:C:2019:221).

[158] Case T-458/17, *Shindler v. Council* (EU:T:2018:838) para. 58.

The proceedings in *M.A. et al.* raised, inter alia, the question of whether the imminence of Brexit had any impact on the handling of an application for international protection, where the United Kingdom was the responsible Member State under the Dublin III Regulation, and in particular whether the determining Member State was itself obliged to examine the application under the optional clause laid down in Article 17 of the Regulation.[159] The Court held that recourse to this clause is entirely at the discretion of the determining Member State, though it did add that the transfer of an applicant to the United Kingdom must not take place if there are substantial grounds for believing that the notification by the United Kingdom of its intention to withdraw from the Union 'would result in a real risk of that applicant suffering inhuman or degrading treatment'.[160]

Finally, by contrast to the grave matters raised in the other pre-Brexit cases dealt with by the CJEU, the appeal proceedings in *Alcohol Countermeasure Systems* offer something close to light relief.[161] A trademark issued to Alcohol Countermeasure Systems (ACS) in 2010 was subsequently declared invalid by the European Union Intellectual Property Office (EUIPO) at the behest of a UK company. ACS challenged this decision, but its challenge was rejected by the General Court by judgment of 29 March 2017, that is, the day the UK government lodged its notification of intention to withdraw from the Union. In its appeal, ACS argued that, as of the date of the Brexit referendum on 23 June 2016, UK trademarks could no longer serve as the basis of the cancellation of EU trademarks, and that 'the General Court should have, for reasons of public policy, taken account of the future withdrawal of the United Kingdom from the European Union or ordered a stay of the proceedings' pending the withdrawal's taking place.[162] The Court pointed out that the Union courts could not annul or alter an invalidity decision on grounds which only came into existence after the adoption of the decision.[163]

6. The Court of Justice and the Withdrawal Agreement

A. Introduction

The Court's work on Brexit has not even begun. The Withdrawal Agreement will create a new hybrid legal order, where vast numbers of provisions of Union law will be applied by the Union institutions, the Member States, and their citizens and businesses, to and in relations with a third state, and its citizens and businesses, outside the scope of Union law properly so-called. In turn, the third state

159 Case C-661/17, *M. A. et al. v. International Protection Appeals Tribunal* (EU:C:2019:53).
160 Ibid. para. 81.
161 Case C-340/17 P, *Alcohol Countermeasure Systems (International) Inc v. EUIPO* (EU:C:2018:965).
162 Ibid. para. 108.
163 Ibid. para. 116.

concerned, the United Kingdom, will be obliged to apply provisions of Union law as a matter of domestic law, albeit that it is obliged to give these provisions legal effect which is essentially equivalent to Union law as we know it. This is not entirely novel; under the European Economic Area (EEA) Agreement, for example, the so-called 'EFTA States'[164] apply Union law on the internal market and competition policy as a matter of their domestic law. Nonetheless, not only is the material scope of application of the Withdrawal Agreement of a different order of magnitude to the EEA, but the judicial supervision of the application of the Agreement by the United Kingdom, and particularly provisions of Union law it applies or refers to, will fall ultimately to the Court of Justice, rather than a separate court such as the EFTA court.[165]

B. The Transition Period

Amongst the key provisions[166] of the Withdrawal Agreement is the establishment of a transition period,[167] which commenced on 31 January 2020, and ended on 31 December 2020, not having been extended once by 'up to 1 or 2 years'.[168] During this time, all of 'Union law [was] applicable to and in the United Kingdom', subject to a very limited number of exceptions, such as the protocols excluding the United Kingdom from the Schengen area and certain policy measures on freedom, justice, and security.[169] The Agreement provides that such Union law 'shall produce in respect of and in the United Kingdom the same legal effects as those which it produces within the Union and its Member States, and shall be interpreted and applied in accordance with the same methods and general principles as those applicable within the Union'.[170] It follows that in essence Union law as a whole applied in respect of the United Kingdom during the transition period, and the vast majority of the substantive provisions of the Agreement only come into operation at the end of this period, rather than the date of withdrawal per se.

[164] 'So-called' because not all EFTA States are in fact in the EEA (Switzerland remains out), while all the EU Member States are also in the EEA, along with the Union itself; 'EFTA States' is nonetheless preferred in practice to 'EFTA-EEA States'.

[165] See Opinion 1/91, *EEA Agreement I* (EU:C:1991:490).

[166] See generally Dougan (n. 19); Bradley (n. 68), at 392–397.

[167] On the assumption that an agreement on future relations would be concluded in parallel with the Withdrawal Agreement, the UK had always referred to this as the 'implementation period' (see Dougan (n. 19) at 657 and fn. 139) or even 'IP'; see e.g. European Union (Withdrawal Act) 2018, s. 1A, as amended.

[168] Arts 126 and 132(1) Withdrawal Agreement ('WA') respectively. '[U]p to 1 or 2 years' is somewhat unclear; it appears from Art. 132(2)(c) WA that an extension may be granted for a period which is not a multiple of 12 months.

[169] Art. 127(1) WA.

[170] Art. 127(1) and (3) WA respectively.

Though the Withdrawal Agreement allowed the Joint Committee to take a decision on the extension of the transition period any time up to 30 June 2020, British concurrence in such an extension was rendered illegal as a matter of UK law on 23 January 2020.[171]

C. The New Legal Order

The primary characteristics of the new legal order are established in the opening provisions of the Withdrawal Agreement. Article 2 provides a comprehensive definition of the material scope of 'Union law', while Article 4(1) stipulates that the 'provisions of th[e] Agreement and the provisions of Union law made applicable by th[e] Agreement shall produce in respect of and in the United Kingdom the same legal effects as those which they produce within the Union and its Member States'. The familiar characteristics of Union law are there: direct effect, primacy, the judicial power of disapplication of inconsistent national provisions, and a requirement to interpret provisions of Union law 'in accordance with the methods and general principles of Union law'. The Union and the United Kingdom are bound by mutual duties of sincere cooperation, references to Union provisions include amendments to, or replacements of, those provisions, as need be, and, subject to listed exceptions, references to Member States and their authorities include the United Kingdom and its authorities. The Court may be able to rely by analogy on the corpus of EEA law in order to interpret certain of these provisions, at least as a starting point.[172]

Given its rigorously dualist approach to international agreements, the Withdrawal Agreement applies in the United Kingdom through the conduit of national legislation, and in particular the European Union (Withdrawal) Act 2018, as amended by the European Union (Withdrawal Agreement) Act 2020.[173] It remains to be seen whether 'Brexit law' will be accorded a status in the legal order of the United Kingdom similar or equivalent to that of EU law.[174]

[171] Art. 132(1) WA; European Union (Withdrawal) Act 2018, s. 15A, added by the European Union (Withdrawal Agreement) Act 2020, s. 33.

[172] See e.g. C. Baudenbacher (ed.), *The Handbook of EEA Law* (2016).

[173] The European Union (Withdrawal) (No. 2) Act 2019 is essentially limited to requiring the Prime Minister to request an extension of the deadline for withdrawal to 31 January 2020 and making ancillary arrangements.

[174] See in particular *Miller I, Miller et al. v. Secretary of State for Exiting the European Union* [2017] UKSC 5, para. 90, and Dougan (n. 19) at 656–657.

D. The Jurisdiction of the Court under the Withdrawal Agreement

Under the Agreement, the Court's jurisdiction would cover old cases, one category of new cases based on old facts, and several categories of new cases.[175]

1. Old Cases Based on Old Facts

Maintaining the Court's jurisdiction for cases pending before it when the United Kingdom withdraws from the Union was clearly the most sensible solution both in terms of efficiency—the Court is already seised of the dispute and can almost certainly provide a speedier solution—and justice, in that the law which applied to the facts of the case when they occurred was Union law as interpreted by the Court of Justice. Despite its noisy scapegoating of the Court of Justice just before starting the withdrawal process, the United Kingdom acknowledged the validity of this view quite early on in the negotiations.

The Agreement provides the Court with jurisdiction to decide any case which has been commenced but not completed before the end of the transition period, including direct actions by or against the United Kingdom, that is, essentially annulment actions initiated by the United Kingdom and infringement and enforcement actions against it.[176] This latter represents a minor concession by the United Kingdom, which at one point had suggested that the continuance of 'cases . . . aimed at incentivising compliance with EU law when EU laws will no longer apply in the UK' might be superfluous.[177]

The Court's jurisdiction extends to appeals brought after the transition period against a General Court judgment, and referral proceedings before the General Court, in cases commenced before the end of the transition period, as well as, for example, a request for an Opinion on an international agreement that the Union envisages to conclude. It will also have jurisdiction to provide preliminary rulings on requests from national courts which are referred to it before the end of the transition period.[178] For this provision to have any useful effect, the British courts must be entitled to refer questions to the Court of Justice after Brexit day. This was not the case under the European Union (Withdrawal) Act 2018 as originally adopted, which prohibited UK courts from referring such questions to the Court of Justice, though this rule was subsequently amended by the European Union (Withdrawal Agreement) Act 2020.[179]

[175] In each case, 'old' and 'new' refer to the end of the transition period, rather than Brexit day, unless the contrary is specified.

[176] Art. 86(1) WA.

[177] United Kingdom position paper 'Ongoing Union judicial and administrative procedures', no date or reference (13 July 2017), p. 3, para. 12, 3rd indent; see also Section 6.D.2.

[178] Art. 86(2) WA.

[179] European Union (Withdrawal) Act 2018, s. 6(1)(b), as amended.

The essential complement to the Court's jurisdiction is, of course, the obligation on the United Kingdom to give binding force to its rulings, both those handed down after Brexit day but before the end of the transition period, and those handed down after this latter date in the old cases based on old facts described above.[180] While the United Kingdom is explicitly required to comply with a Court judgment finding it is in infringement of its obligations, the enforcement mechanisms of Articles 260(2) and (3) of the Treaty on the Functioning of the European Union (TFEU) are not applicable.

2. New Cases Based on Old Facts

For a period of four years after the end of the transition period, the Court will have jurisdiction in respect of new infringement actions, and state aid proceedings, against the United Kingdom based on old facts, that is, facts which occurred prior to the end of the transition period, where the proceedings are only initiated at the Court after that date.[181] The alleged infringement may concern obligations under either the Treaties or the provisions of the Agreement concerning the transition period itself. Only the Commission, and not the Member States, may initiate such infringement proceedings. The Commission may also initiate infringement proceedings for the United Kingdom's failure to comply or ensure compliance with any decision adopted in administrative proceedings which were completed before the end of the transition period, or which were commenced before that date but only completed subsequently.[182]

The Court's jurisdiction in this regard was seen as particularly important as a means of discouraging the United Kingdom from flouting the rules of Union law in the long period between the decision to leave the Union and the actual withdrawal from the Union itself. In the immediate aftermath of the referendum in summer 2016, it was reported, for example, that the United Kingdom was considering offering financial inducements to certain third-country car producers in order to persuade them not to move production outside British territory. Such purported financial inducements might, possibly, have been investigated from the perspective of compliance with the Union's rules on state aid.

The decisions of the Court of Justice in new infringement actions based on old facts would also 'have binding force in their entirety on and in the United Kingdom'. The same is true of decisions addressed to the United Kingdom or companies or persons resident in the United Kingdom, which are adopted under ongoing administrative procedures. The Court would have exclusive competence to review these decisions.[183]

[180] Art. 89(1) WA.
[181] Art. 87(1) WA.
[182] Art. 87(2) WA; see also Art. 95 WA.
[183] Respectively Arts 89(1), 95(1), and 95(3) WA.

3. New Categories of Jurisdiction

The Agreement bestows new jurisdiction on the Court of Justice in certain circumstances.

The most important new head of jurisdiction concerns requests for preliminary rulings from British courts on citizens' rights. Part Two of the Agreement preserves certain residence and social security rights of EU27 citizens who are resident in the United Kingdom at the end of the transition period and who continue to reside there after that date. The Court will be able to provide preliminary rulings on questions of citizens' rights arising in any case concerning Part Two which are commenced in the United Kingdom courts before 31 December 2028. The legal effects of any such rulings 'shall be the same as the legal effects of preliminary rulings' provided under the Treaty.[184] The proper application of Part Two in the United Kingdom will also be subject to the supervision of an independent national authority with extensive powers to investigate and pursue alleged infringements by the UK authorities, through the courts if need be.[185]

The Court will be able to rule on infringement, enforcement, and preliminary ruling proceedings concerning the application and interpretation of the rules of the Agreement regarding the Union's own resources and the implementation by the United Kingdom of Union programmes without limitation of time.[186] This is an integral part of the deal the negotiators reached on the so-called financial settlement, which had threatened to derail the negotiations on the Agreement even before they had got off the ground. On one occasion, the Foreign Secretary of the day, the mercurial Boris Johnson, had indicated in the House of Commons his agreement with the view that if the Union thought the United Kingdom was going to pay any money to the Union after Brexit, it could 'go whistle'.[187] Commenting on the state of negotiations on the financial settlement just over a year later, he declared that '[t]he UK has agreed to hand over £40bn of taxpayers' money for two-thirds of diddly squat'.[188]

The Protocol on Ireland/Northern Ireland applies large swathes of Union law to Northern Ireland. The jurisdiction of the Court is limited *ratione materiae* to the customs treatment of goods imported into Northern Ireland, the placing of goods on the market in Northern Ireland, and the exchange of information on the application of these provisions; within these limits, however, the usual panoply of jurisdictional clauses apply, with an explicit reference to the preliminary

[184] Art. 158 WA.
[185] Art. 159 WA.
[186] Art. 160 WA.
[187] *The Guardian* online, 11 July 2017.
[188] Johnson, *The Daily Telegraph*, 3 September 2018; he had used the same colourful expression to describe the 'New Settlement' for the UK agreed with the European Council on 19 February 2016 (*ITV news* online, 24 April 2016). As Prime Minister, Mr Johnson had the opportunity himself to sign up to precisely this bargain on 24 January 2020.

ruling procedure.[189] The Court also has jurisdiction under the Protocol on Cyprus.[190]

Finally, the special position of the United Kingdom as a newly departed ex-Member State is recognized by the invitation to the Court to establish a 'regular dialogue' with the highest courts of the United Kingdom 'analogous to the dialogue in which the Court ... engages with the highest courts of the Member States'.[191] This dialogue is designed to facilitate the consistent interpretation of the Agreement in the two jurisdictions. While much of the Agreement is time-limited, the dialogue could prove useful well into the future, particularly as certain other parts will be applicable for many years to come.[192]

E. Dispute Resolution under the Withdrawal Agreement

In respect of the settlement of disputes on the interpretation and application of the Withdrawal Agreement, the Union negotiators had to ensure the preservation of the monopoly that the Court of Justice claims to provide the authoritative interpretation of provisions of EU law applicable within the territory of the Member States.[193] The Court has no problem in principle with the Union signing up to an international agreement which creates a new court charged with interpreting the provisions of that agreement. The matter gets a little more complicated when the agreement incorporates provisions of Union law, as the Withdrawal Agreement does on an industrial scale. In these circumstances, the Court insists that it, and it alone, can provide an interpretation of these 'incorporated provisions' for the Union and its Member States.[194] In its draft text of 19 March 2018, the Commission had proposed not only compulsory jurisdiction for the Court of Justice for the resolution of such disputes, but also, under certain circumstances, the suspension of the United Kingdom's internal market benefits under the agreement, in situations where it failed to comply with an infringement judgment of the Court or an enforcement order during the transition period.[195]

In its final form, the Withdrawal Agreement includes both political and legal dispute settlement mechanisms which have been tried and tested in previous agreements. The former comprises a Joint Committee, made up of officials from

[189] Art. 12(4), Protocol on Ireland/Northern Ireland.

[190] Art. 12, Protocol Relating to the Sovereign Base Areas of the United Kingdom of Great Britain and Northern Ireland in Cyprus.

[191] Art. 163 WA.

[192] In practice, the Court already maintains a similar dialogue with supreme courts of a number of third states, including SCOTUS.

[193] Halberstam, '"It's the Autonomy, Stupid!" A Modest Defense of Opinion 2/13 on EU Accession to the ECHR, and the Way Forward', 16 *German Law Journal* (2015) 105.

[194] See most recently, Opinion 1/17, *CETA* (EU:C:2019:341), and particularly paras 106–111.

[195] Draft withdrawal agreement of 19 March 2018, Arts 162 and 165.

the two parties, which would be primarily 'responsible for the implementation and application of the Agreement'.[196] Disputes must first be referred for consultations to the Committee; failing a solution within three months, the parties may move to an arbitration procedure at the request of either one of them. For the latter, the Agreement provides for the establishment of a permanent arbitration panel, comprising 25 persons, of whom 10 are proposed by each of the parties, and five chairpersons proposed jointly by the parties. Members are required to have the same qualifications as for appointment to the Court of Justice[197] and to 'possess specialised knowledge or experience of Union law and public international law'. The requirement of specialized knowledge of Union law is not expressly laid down for members of the CJEU, though the Article 255 panel does require that candidates 'demonstrate they are able to rise to the challenges involved in the application of European Union law'.[198] The arbitration panel is normally required to conclude its work within 12 months, except in urgent cases, when it is expected to conclude within six months.

Three types of dispute may require the involvement of the CJEU: those concerning the interpretation of a 'concept' or a provision of Union law; the proper compliance by the United Kingdom with a Court judgment finding it in infringement of its obligations under the Treaty or the Agreement; and the conformity with the Agreement of measures taken by a party to comply with a ruling of the arbitration panel which raise a question of the interpretation of Union law.[199] The arbitration panel 'may not decide on any such question … [but] shall request the Court of Justice to give a ruling', which ruling is then 'binding on the arbitration panel'.[200] Either party may challenge the panel's initial determination that a ruling of the CJEU is necessary, and the panel must provide a reasoned decision on the challenge. As the rulings of the arbitration panel are in turn binding on the parties, the United Kingdom can rightly claim that in this regard it is not subject to the 'direct jurisdiction' of the CJEU; at the same time, this mechanism is clearly designed fully to safeguard the autonomy of Union law.[201]

Despite its singular importance for the actual withdrawal of the United Kingdom from the Union, much of the Withdrawal Agreement will have a limited shelf life compared to the future relationship agreement, should one be concluded and enter into force. Already, however, the parties have acknowledged 'the [CJEU] as the sole arbiter of Union law [with competence to provide] binding ruling[s] as regards the

[196] Art. 164(4) WA.

[197] Art. 253, first para. TFEU.

[198] Fifth Activity Report of the panel provided for in Article 255 TFEU, Brussels, 28 February 2018, section III.1, p. 26.

[199] Art. 174(1) WA; on infringement proceedings, see Art. 89(2) WA and s. 6(d)(i).

[200] Art. 174(1) WA.

[201] Though it has not (yet) received the imprimatur of the Court; I am grateful to Maciej Szpunar for pointing out this small but important detail.

interpretation of Union law' in their future relations,[202] though whether that will survive the rough and tumble of negotiations on any such agreement remains to be seen.

F. Judicial Mandates

A number of the provisions of the Withdrawal Agreement deal, albeit somewhat obliquely, with the issue of the mandates of the members of the CJEU nominated by the UK government. While references in Union law to 'Member States' are, in general, to be interpreted as including the United Kingdom, those concerning 'the nomination, appointment or election of members of the institutions ... of the Union [or] the participation in the decision-making and the attendance in the meetings of the institutions' are expressly excluded.[203] Exceptionally, this provision applies even during the transition period; moreover, the Preamble to the Agreement refers to 'the end, on the date of entry into force of this Agreement, of the mandates of all members of institutions ... nominated, appointed or elected in relation to the United Kingdom's membership of the Union'. The same position is echoed in the Preamble to Council Decision (EU) 2020/135 concluding the Withdrawal Agreement on behalf of the Union and the European Atomic Energy Community.[204] A declaration of the Conference of the Representatives of the Governments of the Member States of 29 January 2020 states bluntly that the mandates of members of the institutions 'automatically end ... on the date of withdrawal', and notes that the 'permanent post of Advocate-General which was assigned to the United Kingdom ... will therefore be integrated in the rotation system among the Member States for the appointment of Advocates-General'. The declaration envisages that the post occupied by Advocate General Sharpston on 31 January 2020 would be filled by a Greek national.

G. The Role of the Court in the Withdrawal Agreement: An Overview

While the jurisdiction of the Court has been preserved in a number of areas, notably certain categories of pending procedures and disputes concerning citizens' rights, it should be recalled that, for those seeking to enforce their entitlements in or with respect to the United Kingdom, the nature of these rights has been subtly

202 Revised Political Declaration (n. 63), para. 131.

203 Art. 7(1)(a) WA.

204 Respectively Art. 128(1) WA, 8th para. of the Preamble to the Agreement, and para. 4 of the Decision, OJ 2020 L 29/1.

altered even if their substantive content remains the same in principle. They are no longer rights deriving directly from the Treaty or Union law, but from an agreement between the Union and a third state, from which they may only benefit in accordance with UK domestic law, and which are, for the most part, enforceable before its domestic courts.[205] Moreover, many of the rights accorded under the Withdrawal Agreement are limited in time and even those which are not, such as citizens' rights under Part Two, are subject to a degree of judicial and non-judicial protection which will diminish over time.

The potential for the qualitative degradation of rights originally created as Union rights is illustrated, for example, by the exclusion of the jurisdiction of the Court to rule on requests for preliminary rulings relating to facts occurring before the end of the transition period, but which could not be referred to the Court until after that date.[206] In such cases, Union law as interpreted by the Court of Justice is in principle applicable to the facts, yet the United Kingdom refused to accept the Court's jurisdiction—the exclusion of which, under one view, fails fully to vindicate the parties' right to an effective judicial remedy.[207] Similarly, Article 2(1) of the Protocol on Ireland/Northern Ireland requires the United Kingdom to 'ensure that no diminution of rights, safeguards or equality of opportunity, as set out in [the relevant] part [of the Belfast/Good Friday Agreement] results from its withdrawal from the Union, including in the area of protection against discrimination'. However, the exclusion of this provision from the jurisdiction of the Court could arguably be seen itself as a diminution of those rights, in so far as the Court had any jurisdiction to review respect of these rights when the United Kingdom was still a Member State.[208]

The Union had also proposed that the Court have infringement, enforcement, and preliminary ruling jurisdiction for all the matters covered by Part Three of the draft Agreement, that is, the so-called 'Separation issues'. These would cover essentially proceedings concerning activities or procedures which commenced before the end of the transition period but which were still ongoing after that date, such as the treatment of goods placed on the market, ongoing customs procedures, the protection of intellectual property rights, and so on. Again the Union gave way in the face of the United Kingdom's hostility to the Court.

The position of the Union and the United Kingdom on the question of judicial mandates contrasts with that which, some have argued, arises from the Court's

[205] See Smismans, 'EU Citizens' Rights Post-Brexit: Why Direct Effect beyond the EU is Not Enough', 14 *European Constitutional Law Review* (2018) 443; while the article refers to a draft of the withdrawal agreement, many of the points made remain valid.

[206] Art. 83(2), draft withdrawal agreement of 19 March 2018.

[207] N. Fennelly, 'Dispute Settling between the EU and the UK', Conference presentation, September 2017, on file with the author.

[208] Art. 12(4), Protocol on Ireland/Northern Ireland.

Statute.[209] This provides that a member of the Court 'may be deprived of his office ... only if ... he no longer fulfils the requisite conditions or meets the obligations arising from his office'. While the mandates of the UK judges at the Court of Justice and the General Court had already expired by 31 January 2020, this was not the case for the Advocate General nominated by the UK government, whose six-year term still had some 21 months to run.[210]

While some or all of these impacts on Union rights, and on the role of the Court and its members, might, arguably, be considered an inevitable consequence of the unconstrained right of withdrawal allowed by Article 50 TEU, they nonetheless pose a challenge to Union legality as it existed prior to the United Kingdom's withdrawal from the Union.

7. Conclusions

The introduction into the EU Treaties of an exit clause is fundamentally antithetical to the idea of European integration, and challenges the expectation of Union legality that rights conferred on individuals under Union law become 'part of their legal heritage'.[211] That said, the addition of a withdrawal procedure might be considered a rational choice; it was argued many years ago that it would be better that a recalcitrant Member State be able to leave the Union, than it stay in and hinder the Union's activities.[212]

The principal problem in this context is Article 50 TEU itself. It was conceived from a perspective which takes account neither of the specificities of the Union Treaties, nor of those of international law. It undermines the notion of the Union Treaties as being 'more than an agreement which merely creates mutual obligations between the contracting states'.[213] Unlike the VCLT scheme, on which it was purportedly based, Article 50 fails to take account of the scale of the impact of withdrawal on the interests of the remaining Member States, their citizens, or the Union, or indeed the fact that withdrawal will have any such impact at all. Whereas the VCLT procedure is designed to prevent its 'arbitrary application for the purpose of getting rid of inconvenient treaty obligations',[214] the Union procedure appears to be designed precisely to facilitate this result. Of course, it could be argued that

[209] Available at https://www.theguardian.com/law/2020/feb/17/british-ecj-could-sue-eu-eleanor-sharpston (accessed 11 November 2020).

[210] See, however, Cases T-180/20 and T-550/20, both *Sharpston v. Council and Conference of the Representatives of the Governments of the Member States*, and Case T-184/20 *Sharpston v. Court of Justice of the European Union* (EU:T:2020:473, EU:T:2020:475, and EU:T:2020:474 respectively). The former two judgments have been appealed as Cases C-684/20 P and C-685/20 P (pending).

[211] Case 26/62, *Van Gend en Loos* (EU:C:1963:1) 12, 4th para.

[212] Weiler (n. 20).

[213] *Van Gend en Loos* (n. 211) 12, 2nd para.

[214] ILC (n. 24), 'Draft Articles on the Law of Treaties', Commentary on Article 39.

in the case of Brexit, failures of governance on the part of the UK government[215] were a major contributory factor in rendering the negotiations on the Withdrawal Agreement slow and difficult, and the outcome suboptimal. That said, any Member State seeking to withdraw is likely to be at least mildly, or perhaps virulently, hostile to the Union; moreover, the exit decision may be domestically controversial too, and there is no reason to assume that the Union will necessarily be dealing with a fully rational or well-governed partner. Article 50 TEU is not designed properly to protect the Union's interests in such situations.

A proper Union withdrawal procedure could genuinely have taken the VCLT provisions as a model—though adapting them to take account of the character of the Union Treaties—by minimizing the negative effects of withdrawal on the interests of other parties and, because it is the Union, other parties and in particular of individuals, and avoiding unseemly rows about financial obligations and border regimes. Indeed, once a right of withdrawal is established, the application of the relevant provisions of the VCLT *mutatis mutandis* could have provided a much more satisfactory procedure than Article 50 TEU. Even the EFTA Convention, which is limited to creating a free trade area of strikingly modest ambitions compared to those of the Union, has a more sensible exit clause, which conditions withdrawal to agreement on 'appropriate arrangements and equitable cost-sharing relating to the withdrawal'.[216]

The combination of an unconstrained right of withdrawal and an unconstrained right of revocation is hard to reconcile with the stability of treaty relations. As matters stand, however, the Union may not, in accordance with its own legal rules, prevent any Member State notifying its intention to withdraw, at any time and for any (or indeed no) reason, and subsequently revoking its notification, again at any time before it actually withdraws. Should it feel so inclined, the Member State may restart the process at will. The requirement that the State comply with its own constitutional requirements for each such decision is unlikely to provide any worthwhile restraint for a Member State which is minded to abuse Article 50 TEU in this way. This is a truly dysfunctional state of affairs.

Nor are concerns regarding the operation of the Union's withdrawal process entirely academic. To take just one example, Poland is currently engaged in an existential, in the sense of membership-threatening, dispute with the Union concerning the organization of its judiciary and its respect for the rule of law. In a statement reported in December 2019, the Polish Supreme Court opined that '[c]ontradictions between Polish and EU law ... will in all likelihood lead ... in the long[ ] run to the need to leave the European Union'.[217] It remains to be seen whether this prediction

[215] See e.g. Dougan (n. 19) 640–641. The Union's impression of the government's approach is forever encapsulated in a photograph taken in the negotiation room, showing the UK contingent with fulsome smiles but no documents, and the Union contingent with sheaves of documents but no smiles (Stone, 'David Davis pictured without any notes at Brexit negotiations', *Independent*, 17 July 2017).

[216] Convention establishing the European Free Trade Agreement (as of 1 July 2013), Art. 57(2).

[217] BBC News, 'Poland May Have to Leave EU, Supreme Court Warns', 17 December 2019, available at https://www.bbc.co.uk/news/world-europe-50828516.

comes to pass, or whether any other Member State in dispute with the Union regarding respect for its fundamental values[218] decides to take the ultimate step and withdraw. In any case the British people, or perhaps their government, may not be alone in celebrating 'national sovereignty as the supreme value in a nation's policy, which needs to be forever defended and strengthened',[219] and approving the Court's reliance on this notion in *Wightman*.

On a more positive note, the Conference on the Future of Europe,[220] should it get off the ground, would provide a precious opportunity, away from the heat of battle, to take stock of the operation of the withdrawal procedure, to amend Article 50 TEU to correct its defects, and to adapt it, as far as possible, to the logic of both Union and international law.

[218] The approval on 30 March 2020 by the Hungarian Parliament of emergency powers allowing the government to rule by decree without limitation in time, and providing stiff jail sentences for 'spreading misinformation', was condemned by many Union personalities, though not immediately by the Commission or Council.

[219] W. Sadurski, *Poland's Constitutional Breakdown* (2019) 12.

[220] See e.g. 'Franco-German non-paper on key questions and guidelines', November 2019, available at https://www.politico.eu/wp-content/uploads/2019/11/Conference-on-the-Future-of-Europe.pdf (accessed 11 November 2020); and Commission Communication, 'Shaping the Conference on the Future of Europe', COM(2020) 27 final, Brussels, 22 January 2020.

Index

For the benefit of digital users, indexed terms that span two pages (e.g., 52–53) may, on occasion, appear on only one of those pages.

Tables are indicated by an italic *t* following the page number. Notes are indicated by n. following the page number.

Note 1: In order to avoid multiple entries under European Union, agreements between EU and other countries have been indexed under the relevant country.

Note 2: Only cases that are discussed at length have been indexed.